Mind-Body Intelligence

How to Manage Your Mind Using Biofeedback & Mindfulness

Glyn Blackett

ISBN:1973845156

ISBN-13: 978-1973845157

To my parents, with love and gratitude

Contents

Acknowledgements

My thanks go to my good friends Colin Mawhinney and Melissa Foks for encouragement, advice and help with editing, and to Nick Janvier for help with cover design. Of course we all stand on the shoulders of giants, and I thank all the numerous people who have taught me, directly or indirectly. Nothing would have been possible for me without my parents, who supported me as I learned, while my business didn't earn much money.

1 Introduction: How To Manage Your Mind

1.1 Introduction

This book is about the mind and how to manage it, or how to be in possession of it, or even how to control it. Happiness and well-being are intimately connected to the mind – to feel happy and well you need to be able to access positive emotions, energy and motivation, and you need to be able to direct or focus the mind at will, and sustainably. These qualities aren't simply givens, but are complex abilities that develop to a greater or lesser extent as we move through life.

In this book I use the term self-regulation to sum up these abilities. I also use the term self-control, though it does have a somewhat negative connotation of "mind control" (on the other hand self-regulation may sound a little mechanistic and even automatic).

The core idea of the book is that self-regulation or self-control is a hierarchical set of skills that can be developed and trained. In its essence, self-regulation is a mind-body skill, which is to say that to manage your mind you need to simultaneously manage the physiology (both body and brain) that is the concomitant of your mental experience. Hence the words used in the title, "mind-body intelligence", are another way to describe the skill-set.

The book is an attempt to lay the groundwork for a practical project of learning or developing mind-body intelligence. I describe the science behind the mind-body connection as an important basis for understanding this project, and then I present a set of models or ways of thinking about self-regulation and challenges to it, and a set of tools and practices for developing and training it.

I see three core domains for the skill-set of self-control:

i.   emotional balance and resilience
ii. energy, drive and motivation
iii. attention, focus and concentration.

1.2   The Problem: Being Out of Control

Being out of control feels bad. When people seek help from a psychotherapist or coach, it's because something feels out of control, or is unmanageable.

1.2.1   Case Vignettes

The following vignettes are made up but they all represent typical problems I encounter in my therapy / coaching practice. Throughout the book I refer to these types of problem collectively as self-control challenges or self-regulation challenges.

Anxiety

Barbara had quite senior job as a manager in a public sector organisation. She was intelligent and capable and for the most part enjoyed her job, except for one thing: giving presentations. As soon as she knew she would have to present at a meeting she would start getting anxious.

In meetings she would feel tense, her heart would pound, her hands would feel cold and clammy and her breathing tight and restricted. She knew she was likely to blush and her voice crack. When she stood up she felt everyone could see she wasn't up to it and expected her to fail, though later when she'd calmed down she knew this wasn't the case.

Barbara did everything she could to avoid having to give presentations but it wasn't always possible. Anticipatory anxiety started to build even days before. She couldn't stop thinking about the coming presentation. She'd try to calm herself down, telling herself she'd done presentations before and always got through them. She'd read books on stress management techniques and could even do them quite successfully – if she didn't have a presentation coming up. But when the heat was on, these skills would frustratingly desert her. Her anxiety was out of control.

Anger

Tim liked playing tennis but his Achilles heel was his temper. On good days he could get into "the zone" and loved the feeling of his body timing shots well. But good days were probably more the exception than the rule. At other times he couldn't understand how he could play so badly when he knew he could and should do better. On bad days his rage would build to a fever of self-contempt. He'd tell himself to focus harder on his grip, or his foot work, but if anything things would get worse. His temper explosions had led to physical damage on more than one occasion, and tennis racquets weren't cheap. Socially he was aware that other people at his club didn't like to play with him.

If he was honest, it wasn't just tennis where Tim's temper was making things hard for him. He knew all about road rage. He was afraid of getting himself the sack by screaming at his boss. Tim's attempt to keep a dam on his rage always seemed to fail.

Craving

Jane wanted to lose a few pounds in weight so she decided to stop eating chocolate for a few weeks at least. Jane had always loved chocolate and she knew from experience that if she had one piece she'd finish the bar. So she resolved to go cold turkey – no more chocolate.

Evenings at home were the danger time. Thoughts of chocolate would frequently pop into her mind as she watched TV. She'd try to dismiss them from her mind, but they'd just creep back in again in an unguarded moment. In fact it seemed the more she resolved to resist, the more persistent her cravings became.

Addiction

David had a well-paid job, a loving wife and two children, but his gambling habit risked wrecking everything. His work as a travelling salesman gave him the resources to burn, and opportunities to visit bookies and even casinos. He loved the buzz, the adrenalin rush, that gambling gave him. Of course he'd tried to give it up before but life just seemed flat and tedious. He felt most alive when he was listening to the racing commentary or watching the roulette wheel spin. But win or lose, he never felt satisfied and soon started to think about the next bet.

Procrastination

Alejandra had a deadline to submit her Ph.D. in just a few months, when her visa would expire and she'd have to leave the country. She'd collected most of her data and really only had to write it up. Each day she arrived at the office resolved on writing a chapter or even a section, but it wasn't long before she was browsing Facebook or catching the latest news. Alejandra was staring to feel anxious about the prospect of finishing in time but this seemed to make things worse. When she'd put in an hour of work she felt relaxed enough to reward herself with a few minutes of surfing but that would turn into an hour. And even her work time was more likely to be spent reading one more research paper that she knew she didn't really need to read – anything but writing.

Concentration

Alison was a manager in a large company who could never seem to wake up feeling sharp and clear headed, however long she slept. Her performance at work was flagging. She attended lots of meetings and listened to lots of presentations but struggled to concentrate. No matter how hard she tried she drifted off into daydreams or even just blankness. It wasn't just concentration that was a problem – just holding things in mind was hard. In conversation she'd think of a constructive thing to say but often, by the time the other person had finished speaking she'd forgotten what it was. At home she found herself at times going into the kitchen and wondering what she came for. She described her state as "brain fog".

Insomnia

As the owner of a small business, James' life was inevitably rather stressful but that didn't seem to justify his inability to sleep. James often arrived home from work feeling exhausted and sometimes even dosed off in front of the TV. Even so he would often find himself wide awake as soon as his head hit the pillow. His mind would start to think of all the things he had to do tomorrow (inevitably too many). It wasn't all worry – sometimes he would have good ideas about how he could improve his business, and his mind would soon be racing, buzzing – and still would be, two hours later. James just couldn't seem to switch off the mind-chatter.

Obsessiveness

Mary was a worrier. No matter what she was doing, she couldn't help thinking about all the things that might go wrong. Even holidays which she should have looked forward to became threats to her equanimity. She was frustrated because it wasn't even helpful – it would be the same old worries going round again and again. She'd get stuck on thoughts even she knew were simply irrational. All this catastrophising made her feel anxious, and as a result of her attempts to avoid trouble her life was extremely rigid and constricted. For example she wouldn't drive on motorways. Even just the idea of change, doing anything out of the ordinary, would send her into a kind of mental panic. Mary just couldn't seem to let go.

Depression

Nigel had been diagnosed with depression by his doctor and recommended anti-depressants, but he didn't agree. He didn't see his problems as emotional – in fact in his job as an accountant he prided himself on his cool headed stability. Rather his problem was one of energy – he just didn't feel like doing anything any more. He wasn't able to enjoy anything in life any more. His last (short-lived) relationship had ended some months ago – in fact he'd had a string of unsuccessful relationships and he didn't know why. His ex-partners would have told a different story. They found him rigid, obstinate, and above all emotionally cold – more than that, he just didn't "get" emotions. Nigel didn't seem to realise what he was missing – positivity.

1.2.2   Underlying Themes

Let's draw out the patterns underlying these case vignettes. Aspects of our minds that can feel out of control are:

- emotions – unbridled negative emotions and absent, out-of-reach positive emotions
- desires and cravings – overwhelming us and working against our longer term interests
- motivation and energy – lacking or faltering
- focus and attention – mind too busy and racy, or perhaps too foggy
- thoughts and thinking patterns – unrestrained mental chatter or negativity.

Self-control Dynamics

Looking a little deeper at self-control challenges we can discern three broad patterns:

- **Inner Conflict** – the mind is divided against itself. We experience a part of ourselves that we don't want, we'd like to reject – a destructive emotion, an impulse that goes against our higher level goals and values, or racing thoughts when we'd rather have some mental stillness. Throughout the book I refer to the experience of inner conflict as resistance, and sometimes as experiential avoidance.

- **Inaccessible Inner Resources** – there's some state of mind or body that we know we're capable of, but we can't do it now. We sleep every night, but can't right now, or we need the mind to be clear and focused, only it fogs out, or races away with us. Or we'd simply like to relax like we have done before, but the harder we try the more agitated we get.

- **Lack of Self-awareness** – if you're not aware of something you can't control it – just as your central heating system won't be able to control room temperature without a functional thermostat to sense current temperature. A lot of the mind's functioning goes on at a sub-conscious level, which can be very convenient for us but can also lead to problems. Nigel the "depressed" accountant is an example – for him emotions were a "blind spot" but just because he didn't feel them didn't mean they weren't operating. Lack of self-awareness is one reason inner resources can be inaccessible, and can also obscure inner conflict.

Some of our self-regulation challenges involve all three of these dynamics at the same time.

Dis-integration

In his excellent book "Mindsight"[1], psychiatrist Daniel Siegel takes a systems view of the mind. A system is a set of distinct elements or parts that are connected. In a healthy system (or a healthy mind) the parts work together smoothly and harmoniously for a common purpose. Siegel calls this integration, and in the case of a human mind it is the hallmark of well-being. When integration breaks down, the result is either chaos and instability on the one hand, or rigidity, inflexibility and "stuck-ness" on the other. We can see these themes at play in our case vignettes.

Instability and chaos can manifest as emotional volatility – explosive anger, or panic for example – or as distractability (unstable focus) or impulsivity (unstable purpose or motivation).

Too much stability leads to rigidity, feeling stuck. This happens in many cases of depression for example, which can be an emotional or motivational stuck-ness. Insomnia is a mind that is stuck in the waking state. Obsessiveness, craving and addiction are more examples of rigidity.

Inner conflict is a form of dis-integration too – the parts of the system lack unity of purpose. Inaccessibility of resources is the result of loss of connectedness or communication between parts of the system.

Mind-Body Dimension

The mind-body connection is the idea that our subjective experience is reflected in our body and brain physiology, and vice versa. By 'physiology' I mean:

i.   the set of processes by which energy and substances are created, used, broken down, and transported around the physical body, and

ii. the activity of the body's multiple communication and control systems which regulate (i) above, maintaining healthy,balanced functioning, including the nervous system and the endocrine (hormone) system.

We can discern the mind-body connection in each of the examples. Destructive emotions play out in the body – a pounding heart and clammy palms in anxiety for example. Cravings are rooted in biological drives – we all need to eat and if we go without food for long enough any of us will be hungry. Sleep is a biological necessity, and if we don't get enough we'll struggle to concentrate. Our sense of mental energy and motivation is conditioned by the body's ability to produce physical energy at the cellular level.

I'm not espousing a simplistic reductionism here – I don't want to say we are defined by our biology – rather there is a two-way conditionality. Our choices affect our physiology.

1.3 The Solution: Mind-Body Intelligence

If the problem is a mind out of control, then what's needed is the ability to control the mind – or rather more or better control. This is what I'm calling self-regulation – but what exactly does this term mean?

We can divide our experience into things we do (e.g. I decided to write this book) and things that just happen to us (e.g. a belly ache). For the things we decide to do, we may have to expend effort in bringing them about. This distinction extends even to inner life – for example thinking can be directed, purposeful, even effortful, or thoughts can just pop up in the mind unbidden and wander aimlessly.

A first pass at defining self-control might be the exercise of rational conscious choice or free-will, allied to the application of effort. But some experiences feel very much "in-control" yet have little to do with choice, free will or effort, as we'll see in the next section.

1.3.1 Self-control as Flow

Consider the following examples of self-control.

- A professional violinist and member of an orchestra takes part in a concert performance. She doesn't choose the programme. Since she's not a soloist, it's about playing in close harmony with her fellow musicians rather than personal interpretation. She gives her best, and becomes deeply absorbed in the music. The result is an excellent performance. She finds the experience very gratifying.
- A computer programmer has been given a project to do. He understands what is needed and applies his mind to logically, efficiently delivering a solution. He makes decisions but it's a matter of seeing the best way to solve problems rather than expressing his personal preferences.
- A swimmer competes in a race. She pushes herself hard, overcoming the pain of muscle fatigue, but not so hard she'll

run out of steam before the end. She wants to win. She allows her body to cut through the water gracefully and efficiently.

- A man is sitting absorbed in meditation practice. Outwardly he is quiet and still, looks calm and serene. Inwardly his mind is stable, clear, bright, intensely awake. His attention is rapt and one-pointed. He feels fully self-possessed.

These are examples of a class of experience that psychologists call flow states[2]. Flow states are peak experiences, when we feel at our very best, fully ourselves. People experience flow when they're doing something they really enjoy, something they can lose themselves in. More everyday examples are watching a really good film or reading a novel or playing a video game.

In some sense they are the epitome of self-control, yet in essence they aren't really about the exercise of choice or effort. They're creative, but not necessarily about producing something new and unique. One of the most definitive features of flow is a sense of effortlessness – you're doing it, you're actively engaged, but not trying – you somehow let go, allow something to happen, as though from a deeper part of yourself.

Successful people have abundant drive and energy – they exert effort in achieving goals. But if the only way you know to solve problems is to make effort, try harder, then you have a serious limitation – you only have one tool in your locker – and it's not always going to work. Successful people have options. They are flexible and adaptable. The idea that there are other ways to achieve besides effort will emerge as a major theme of the book.

1.3.2 Self-control as Integration

Another key characteristic of flow states is concentration – our attention is fully engaged, even to the point where we forget ourselves – there is just the doing of the activity. All our energies are flowing together, the different aspects of our minds are temporarily unified. In other words flow is a state of *integration*.

Earlier I described integration as Dan Siegel's defining characteristic of a healthy mind[3]. It is the river that flows between the banks of chaos and rigidity (both of which are a loss of flow). Integrated flow has five features:

- flexible – the mind can easily shift state, for example from waking to sleep, or from work to play
- adaptive – these shifts happen appropriately, at the right time – for example falling asleep in bed, not while driving
- coherent – parts of the mind (and brain) work together in a consistent and harmonious way
- energised – vitality is a quality of the healthy mind
- stable – the balancing counter-part of flexibility.

At a higher level we can speak of an integrated personality – you act and behave in a consistent way, as though there were some guiding principle behind your actions, and you own and take responsibility for what you do, even though you make mistakes at times and you don't always feel perfectly self-possessed.

1.3.3   Self-control as a Skill-set

Another thing my flow examples share is the expression of skills. There are specific skills, such as the violinist's manual dexterity in her fingers or the programmer's knowledge of computer languages and concepts. But they share more general skills, skills of managing the mind – for example keeping the focus steady and calming agitation.

So self-control is a complex capacity, not easily defined. I'm proposing we look at it as a set of skills. As a first pass, here are some of the high-level skills:

- ability to easily and regularly access flow
- stable and flexible attention
- emotional resilience – the ability to quickly recover from set-backs
- emotional intelligence – awareness of and understanding of emotions, how they develop and what influences them, in ourselves and others

- purposefulness, commitment and perseverance, or consistent motivation, or even willpower.

High-level skills such as these are founded on more fundamental skills. Perhaps an analogy will serve. Ability to play tennis is a set of skills: service, forehand, backhand, volleying etc. These skills are built on a set of more fundamental skills, such as timing, court mobility, anticipation, concentration. Similarly all complex mental activities rely on core mental abilities.

Some core skills of self-control are:

- refined self-awareness – of body, mind and the connection between the two (awareness seems to be a prerequisite for control)
- ability to reduce physiological arousal (calm the body)
- ability to activate the mind (and brain), to intensify awareness and focus
- ability to access positive emotions such as hope, appreciation and interest
- ability to suppress distracting thoughts and other influences.

1.3.4 Training, Development and the Growth Mindset

Want to learn to play piano? You can go to lessons or read a how-to book, but you won't get anywhere till you sit down at a keyboard and practice, or exercise – starting with basics. If you want to improve your tennis game, the same applies – you need a context for practising your skills. Same for woodwork, painting, learning a foreign language.

Yet if you have problems with out-of-control emotions or wandering focus, our society's solution seems to be, take some mind-altering substances, or perhaps pour your heart out to a counsellor. My point here is not to disparage either psychiatric medication or counselling – both have a useful role to play – but to show an anomaly in our mindset: we don't really think in terms of training the core capacities of the mind – emotional regulation, concentration, motivation etc.

Psychologist Carol Dweck's decades of research into achievement and success[4] led her to a simple but profound and important insight: that what matters most is what she calls a growth mindset: the view that ability is not a matter of the talent you're born with (or without) but is developed through commitment and the hard work of training. All complex skills are by their nature learned, and honed over time through practice and training. The skills of managing the mind are no different.

A new-born baby has almost no self-control, but is eminently equipped to develop it. Children have some control over their minds but much less than most adults. Development clearly happens. We can also say that some adults are not as good at self-control as others (think of addicts, or people sentenced for crimes of passion). Yet when it comes to the everyday problems of managing the mind, especially emotions, many of us seem to have lost the growth mindset.

For human beings learning is natural and spontaneous and we're very good at it (fortunately, since they don't teach you to control emotions and desires at school). But to reach our full potential we still need a context for learning and practising. This book aims to show you how to develop the skills for managing your mind, concentrating on core mind-body regulation.

1.3.5 The Mind-Body Connection

We've already seen how the mind-body connection (the relationship between subjective experience and objective physiology) shows up in various mind-body problems. For example, feelings of anxiety can be reflected in muscle tension and a racing heart, while tiredness and inability to focus are seen in an unstable activation of the front part of the brain, the Prefrontal Cortex (more on this in chapter three).

If you learn to play violin, the brain regions that sense and control the fine movements of the fingers will change and develop (it's called neuroplasticity – now established science). The finger muscles themselves will also strengthen. So as a matter of practical reality, it is possible to change our physiology. It's not hard, and doesn't take long – brain imaging studies have demonstrated change in just weeks or even days.

The mind-body connection is a core principle that underlies the whole book, and it has considerable practical import: if we want to manage the mind effectively, we have to take into account the body. A key part of our strategy for developing self-control is to create the physiological "terrain" that supports positive, resourceful and creative mental states. Developing skill in influencing the physiology side of the mind-body connection is central to our project.

Mind-Body Adaptability

In speaking of physiology I don't mean to suggest there is a single optimum state that is the answer to all problems. Rather, the goal is flexibility or adaptability: the capacity to rapidly and easily shift physiological state in order to meet the demands of the present context, whatever they may be. Suppose you're concentrating on a rather technical presentation or text – your optimum physiology is not the same as when you're having a social drink with colleagues after work. When you get into bed ready for sleep at night, that's another shift of physiology. If you you can't make the shift, if your physiology is stuck, problems such as insomnia will arise.

1.3.6   Key Tools for Training the Mind

To summarise so far: the ability to manage your mind is key to well-being. A mind that feels out of control is a mind that feels bad. Self-regulation is not a simple state but a set of skills and abilities. Like all abilities, the skill-set of self-control can be trained and developed. At its heart is mind-body regulation, or the ability to guide your physiology towards states supporting positive, resourceful and creative states of mind.

In my professional practice I coach people in developing these skills. The core of my approach is a combination of two tools for training the mind: mindfulness and biofeedback.

Mindfulness

Mindfulness is a form of mind training (more specifically, attention training) that first developed in the ancient eastern spiritual traditions, particularly Buddhism. More recently mindfulness has been gaining prominence in western psychological health services, thanks to a growing body of research attesting to its efficacy in improving outcomes in cases of depression, anxiety and many other health conditions. But it's a mistake to think of mindfulness as a therapy – in the Buddhist tradition it is a means of transforming the mind, appropriate to anyone.

Mindfulness is simply a way of actively paying attention to immediate experience, with openness, interest and acceptance. It can be practised in almost any context of everyday life, or more formally in meditation (where often, though not always, there is a specific object of focus such as the breath). The intention is simply to be aware of and open to sensations, thoughts and emotions, in the present moment, neither resisting unpleasant experiences nor craving and grasping after pleasant experiences.

How exactly does mindfulness transform the mind? With regular practice you can develop stillness, sensitivity, clarity, openness, stability and balance, perspective, contentment, and a sense of freedom. In short, mindfulness expands, enriches and purifies awareness. Ultimately, at least in the Buddhist tradition, mindfulness opens us up to seeing the true nature of reality and experience – a spiritual insight equivalent to enlightenment. (For any reader getting uncomfortable at this point, let me say spiritual practice is beyond the scope of this book and I won't be discussing it further.)

In a sense the *intent* of mindfulness is not to develop any of these qualities, but simply to stay open to your present-moment experience, on the one hand without getting so involved with feelings and thoughts that you lose self-awareness, and on the other hand without getting caught up in resisting, struggling with, or attempting to suppress or avoid certain other thoughts and feelings. In this space, positive qualities arise naturally.

Biofeedback

Biofeedback is a method of training the mind founded on the mind-body principle. Biofeedback measures physiological changes that accompany (or *embody*) thoughts, feelings and other subjective experiences. For example we can measure muscle tension, breathing and heart rate changes that are perhaps reflective of anxiety. This measured information is fed back to the trainee via computer in real time, either visually (as a changing graph) or through sound feedback. This conjunction of external feedback and subjective experience is a means of developing greater awareness of your own responses, particularly in their mind-body aspect. You can see how your body responds to even fleeting thoughts and images.

At times in the book I refer to neurofeedback, which is just a particular kind of biofeedback in which the measurement is directly of brain activity (e.g. EEG or brainwaves).

This enhanced mind-body awareness is then the basis for developing the ability to guide physiology towards a more favourable state. Biofeedback is a tool to support learning. It doesn't do anything to you or for you – it simply provides feedback – lets you know how you're doing. You actually need feedback to learn anything. In piano playing you can hear your wrong notes, and in tennis you can see when you missed the ball or sent it into the net. But in mind-body regulation challenges (e.g. trying to control your emotions) the feedback is not so apparent. It's easy to miss breathing changes or heart rate changes, even muscle tension changes. Biofeedback just gives you some objective help.

Besides being a vehicle for skills development based on insight into the mind-body connection, biofeedback is a tool for building "fitness" in the brain and nervous system. Just as you can build muscle mass through weight training, consistent biofeedback practice can strengthen the "muscles" of the nervous system.

How Biofeedback Supports Mindfulness

I consider mindfulness and biofeedback an ideal partnership. Using them together enhances both. Mindfulness practice provides an excellent context for working with biofeedback. Indeed I use biofeedback in my own meditation on an almost-daily basis, and have done for years. Yet I'm well aware that many mindfulness practitioners would not agree. At first sight, biofeedback and mindfulness seem to be incompatible – biofeedback is goal-focused and even "judgemental" in a sense, while mindfulness is not. So I've got a case to make. I shall develop my argument fully in later chapters, but for now I'll summarise some of the advantages.

Biofeedback Enhances Sensitivity.

In mindfulness we're directed to be aware of the body, and as you pay open attention you'll naturally find yourself become more sensitive, increasingly aware of the richness of sensory experience. But we also have blind spots, and by their nature we can't see them – without some help. Biofeedback gives us that help. I've worked with some extremely experienced meditators who carried a baseline of muscle tension without being aware of it, or being able to let it go. An analogy: you're sitting in the kitchen, and you think it's quiet, until the fridge switches off. Muscle tension can be like that – you're not aware of it till it falls away.

Insight into the Mind-Body Connection

Biofeedback highlights the mind-body connection, which I believe is at the heart of mindfulness, even though it's not necessarily explicitly taught in the mindfulness tradition. Mindfulness aims to lay bare the true nature of experience, and part of that is the relationship between thoughts and mental imagery on the one hand, and sensations and bodily feelings on the other.

Biofeedback as a Distraction Detector

In mindfulness practice, sooner or later we lose ourselves in distraction. Eventually we notice, and bring the mind back to the object of focus. The practice is to keep on coming back, without getting disheartened or self-critical. The hard part is noticing. If you're like me it's quite possible to spend several minutes at a time day-dreaming when you're "supposed" to be focusing on the breath, and however non-judgemental you'd like to be, that can feel like a waste of time.

To the extent that distractions manifest as physiological changes (and the mind-body principle would suggest they will), and to the extent that biofeedback devices are capable of detecting these changes (which can be subtle), we can use biofeedback to flag these departures from the optimal psychophysiological zone, e.g. by ringing a (computer-generated) bell. For instance, if the mind takes up a habitual worry, the brow may start to furrow slightly, which is detectable as a change in muscle tension. By flagging up distractions, biofeedback helps you stay focused.

Making Mindfulness More Gratifying

Mindfulness courses are increasingly common these days. In my personal experience, many participants don't persist with a regular mindfulness practice beyond the end of their course, even when they have benefited. On the face of it they lack the self-discipline needed but I think a deeper, more fundamental explanation is called for. I suspect that, because their minds are so distracted, they don't really *enjoy* mindfulness practice (at least, not enough to stick with it). If you spend most of your time day-dreaming, worrying or planning what you're going to do later, or just plain dosing off, there won't be much opportunity for qualities such as stillness, clarity and serenity to emerge. Purists might argue that whether mindfulness is gratifying, peaceful etc. is beside the point. But for practical intents and purposes, if we don't find it gratifying we won't stick with it.

Biofeedback, by reducing distracted time, and helping move the physiology into a state more conducive to stillness, clarity, etc., makes mindfulness practice more gratifying.

1.4   Overview Of The Book

1.4.1   How to Use This Book

The book is essentially practical: I hope reading it will help you develop your own mind-body intelligence or self-regulation capacity, and help you overcome some of the self-control challenges you face in your life.

Yet it is not quite a self-help book. Clearly you can't learn to ride a bike by reading a book about it. The same is true of both mindfulness and biofeedback – at some point you have to get on and do it. You can't become an electrician by reading books, but on the other hand it will help if you understand something about the nature of electricity – the "theory" if you like. At the outset of a journey, you need to understand where it is you are trying to get to, and something about the nature of the journey ahead, what you're going to need on the way. So this is what I hope the book will give you – a better understanding of where you need to get to and how to get there. It's more like a manifesto for biofeedback and mindfulness rather than a true self-help book (actually there are plenty of good mindfulness self-help books on the market, though not many for biofeedback). If you do go on to take a course in mindfulness or biofeedback (and I hope you will) the book should help you along the way. If you decide biofeedback is not for you I hope you'll still gain some useful insights.

As a professional biofeedback and mindfulness coach, I wrote this book with my clients in mind – I wanted to make the learning as cost-effective as possible. By making this sort of material available for people to take in in their own time, we can minimise the need for expensive face to face time and at the same time make it as productive as possible.

I've tried to keep the book as short and succinct as possible, but without oversimplifying. In places I go into some rather technical detail, which is probably not strictly necessary, but I hope this material is still interesting and relevant. Of course you may wish to skip over some of it, and I try to let you know when you can safely do so. Chapters three and four contain the main content on biology and physiology, and chapter ten on biofeedback. In any case I (intentionally) repeat myself rather a lot – after all, repetition is the key to learning. Each chapter has a summary of main points at the end.

1.4.2   Who the Book Is For

This book is for anyone who wants to improve their mental performance or brain performance – which could be just about anyone. It's not aimed at people with a medical condition – but that doesn't mean that you can't benefit from it if you have a medical condition. It just means that you shouldn't consider what I'm offering as medical treatment, and certainly not a substitute for professional care. If you have a medical condition and want to try biofeedback, I'd advise you to discuss it with your doctor or therapist first. For my part, I consider myself a health practitioner but not a medical practitioner.

1.4.3   Outline of Contents

In part one we lay the foundations by developing the concepts and "background knowledge" we need to fully understand our project of training the mind in the skills of self-regulation. Chapter two starts us off with a consideration of what it is we're training – the mind. In particular we'll unpack the rather vague and general concept of emotion. From our discussion the significance of the mind-body principle will emerge: to understand the mind we need to understand its relationship to the body and its embodiment in brain and nervous system physiology. Chapter three takes this theme further with a closer look at the biology of the mind-body connection. Chapter four continues this exploration with a detailed consideration of the psychophysiology of breathing, a topic of great practical significance.

Part two builds on this foundational knowledge and develops it into a practical framework for understanding the problems of self-control and how they might be addressed. In chapter five we pose the question of what it means to be in control of the mind, or what kind of control is ultimately possible. We'll explore the dynamics of self-control challenges: (i) inner conflict or resistance and (ii) inaccessibility of inner resources. We'll see how applying ourselves in the wrong way can actually make things worse rather than better.

Chapter six presents practical models as ways of understanding the mind-body connection and how to apply the mind effectively, to overcome the problems of resistance and inaccessible inner resources. Chapter seven looks at how to access the hidden resources of the mind. Chapter eight looks at how to reduce arousal levels and stress.

Part three is a detailed look at the tools for the project: first mindfulness (chapter nine) then biofeedback (chapter ten). Chapter eleven considers how these two mutually support each other, and resolves the surface-level incompatibility between them.

In part four we revisit each of the main domains of self-regulation challenge – attention (chapter twelve), motivation (chapter thirteen), thinking (chapter fourteen) and finally emotion in chapter fifteen. I hope to give you a clear sense of how biofeedback and mindfulness are relevant in these domains.

Chapter sixteen is the conclusion and reviews the skill-set of self-regulation, showing how mind-body regulation is the foundation for the high-level abilities.

1.5   About the Author

My personal journey started with mindfulness meditation. As a Cambridge University student I was captivated by the idea of total transformation of my mind. Fast forward ten years or so, and

I'd realised my experience of meditation hadn't lived up to my hopes, even though by this stage I had given up my job in the IT industry in order to live and work at a meditation retreat centre in North Wales. In fact I was still struggling to focus my mind in the most basic way – my experience of meditation was mainly one of distraction and mind-chatter. Even the occasional experiences of serene concentration, though they served to keep me going, didn't seem to make any lasting difference.

It was at this point that I began to read around to see if there were a way to make things easier. As a scientist by temperament and training, I wondered if technology could help. My first idea was brain stimulation. Reading a book "Megabrain", by Michael Hutchison[5], I first encountered biofeedback. Of all the methods Hutchison discusses (including various brain stimulation techniques, which I also tried out) biofeedback really captured my imagination because by nature it's a tool for learning, and for enhancing awareness.

I began a hands-on investigation, buying a few simple biofeedback devices. My early experiences were of Electrodermal Activity (EDA) and Heart Rate Variability (HRV) – two biofeedback parameters covered in chapter ten. From the beginning I used biofeedback in the context of my meditation and found it added a new dimension to my awareness, rejuvenating my enthusiasm for practice. But soon I came up against frustrations: I felt the software gave feedback that was too basic and simplistic and at the same time too obtrusive. In particular I didn't want to have to keep looking at the screen.

It wasn't long before I began thinking in terms of making a career out of biofeedback. I realised biofeedback was a tool rather than a therapy in itself, so in 2001 I began training in psychotherapy. When I began looking for professional training in biofeedback and neurofeedback, I found there were precious few practitioners in the UK, and even less in the way of training, so I mostly had to go abroad for courses. I established my current practice, first as York Biofeedback Centre, in 2005.

I had also invested in professional grade biofeedback equipment and software, but even though it was much more powerful than the consumer products I'd started with, I still felt there was a lot of untapped potential. HRV biofeedback in particular seemed to offer a depth and richness that the software didn't fully bring out. Having been a programmer in my early career, I began to tinker with creating my own customised software, and so began a process that years later produced a saleable product, Mind-Body Training Tools (available from my website). Actually in the beginning I wasn't thinking of marketing anything, but my intent was to create feedback I could use in the context of meditation practice – indeed I still personally use the software on an almost-daily basis.

In my professional practice I could see that I was helping my clients with weekly sessions of biofeedback, but I knew they could benefit more with more consistent practice in their own time. I began renting out simple devices along with my Mind-Body Training Tools. I taught them to practise mindful awareness while using the device, just as I was doing for myself at home.

The idea for this book first came out of the limitation of being located in one city. Only clients who could come to my office and pay for sessions were benefiting from what I had to say. Clients who rented from a distance didn't get the best out of biofeedback because they didn't appreciate how to approach it.

I developed a programme for my clients including those at a distance consisting of (i) online video teaching material, (ii) biofeedback device rental (for home training), and (iii) one-to-one coaching. Please visit my website (*www.stressresilientmind.co.uk*) for further information on the services I offer.

The book forms a useful preparation or background reading for the programme, but that said, it's certainly not intended as a sales pitch for my services, and I hope many more people besides my clients can benefit from it.

1.6 Summary of Key Points

- The three core domains of mind-body intelligence are (i) emotional balance and resilience, (ii) energy, drive and motivation, and (iii) attention, focus and concentration.
- Three underlying dynamics of self-control challenges are (i) inner conflict, (ii) inaccessible resources, and (iii) lack of self-awareness.
- The mind-body principle is the idea that subjective experience is reflected in (body and brain) physiology, and vice versa.
- Self-regulation goes beyond the exercise of conscious rational choice or volition.
- Flow states are peak experiences characterised by intense, clear focus, absorption and effortlessness. In a sense they are the epitome of self-control but aren't about conscious choice.
- Self-regulation creates *integration*, in which energy and information flow coherently and harmoniously. The opposites of integration are chaos and rigidity.
- Self-control is a hierarchical skill-set founded on mind-body regulation.
- Mind-body intelligence can be developed through training and exercise.
- There is no one optimal mind-body state, but rather the goal is flexibility, or the ability to adapt to meet the needs of the present context.
- Key tools are mindfulness and biofeedback, which mutually support each other.

Part 1

Foundations of the Mind-Body Connection

2 What Is the Mind?

2.1 Introduction

We're exploring the project of how to manage your mind more effectively, and we've seen that means managing emotions, desires, motivation, attention and thinking. In this chapter we'll lay some foundations for developing the concepts of self-regulation and mind-body intelligence more fully.

'Mind' is one of those words that is very hard to pin down to a succinct definition, but that everyone more or less knows what it means anyway. My intention is to be pragmatic – I won't attempt a definition but will simply touch upon a few aspects of mind:

i. mental contents
ii. appetites, needs and motivation
iii. faculties.

2.2 Mental Contents

Mental contents are what we can be aware of. The main types are:

- Sense perceptions – the process of seeing, hearing, smelling, tasting and feeling things – either things in the external world or internally generated (imagined) perceptions – mental "images". Examples include an image of your front door and the sound of the sea shore.

- Feelings and sensations – sensations are perceptions of the body – for example a tingle in the foot or the sun on my skin. Feelings are similar but are more vague, less tangible, perhaps more metaphorical in nature – for example a feeling of warmth or expansiveness in the heart. I'm using the word differently from 'emotion', which I'll cover later.
- Memories – these are stored sensations, perceptions or feelings that can in some sense be "replayed".
- Impulses or urges to act – for example the urge to light a cigarette or to stretch my legs.
- Thoughts – in this book I use 'thought' to refer to a mental process taking the form of words (internal dialogue). Thoughts have a content that might be true or false. Examples are, "people will think I'm stupid" or "applying for the job is a waste of time". Thoughts can be subtle, or less clearly inner dialogue. I'm not including mental images – they would be internal sense perceptions – though clearly mental images can often accompany thoughts.
- Beliefs – these are thoughts we feel to be true and are likely to recur frequently in the mind, such as "I'm not very intelligent" (an example of a negative or unhelpful belief). Some beliefs operate as (perhaps unconscious) assumptions about the world, ourselves and other people, and so condition how we perceive things (they work like attentional filters).
- Emotions – these are rather complex and composite things, and get their own section (section 2.5 below).

2.2.1 Pleasure and Pain

Anything that is sensed can have the quality of being either pleasant / pleasurable or unpleasant / painful. These are two fundamentals of inner life, that don't need definition. Think of them as qualities of sensations (or even thoughts and ideas) rather than as things in their own right.

2.3   Appetites, Desires and Motivation

Here I'm including:
- basic physiological appetites and drives such as hunger, thirst, keeping warm and sex drive
- more complex social needs such as the need for human contact, (both physical and emotional) and the need to be challenged or stimulated.

Desire and motivation are related; both tend to move us toward action. Perhaps the difference is that motivation has a stronger connotation of action or movement than desire, which is more about subjective feeling. Motivation is more internally driven, while in desire we are pulled from the outside.

Desire and motivation are intrinsically connected to pleasure and pain, but at the same time distinct from them. Anything that holds out the promise of future pleasure or feeling good, tends to kindle desire. Similarly we desire to avoid pain. As we'll see in the next chapter, pleasure and desire have distinct biological substrates.

Things that we crave don't necessarily deliver on their promise of pleasure. Conversely it's possible to feel pleasure and yet remain free of desire and craving.

2.3.1   Volition

Inner life encompasses things we do and things that just happen. The experience of volition or choice is intrinsic to the human mind, but philosophically it's a very slippery concept. Generally we choose to do things we want to do, but we didn't choose to want them in the first place, so did we really choose? Yet the experience of free-will seems to be undeniable. In this book we'll stick to the practical issues, such as the problem of conflicting motivations.

2.3.2 Energy

Energy (in the sense of mental energy) is a rather vague concept. When we speak of having energy, we usually mean we have the motivation to act, and to sustain activity in the pursuit of goals. It can also mean the experience of positive emotion, but that's also quite a vague concept (covered in section 2.5 below).

2.4 Faculties

Faculties are our internal tools and means by which we do things, achieve things. We can use our faculties to influence our own mental contents. Again I'm not going to attempt any definitions, just list some examples. The following is by no means a complete list.

- Imagination – the ability to bring to mind what is not immediately present, through either the senses or through thought. The ability to conceive of change.
- Attention or focus – meaning directed awareness. It's the ability to maintain our focus stably on a content of our choosing, and to flexibly shift focus when appropriate.
- Empathy – the ability to put ourselves in the position of someone else and imagine what it's like to be them – what they want, expect and intend. This is a key aspect of social intelligence.
- Executive function – this is a psychological term that includes the ability to formulate goals (intentions), to plan how to achieve them, and to stick to plans in the face of distracting influences.
- Physiological self-regulation – the ability to appropriately adjust physiological arousal level, for example to calm down when it's time for bed and rouse yourself again next morning when you need to get up.
- Self-restraint – the ability to resist or not act upon every little impulse that comes to mind, or express outwardly emotions that we feel inside.

- Distress tolerance – the ability to remain self-possessed and function effectively in the face of painful or unpleasant experiences, e.g. you can sit calmly while the dentist gives you a filling.

2.5   Emotion

Emotions are complex entities. Essentially they are responses to events or perceptions, that evolved to serve some purpose. They predispose us to act in certain ways and also prepare our bodies accordingly. For example fear serves the purpose of keeping us out of harm's way, and primes us to fight, flee or freeze.

Emotion has been studied extensively in recent years. Anthropologists believe that basic emotions are universal to all cultures (and even animals)[6]. A lists of primary emotions usually includes: fear, anger, sadness, joy (or happiness), surprise, disgust. Secondary emotions are more complex, having a more cognitive component, and are usually social in nature – for example guilt, gratitude or envy. They may be specialisations of primary emotion – e.g. contempt is a kind of disgust. There are lots of secondary emotions.

We speak of positive and negative emotions, but what makes an emotion positive or negative? Negative emotions tend to feel bad or painful – examples are anxiety and fear, anger, frustration, hatred – but it's not always clear that's what makes them negative – for example remorse or grief feel bad but aren't negative from a moral perspective. I will use 'negative emotion' to mean emotions that are destructive, harmful, unhelpful or inappropriate to either self or other, with the understanding that any particular emotion like anger isn't universally negative in this sense – sometimes anger, fear, etc. is appropriate (after all, negative emotions too evolved to serve some function such as keeping us safe).

Positive and negative emotions aren't simply opposites of each other, they are distinct processes underlain by distinct biology as we shall see in chapter three.

A related distinction is between "approach" and "withdrawal" emotions. Most of the positive (or feel-good) emotions help us become more outward-going (especially in the social sense), while most of the negative emotions are associated with avoidance or withdrawal (e.g. anxiety, sadness). Anger is an exception – it is more of an approach emotion.

The words 'emotion' and 'feeling' are often used synonymously, but I think it's useful to draw a distinction: emotion is an active response or set of responses while feeling is the perception or sensation of those responses[7]. We'll return to this in the next chapter.

2.5.1   Components of Emotion

Bodily Responses

Emotional triggers entail physiological changes. For example in fear: heart pounding, sweating, blanching, muscles tightening or developing tremor, breathing feeling short and rapid and tight. Or an embarrassing situation may trigger blushing.

Facial Expressions

A particular kind of body response is facial expression. Primary emotions especially have their own characteristic facial responses, which are easily recognisable, even across cultures. A smile indicates joy, while a frown suggests frustration or anger. Secondary emotions too involve facial expression.

Body Posture or "Body Language"

In disappointment and despair we slump and cast our gaze downwards, maybe cramping up our chest. In joy we can be (literally) uplifted, and we open out. In a similar way emotions change how we move about. When we're low we tend to move less, or our gait may be sluggish and laboured while in positive moods we are sprightly.

Thinking

Often people recognise their own emotions by a tendency to think in certain ways, firstly along certain lines of content, and secondly in particular styles. In anger the content is e.g. that someone has done something against us, and how to get back at them. The style tends to be quick or "staccato", and black-and-white. In sadness, we think about what we have lost, in a slow and perhaps repetitive way.

Motivation and Action

Emotions typically move us to act and behave in certain ways. In anger we may yell or even hit out physically. In sadness we may cry, and stay at home (a behaviour taking the form of inaction). In fear we may either flee or freeze. Love moves us to do caring things. Gratitude moves us to help other people in turn.

Attention or focus

When we become emotional we tend to focus in certain ways – again in terms of both style and content. For example in anxiety we focus on what can go wrong, or signs of anxiety in the body, often in a very narrow or tunnel-vision sort of way. In sadness and despair our focus is withdrawn, often internal, often in the past.

Conversely positive emotions direct our focus outward and broaden it, enabling us to see the bigger picture, both conceptually and literally. Research shows we literally take more in – our peripheral perception is heightened[8].

2.5.2 Timescales

Emotions in and of themselves are responses to stimuli and as such they are brief in duration. Think of a phobic response for example – you can go from zero to sixty (in terms of arousal level) in a split-second. Calming down again takes longer, but is still often just a matter of seconds or minutes.

Sometimes emotions appear to last longer, because we have a recurring experience of them, and we infer that the emotion was there all along. (Sometimes when you're going round in circles it can look as though you're stuck in one place.) Take anxiety, for example – suppose you're worried about a presentation you have to give next week. Every so often a thought pops into your head reminding you about it, and it brings with it an emotional reaction. But you manage to distract yourself – only for the thought to return later. Sometimes people say they "have" anxiety of they "have" depression – as though they are carrying it around with them. This way of thinking can distort the nature of emotions as processes. In reality our emotional experience is constantly changing.

However it's also true to say we have "background" states that have an emotional quality. We can them moods. Being in a positive mood means that you're more likely to experience positive emotional responses to events (e.g. someone smiles at you – you appreciate it and smile back – whereas in a bad mood you might hardly even notice it). You're also more likely to be outwardly and broadly focused.

When background emotional states are really stable we call them temperament or disposition (as in "sunny disposition").

Overall, it's important to recognise the constantly changing nature of emotional states. Knowing this, and knowing that emotional responses, left to their own devices, will start to fade away quite quickly, is an important aspect of emotional intelligence.

2.5.3 Circumplex Model of Emotion

The circumplex model of emotion, first developed by James Russell[9], views emotion in terms of a two dimensional map, defined by axes of arousal and valence as shown in figure 2.1. Valence is a term borrowed from chemistry to refer to the intrinsic attractiveness or aversiveness of emotions. Arousal means principally physiological arousal. Some emotions, such as panic, are highly aroused – they come with racing or pounding heart, rapid breathing, taught muscles, etc. – while others such as serenity are quieter.

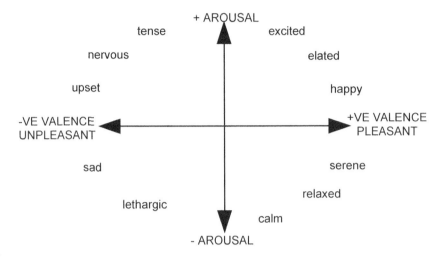

Figure 2.1 Circumplex model of emotion – clearly not all emotions are shown

Whilst it doesn't capture the whole nature of emotion, the model is useful in characterising particularly primary emotions, and particularly in their bodily aspect (the mind-body connection again). A practical application of the model immediately presents itself: if we know how to change physiological arousal, we have a way of changing emotion – both those already arisen and those which might arise. A weakness of the model is that a single dimension for arousal is too simplistic for capturing the breadth of emotional experience. Serenity for example is shown as having slightly negative arousal (as it is in terms of its bodily expression) but it may at the same time be intensely and vividly awake, which is in some sense a kind of brain arousal. We'll return to this topic in chapter three.

2.5.4   Positive Emotion

What makes an emotion positive? If emotions evolved to perform some function (for example fear keeping us from harm), what do positive emotions do?

It turns out positive emotions are more than just pleasurable. Positive psychology researcher Barbara Fredrickson has proposed a "broaden and build" theory: positive emotions broaden our senses and our thinking[10]. As I mentioned earlier, her work shows that in a positive emotional state we literally take more in – our peripheral perception is heightened. The open mindset of positive emotion leads to outward-going behaviours that build skills and resources. Joy brings out creativity and playfulness, love and gratitude help us to build strong relationships. Curiosity leads to exploration and discovery.

In her book, "Positivity", Fredrickson presents a list of ten emotions which cover the spectrum of positive emotional states. They are:

- love
- gratitude
- interest
- joy
- hope

- amusement
- pride
- inspiration
- awe
- serenity

I think Fredrickson's list does a pretty good job of covering the spectrum of positive emotions. There are clearly other positive emotional words but most are a close variant of something already on the list – for example curiosity is a form of interest. Others are more like combinations – one such is enthusiasm, or anticipatory enthusiasm. This seems to combine elements of hope, interest and desire (in the more psychological sense of drive or motivation).

Looking at this list in light of the circumplex model, we can see that some are in a sense more "activated" or engaged or aroused states, while others are less so. Serenity is peaceful and calm (low arousal), while interest is more energetic. Inspiration is similar to awe in that they are triggered by impressiveness, but inspiration moves us to action (i.e. is arousing) while awe stops us in our tracks.

Confidence

Confidence is undoubtedly one of the most important and valuable inner resources. Lots of people suffer from lack of it. Yet it's not on Fredrickson's list. Should it be? Does it count as an emotion?

I think confidence very much has an emotional tone, but is not a pure emotion. Having confidence entails a cognitive appraisal of your capabilities in any given context, or perhaps of someone else's capabilities. Confidence is a knowing as much as a feeling. The word isn't really meaningful taken out of context. I'm confident I can drive home after work. I'm not confident I can win Wimbledon. When my clients speak of lack of confidence, the first thing is to ascertain confidence in doing what exactly?

On the feeling side, confidence connotes feeling safe, secure. Curiously there doesn't seem to be a word for the emotion of feeling safe, protected, nurtured, soothed. I'm not just talking about absence of threat here – in chapter three, where we explore the nature of the mind-body connection in more detail, we'll see that there is a definite physiology that's not just the absence of threat.

2.5.5 Negativity Bias

Positive and negative emotions are really quite different fish. They aren't simply opposites. Positive emotions involve less dramatic physiological changes, and negative emotions seem to be more easily triggered. This latter pattern is an aspect of negativity bias – the tendency for human experience to be more often negatively tinged than positive[11]. For example we're more likely to notice negative stimuli than positive, and we remember negative emotions more easily than positive. Furthermore we tend to be more motivated to avoid the negative than to experience the positive. Negativity bias makes sense in the light of evolution, where one missed danger signal is often fatal – rather more consequential than a missed opportunity for positivity. Even so it isn't universally true, or doesn't have to be. With training we can shift the balance.

2.5.6   Emotional Needs

Again, emotions evolved to serve some function – in general, to move us to meet our needs. Besides our basic physical needs, we have needs that are more psychological. Negative emotions arise when these needs aren't met, and positive emotions arise when we do meet them, or have an opportunity to meet them. Here is my version of a fairly comprehensive list of psychological needs:

1. Safety, security
2. Autonomy, control, freedom of choice
3. Stimulation and challenge – opportunity to learn and develop, and contexts for experiencing flow.
4. Sense of competence / achievement – growing out of 3 above
5. Social connection – having these elements:
   - giving and receiving attention
   - giving and receiving affection
   - understanding and acceptance (warts and all)
   - sense of belonging (to a family or community) – feeling part of something greater than yourself
   - having status and respect – being valued within the group.

2.5.7   Positive Emotions and Values

Does kindness count as a positive emotion? Does trust? What about honesty? They're not on Fredrickson's list, and I think the reason is that they're best described as values, or virtues, or even character strengths. A value is something you aspire to live your life by, and act on the basis of, even at times when you don't feel like it. You can express kindness, trust and honesty in what you do, even when you don't feel very positive emotionally. Certainly values and positive emotions are connected, and you can usually expect that acting on the basis of your values (e.g. being kind) will engender positive emotions. Gratitude by contrast is a response to another person's actions – you can't just decide to "do" gratitude.

Values don't have to be particularly virtuous. Values are just what matters to us, and don't require any justification (indeed it's important not to be judgemental about your own or anyone else's values). For example, financial security and receiving affection are values you may not be particularly proud of, but note they both relate to the needs we listed in section 2.5.6 above.

2.5.8   Emotional Resilience

Research shows that what counts in life is emotional resilience or "bounce-backability". No-one can avoid negative emotions like anxiety and anger – they are natural responses to set-backs not pathological processes. But successful people can quickly turn negative emotional experience into positive, so that positive emotions far out-weigh the negative. Positive emotions can quickly reverse the physiological changes associated with destructive emotions. Fredrickson's research suggests that a ratio of at least three to one is something of a tipping point – at this ratio and above, people really thrive and flourish in life, as opposed to merely coping[12].

Emotional resilience is a key part of mind-body intelligence, and is itself a composite of two core skills: firstly, the ability to let go of destructive and painful emotions, and secondly the ability to rapidly and reliably access positive emotions.

2.6   Summary of Key Points

- Mind as a term is difficult to define but covers (i) mental contents such as thoughts and images, (ii) appetites, drives and motivation, and (iii) faculties, or abilities to alter mental contents or our relationship to them.
- Emotion is a complex, composite term covering bodily responses, ways of thinking, ways of paying attention, and impulses to act.

- The circumplex model characterises different emotions in terms of two dimensions, arousal and valence.
- Positive emotions broaden our senses and our perspective, and build psychological and social resources and skills.
- Resilience is the ability to quickly let go of negative emotions and access positive emotions.

3 Biology of the Mind-Body Connection

3.1 Introduction

We've seen that an understanding of the mind-body connection is essential to our project of developing the skill-set of self-regulation. In this chapter we'll look at what science has to tell us about the mind-body relationship. Much useful information has been discovered in recent years particularly in the field of the neuroscience of emotion. My account draws heavily on the work of Antonio Damasio[13], one of the foremost figures in the field.

3.2 Self-regulation and Emotion

As Darwin first demonstrated[14], animals show emotion. Emotions *evolved* to serve functions. Any account of emotion needs to be rooted in an evolutionary context. Damasio sees emotion as a development of *homoeostasis* – this is the idea that all organisms act to keep their physiological state within healthy bounds. If I'm thirsty I will drink to take on fluid. If I'm too hot or too cold, my body can tighten and relax small muscles in the blood vessels in the skin to adjust blood flow, thus increasing or decreasing heat loss. All this happens quite automatically, just as similar processes happen in primitive organisms.

Emotion is homoeostasis extended to the psychological and social levels. Just as the body automatically regulates its physiological parameters to keep us alive, the brain creates emotional responses to keep us within healthy psychological bounds – e.g. fear stops me yelling at my boss and getting myself the sack. Anger stops me being exploited.

Damasio posits a hierarchy of regulatory mechanisms: at the lowest level simple reflexes and immune responses; at the next level pain and pleasure responses; then drives and appetites such as hunger and libido; at the highest levels primary emotions and secondary emotions.

Emotions are built out of the same physiological mechanisms as lower level homoeostasis. Let's take another example of a homoeostatically controlled parameter: blood pressure. If the body detects that blood pressure is too high or too low, it can act to bring it back into balance. The heart can beat more or less forcefully, and tiny muscles in the walls of blood vessels can tighten or loosen. When you stand up, the body increases blood pressure momentarily – if it didn't, your blood would wash downwards and you'd feel light-headed due to lack of blood in the head.

Emotions effect similar changes in physiology. In fear, the heart can lurch or pound, and we can blanch or blush as the blood flow in the face changes, mediated by the same muscles in blood vessel walls. Fear can make your hands sweat, just as being too hot does.

3.2.1 Homoeostasis and Feedback

Many of the examples of homoeostatic regulation that I've just mentioned involve feedback control. In a feedback system, information about the effects of what the system just did is used to adjust what the system does next. A very basic example is a central heating system, which has two parts, a thermostat and a boiler. When the thermostat detects that the current temperature is too cold (i.e. below target), the boiler is turned on. When the thermostat detects the temperature is now good, the system turns off the boiler.

Feedback systems abound in biology. An example: you become dehydrated, and your system detects this and increases your thirst which moves you to take on fluid. As you take on fluid, your thirst is slaked, meaning that the system has detected the correction in hydration level, and in consequence turned off thirst.

In general terms a feedback system requires two components:

i. a means of *monitoring* the current state of affairs (in relation to some goal state)
ii. a means of *adjusting* or *effecting change*, to reduce the gap between current state and goal state.

These two functions essentially form a *feedback loop:* the monitoring system detects the effects of the change system's actions, and thus the last output forms the next input, and so on.

Self-correcting Versus Self-reinforcing Feedback

In many feedback loops, the system acts to reduce the gap between the detected state and the goal state – as in the central heating and thirst examples. This is self-correcting feedback, sometimes known as negative feedback. Elsewhere the feedback serves to create more of the behaviour that produced it. An example: suppose your child does something you like, such as he acts generously towards his sister. So you reward him with encouragement. Hopefully the result is, he does more of it. (Another example of negative feedback would be punishing your child for doing things you don't want e.g. hitting his sister).

Feedback and Learning

If you think about it, feedback plays a huge part in our lives. When you learn any skill, you rely on feedback. Take tennis as an example: you play a shot, and you can see and feel whether you mistimed it or hit it into the net or out of the back of the court, etc. – that's feedback. Gradually you learn to reduce the gap between where you are and where you want to be.

In this light we can see that using biofeedback isn't a radical departure from the normal way of things – it just gives you a bit of extra help in cases where the "natural" feedback is lacking. In one sense it helps you to tune in to your internal feedback.

3.2.2 Homoeostasis Versus Allostasis

Allostasis is a kind of dynamic version of homoeostasis. Homoeostasis is the idea that the body maintains balance, or keeps physiology within healthy limits. Allostasis is the notion that the body adjusts physiology to most appropriately support what I'm trying to do currently. For example the body maintains blood pressure at a healthy level, but the actual level depends on what I'm doing – if I'm playing a tennis match, it's going to be a lot higher than when I'm sitting watching TV. Health is not just a single state but an ability to respond flexibly to demands.

Emotional life is a social and psychological allostasis rather than homoeostasis Emotions help us achieve goals. If I'm watching a horror film, it's a good idea to experience some fear, otherwise it's going to be a pretty boring film. If I want to have helpful and supportive friends it's a good idea to feel friendly towards others and act on the basis of it.

3.3   Three High-level Emotion Systems

How can we summarise in broad terms the functions that emotions play? What did emotions evolve to achieve?

All self-regulation systems in all organisms serve to furnish the organism with what it needs to thrive and grow (e.g. nutrients) while avoiding sources of harm (e.g. toxins, predators). Emotions fit this pattern. Firstly they help us acquire the resources we need to thrive, particularly *social* resources (humans are intensely social creatures) in the form of strong relationships. Secondly they keep us safe from danger, including psychological and social danger.

Psychologist Paul Gilbert in his book "The Compassionate Mind"[15] outlines three high-level regulation systems, rooted in physiology, in the light of which most emotions can be understood.

The first is the threat-detection and self-protection system. The emotions anger, disgust and fear can clearly be seen as part of this system. They increase physiological arousal (in preparation for action). In a way sadness can also be related to this system, insofar as it promotes withdrawal (from danger) and perhaps rest and recovery.

The second system is the incentive or resource-seeking system. This system motivates us to move outwardly to seek what we need, gives us the energy we need to do so, and rewards us when we are successful (or at least offers us the promise of reward). The basic physical resources we need are nourishment, warmth, shelter, safety. Psychological resources include skills and abilities (which we can learn from others, and which as children we acquire socially, often through play). Social resources include caring relationships, and respect and trust from other people.

The third system is the soothing and contentment system. This is harder to explain. Contentment is what we feel when our needs are met, and we don't have anything we desperately need to achieve. It allows us to rest, restore and rejuvenate. Soothing is what we need when we are distressed. As children we need it from others, and love is what moves parents, friends etc. to give it. As we grow older we learn the ability to sooth ourselves, to ease our own distress and suffering – depending on the quality of our parenting (not everyone develops these abilities to the same level).

Positive emotions come under the second and third systems. Recall Barbara Fredrickson's list from chapter two. Interest and hope are incentivising and resource-seeking. Gratitude helps build and maintain social resources (relationships) so is also linked to the resource-seeking system. Serenity is linked to the contentment system.

3.4   The Brain and Self-regulation

The brain can be seen as an enormously complex self-regulation system – it keeps us safely within our operating norms and helps us meet our goals, on all levels from basic physiology through to personal development.

To perform its functions of self-regulation or allostasis, the brain needs to monitor the current state of affairs and detect changes, and then effect adaptive responses – in other words the monitoring and adjusting functions we outlined in section 3.2. The brain has many feedback loops operating, for example the fear system, which:

- first detects threat or danger
- then moves us to avoid or reduce that danger
- then sees the danger has passed and deactivates the fear response.

3.4.1   Brain Input and Output

It's useful to think of the self-regulation process in terms of inputs and outputs. Inputs are needed to carry out the monitoring function while outputs are needed for the adjusting function. On the input side, we need to detect emotionally salient information in the external world (e.g. there's a spider on the wall, or my boss frowned when he read my report) and also imbalances in body state (e.g. I'm too hot).

Outputs range from the physiological (e.g. quickening of heart rate) to behavioural (e.g. lashing out with fists).

Note that (emotional) outputs are often automatic and non-volitional. Inputs also can be below the threshold of consciousness awareness.

3.4.2   Feeling Versus Emotion

Damasio makes a useful distinction between two words commonly used as synonyms: feelings and emotions. (I mentioned this in the chapter two.) In Damasio's thinking, emotions are sets of responses, or physiological and behavioural actions (brain outputs), while feeling refers to the brain's detection or sensing of those responses (on the input side of the process). (Note this means that, perhaps counter-intuitively, the actual bodily changes come *before* the feelings.) In the brain, the two processes are relatively distinct, although some brain structures are involved in both.

3.4.3 Emotional Feedback Loops and Chain Reactions

When emotions work well, we can see them as self-correcting or negative feedback loops, meaning that the outputs (emotional responses) reduce the gap between current state of affairs and desired state of affairs, and perception of this turns off the emotional response. The output is the basis of the next input, which then generates a new output, and so on.

However it's also possible to create a self-reinforcing feedback loop which can amplify emotion in a sort of chain-reaction. For example, as I begin my presentation I notice my heart is racing and I'm sweating. Realising I'm a little anxious, my attention is drawn to the feelings in my body, and then I forget what I was going to say next. In the embarrassing pause, I blush. I'm very self-conscious by now, and I believe my blushing will be perceived as evidence of incompetence, and that makes me feel even more anxious, and so on. This example is something of a vicious cycle, but it doesn't have to be like that. Effective skills of emotional self-regulation enable you to break out of the spiral.

3.4.4 Brain Structures

Figure 3.1 shows a schematic of emotion and feeling as a self-regulation process, showing some of the key brain structures involved. Output flows are shown on the left side, while input flows are shown on the right. You can see that many of the structures are involved in both emotion generation and feeling (perception of emotion)[16].

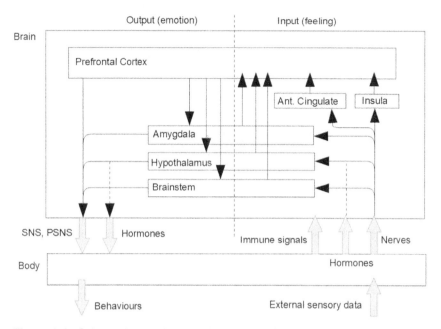

Figure 3.1 Schematic showing brain centres involved in emotion and feeling, and their inter-connections. SNS denotes the sympathetic nervous system and PSNS denotes parasympathetic nervous system.

Let's take a closer look at the roles these structures play.

Amygdala

This nucleus plays the role of look-out and trip-wire. It monitors incoming sensory information, looking out for threats and other emotionally salient material. When it detects a threat it stimulates other brain structures to bring forth a cascade of responses. (In other words it's part of Paul Gilbert's threat detection system.) More generally it tags experiences with emotional significance.

The amygdala's alarms can sometimes translate into rapid involuntarily reactions. I experienced this for myself some years ago. I was walking in some woods in California, chatting with a friend, when suddenly my heart seemed to skip a beat and I was stopped in my tracks. Looking down I saw a snake lying still across the track – I would have put my foot right on it. I had reacted before I even had time to realise what was going on. The amygdala had picked up the visual information before my conscious, rational cortex did, and initiated a fast, crude and automatic response, which overrode my planned behaviour.

The amygdala is pretty old from an evolutionary perspective, but still plays a role (albeit one that doesn't always serve us well).

Brain imaging studies show that in depressed and anxious people the amygdala over-reacts to negative stimuli[17].

Hypothalamus

A small structure near the base of the brain, the hypothalamus is an interface between brain and body. It has two halves, one of which executes the bodily changes triggered by signals from the amygdala, while the other half monitors the state of the body, for example it monitors blood sugar levels (which contribute to our feelings of hunger and even tiredness and fatigue). Besides emotion, the hypothalamus is involved in homoeostasis or regulation of the body's physical parameters (in keeping with Damasio's theory that emotion is a development of the biological machinery of self-regulation).

The hypothalamus outputs to the Autonomic Nervous System (see section 3.4.4 below), and in addition signals the pituitary gland which is located very close by. The pituitary secretes hormones into the blood stream – these are signalling molecules which are picked up elsewhere in the body. The pituitary has been dubbed the master gland because it influences many other glands in the body, including the adrenals and thyroid, which produce yet more hormones (covered in section 3.7.1 below). In reality the brain is the master gland.

Both the hypothalamus and amygdala are part of what is termed the brain's limbic system.

Autonomic Nervous System (ANS)

The ANS extends beyond the brain and is one of the brain's main interfaces to the body. It has two branches, known as the

Sympathetic Nervous System (SNS) and the Parasympathetic Nervous System (PSNS), which work like accelerator and brake in adjusting the body's arousal level.

- **Sympathetic Nervous System** – is the accelerator side of the ANS which revs the body up, preparing it for action. It's a major instigator of what's known as the "fight or flight" response – part of Paul Gilbert's self-protection system. Its effects overlap those of adrenalin (and indeed it actually controls the release of adrenalin). For example it speeds the heart, causes blood sugar levels to surge (which can make us feel wired) and ramps down digestive processes.
- **Parasympathetic Nervous System** – has the opposite action to the SNS, i.e. it calms the body. The PSNS mediates the "rest and digest" response – for example it slows heart rate and activates normal digestion. It plays a major role in Paul Gilbert's soothing system.

We'll take a more detailed look at the ANS in section 3.7.1 below.

Brainstem

The brainstem is evolutionarily the oldest, most primitive part of the brain and has lots of functions, most of them a form of biological house-keeping (keeping us alive). This role is entirely automatic, and although it profoundly influences our consciousness (e.g. it regulates the sleep-wake cycle) it does not require conscious awareness to do its job. Another example of a brainstem function is breathing regulation (covered in more detail in chapter four).

Several nuclei in the brainstem produce neurotransmitters (or more precisely neuromodulators[18]) such as serotonin, dopamine and noradrenalin[19]. These are chemicals which are distributed widely over the brain's cortex, and modulate its functioning, changing the way we feel and think. (The cortex is the more recently evolved outer layer of the brain, associated with "higher" functions.) Serotonin seems to play a role in mood or background emotional tone. Noradrenalin plays a role in heightening alertness, as does dopamine, which is additionally involved in the brain's reward system. Although largely automatic in its functioning, the brainstem does respond to triggers coming down from higher level brain structures. A squirt of dopamine for example may be triggered by the sight of something attractive, and rouses our attention, spurs us to action, gives is a promise of reward, makes us desire.

If you read popular literature you might be forgiven for thinking that neurotransmitters and other brain chemicals are the main story in the biology of emotion, and indeed they can have a profound influence, but they are just one component of a complex multilevel process.

Insula Cortex

For the brain to regulate the internal body state, it must receive information about what is actually happening (just as any self-regulation system needs a monitoring component). Many of the nerves coming from the body to the brain terminate at the insula cortex, and in particular those coming from the interior body or viscera. The insula thus creates a sort of map of the body's visceral state. It's involved in homoeostasis (described above) and in particular *feeling* – in Damasio's sense of the term as perceiving our own emotional state.

Brain imaging studies of emotional imbalance tend to highlight the insula, and moreover the practice of mindfulness (which involves training an expanded awareness of the body) has been shown to physically impact the insula (in meditators the insula is thicker and more active)[20].

The insula has strong reciprocal connections to the amygdala, and can inhibit reactivity in the amygdala, which is one possible mechanism by which mindfulness practice improves emotional balance.

Anterior Cingulate Cortex (ACC)

The ACC is another of the brain centres that Damasio assigns to the role of feeling (sensing of emotional state). Imaging studies show that it becomes active when people detect emotional cues (it is like a higher level version of the more primitive amygdala, and indeed like the insula it has strong connections to the amygdala).

The ACC is also involved in detection of pain (both emotional and physical). In one neurofeedback study (based on a brain imaging method called fMRI), subjects learned to turn down the activation level of the ACC, and in the process reduced their feeling of pain[21].

The ACC has also been shown to be involved in error detection. Brain imaging studies show a difference in the ACC of OCD (Obsessive Compulsive Disorder) sufferers compared to control subjects, and it's been theorised that in OCD the brain's error detection system can't be quieted (like a car alarm that's always going off).

The ACC is intimately connected with the prefrontal cortex (discussed next) and in the function of attention – brain imaging shows differences between ADHD (Attention Deficit Hyperactivity Disorder) patients and controls.

Prefrontal Cortex (PFC)

The PFC is in many ways the top of the tree in the brain – it's at the highest level in terms of information processing, and on the output side it functions as a sort of executive control centre. More highly evolved in humans than in any other species, the PFC endows us with our uniquely human abilities, traits and intelligences – a set of skills known in neuroscience as executive function, and including:

- Focus and concentration
- Emotional regulation and body regulation – balancing over-excitement and under-arousal
- Motivation and emotional drive – the ability to formulate values, goals and purposes

- Sense of self, and self-monitoring – being conscious of what you say and do, and knowing that it is appropriate
- Self-organisation – the ability make decisions, to formulate a considered plan of action, and to hold to it in the face of distractions, as well as to update it appropriately. The ability to check impulsiveness.
- Empathy – the ability to appreciate the minds of other people, and to understand how our own behaviour impinges upon them. Ultimately this is the basis of our moral awareness.

The PFC represents quite a large tranche of brain cortex and has several sub-divisions and sub-systems, which for simplicity I will leave out of the discussion.

The PFC receives input from most of the structures already listed. If the PFC is the chief executive then the anterior cingulate is like its PA, and is the gateway to the PFC, dictating what may grab the attention of the PFC. Another input connects the brainstem to the PFC, via an important centre called the nucleus accumbens. This dopamine pathway, known as the mesolimbic pathway, is like the PFC's power supply – dopamine rouses up the PFC from sleepiness to sharpness.

On the output side, the PFC has connections to many other brain regions, including the amygdala and other limbic structures. The PFC is able to dampen activity in these emotion-triggering centres, and can regulate the ANS. This is key to its role in emotional regulation.

The PFC enables us to *simulate experience* – we can for example simulate future scenarios and what they will be like, and this is the basis for decision-making and planning. In empathy we simulate the experience of other people. This is an important concept that we'll return to in section 3.5 below.

From a practical point of view, a well-functioning PFC is a key goal in our project of creating mind-body intelligence, because it is so intimately involved in attention, motivation and emotional regulation. Indeed, PFC functioning has been found to be compromised in several emotional and neurological disorders, including depression and ADHD. At the same time it's worth remembering that a well-functioning PFC is flexible, rather than stuck in the "on" position – research has shown that creativity is associated with the capacity for the PFC to step back and take the brakes off.[22]

Left-Right Balance

One of the foremost researchers into the neuroscience of emotion is Professor Richard Davidson. In his book "The Emotional Life of Your Brain" (co-authored with Sharon Begley)[23] he outlines six dimensions of what he calls "emotional style" – each dimension having a distinct neurophysiological basis. One of the six is emotional resilience, or the ability to recover quickly from emotional set-backs, which we first encountered in chapter two. A positive emotional resilience is measurable as a slight predominance of activity in the left side of the PFC, while a right side dominance goes with emotional negativity.

Actually this is a development of a well-established research finding: positive or "approach" emotions tend to tilt activity in favour of the left PFC while negative or "withdrawal" emotions shift the balance towards the right PFC.

Several therapies have been shown to shift the balance favourably, towards the left side, including mindfulness. Indeed some techniques, notably transcranial Direct Current Stimulation (tDCS)[24] but also some forms of neurofeedback, deliberately target this change, supposing it to be an actual mechanism for benefits.

Brain injuries that affect the PFC, as you might expect, tend to compromise executive function. The specific effects depend on which side is damaged,, with left side damage being less favourable to emotional well-being.

Emotional Outlook

Another of Davidson's six dimensions of emotional style is emotional outlook, which is a kind of emotional set-point. On one pole is negativity, pessimism, lack of drive and motivation, and at the other, optimism and outward-going positivity. Underlying this, according to Davidson, is the brain's ability to sustain activation of the PFC, mainly via the mesolimbic dopamine pathway (mentioned above). A positive set-point is characterised by sustained activation while in pessimistic people, although they still have an initial kindling of the PFC, the activation fades away relatively quickly.

From a practical point of view the key thing is that this aspect of PFC functioning can be trained or exercised to strengthen it using neurofeedback (see chapter ten).

Inhibition

Imagine you're at a busy networking event, straining to listen to the conversation amongst the two or thee people around you above the background noise of all the other conversations. To achieve this feat of attention, the brain must enhance the signal to noise ratio (to use an engineering analogy) – the signal is your conversation, the background noise is all the other conversations. The PFC has the ability to inhibit activity in some brain circuits while amplifying that in others. Actually this is a normal part of any attentional task. The nature of the brain is that its regions generate spontaneous activity. When resting, and even when sleeping, the brain doesn't shut itself down like a computer, rather it adopts a more disorganised, less globally coherent pattern of activity. Brain imaging studies show this activity in a set of regions collectively known as the default mode network (the PFC meanwhile has reduced activation). Subjectively it's experienced as day-dreaming, or directionless musing, or wandering internal dialogue. When we engage in purposeful behaviour or attention, the PFC suppresses this background activity, while enhancing functioning in those brain circuits involved in the task at hand. A well functioning PFC holds a tonic brake on much of the rest of the brain. A poorly functioning PFC has less of a grip, and its owner is subject to distraction, impulsiveness and random mind-chatter.

We've already alluded to a specific case of this inhibition – the PFC damps down activity in the emotion-triggering limbic structures. Another example is sitting still (for example, in meditation). Again the executive control must quieten the movement generating areas of the brain. In Attention Deficit Hyperactivity Disorder, this inhibition is weak. ADHD is actually more of a low energy state of the inhibiting PFC, more than an excess of brain activity, which explains why stimulating drugs such as ritalin work.

A more general example of PFC inhibition has been termed the "pause-and-plan" response, or more colloquially, stopping and thinking. Suppose you become aware that things aren't going too well (in whatever context). What's needed is to pause, take a step back, view things in a broader context and decide what (if anything) you need to change. To make a conscious choice we first need to pause the auto-pilot.

Psychologically, suppression has a bit of a bad name (it's associated with being blocked, "up-tight" and "anal") but it's actually an essential capability, a core component of mind-body intelligence. At the same time flexibility is the goal at a higher level – at times inhibition is desirable, at other times dis-inhibition is what's needed.

3.5   Simulator Mode

Earlier I described the PFC's capacity to generate *simulated* experience. In Damasio's thinking a key aspect of this is simulating emotion, by projecting out hypothetical or imagined scenarios and then taking in the feeling that results. In other words the brain's feeling centres activate in response to imagined scenarios – this is the somatic equivalent of mental imagery, where the brain's visual processing regions activate without any input from the eye.

We all know that just imagining an experience can trigger some of the same physiological responses as the real thing. I imagine biting into a fresh slice of lemon, and my mouth waters. I think about the presentation I've got to give next week, and I can have some of the anxiety here and now, ahead of the actual event.

Damasio thinks that the brain can simulate feelings without the actual body changes (again the equivalent of mental imagery). In practice I suspect there is at least a vestige of actual bodily change most of the time, but the main point is that emotional experience is essentially somatic – something to do with the body.

I see this as a fundamental feature of the mind. It's as though, for anything we can think of, a part of the brain asks, what would that be like? – and then the brain's emotional machinery gives us the answer.

3.5.1 Decision-making

Damasio first came to emotion via the study of what you might naively think of as the opposite: rational decision making. His research showed that people with a damaged prefrontal cortex had disturbed emotions. He also noted that they made very bad decisions, and yet at the same time had normal intellectual function. How could that be? He realised that real-life decision making depended on emotions just as much as reason.

When we make choices we simulate our emotional reactions to each alternative. Should I choose the steak and chips off the restaurant menu? My mouth starts to water when I contemplate it. But the idea of all that saturated fat gives me a bad feeling. And what will my friends think when they see I've given up on vegetarianism? Another bad feeling. I make the decision based on the relative weights of good and bad feeling. Logic is usually a relatively minor (and secondary) consideration. We tend to use logic and reason to justify to ourselves what we already want.

3.5.2 Simulating the Future

The brain uses its simulator mode again when we think about the future. This is important in planning because it enables us to make decisions ahead of time. When we think about the bad things that might happen, the bad feelings can help motivate us (shall I stay in bed an extra half hour? - I'll be late for work...)

But it can work against us if we're overly focused on what might go wrong. This is exactly what a lot of anxious people do. By simulating the future they can have all the anxiety ahead of time. (Fear of flying? How do you like the idea of going on holiday?)

3.5.3 Empathy

Empathy is the capacity to sense the emotional state of other people. It's a key aspect of emotional and particularly social intelligence. It's the ability to put yourself imaginatively in another person's shoes. In Damasio's account, the brain operates in "simulator mode" again, projecting out the proposition, "what if I were them", then sensing the result in the feeling centres. Brain imaging studies show that these same feeling centres, such as the insula, are indeed activated when we engage in empathy.

The brain contains a set of specialised neurons called "mirror neurons" which have been found to fire whenever we engage in a particular behaviour (such as drinking from a cup). They also fire when we see the same behaviour in another person. It's believed mirror neurons play a key role in empathy. Presumably they form part of the neural machinery of "simulator mode"[25].

3.6   The Biology of Desire and Craving

For most people, eating a piece of chocolate gives us a pleasant sensation, followed by a sense of "do that again!". If not chocolate, you'll be able to think of something else that has the same effect. The experience is inducing a squirt of dopamine in the mesolimbic pathway (connecting brainstem and PFC). Dopamine makes us feel alert, captivated, gives us a buzz of anticipation[26].

When dopamine was first discovered in the laboratory, it was found rats would do anything to get a squirt of dopamine – preferring it to pretty much anything. The researchers assumed it must therefore be the chemical mediator of pleasure, but it proved to be more complex. Rather, dopamine is the brain chemical of desire, not pleasure. It offers the *promise* of satisfaction, not satisfaction itself. It says to us, "do that again, because something good is coming". (Actually, it primes or sensitises the brain's pleasure systems.) It's the feeling that a gambler gets when the roulette wheel spins. (It may be worth adding that dopamine release triggers a stress response, so the buzz has an edge to it.) This dopamine pathway is part of Paul Gilbert's incentive system. It's no accident that most substances that are considered addictive (cocaine, for example) stimulate it.

Conversely, blocking dopamine's action tends to reduce desire. Drugs that do this are called dopamine antagonists, and they're used to treat for example mania and hypersexuality. (Just to prove that desire can't simply be reduced to a brain chemical, these drugs can actually stimulate appetite.)

It's believed that dopamine dysregulation may underlie certain mental health disorders that feature lack of drive and motivation (e.g. depression).

Returning to pleasure – another class of chemicals was found to be more directly associated with pleasure – these are the endorphins and enkephalins. Drugs such as morphine and heroin that act on the brain in the same way as endorphins produce feelings of euphoria, and reduce pain. The feeling is described as warm, relaxed and contented, as opposed to the edgy excitement of cocaine.

The important practical consideration is this: we should not confuse the good feeling that dopamine brings of pleasurable anticipation, the promise of reward, with the contented, relaxed release of satisfaction. Dopamine may not actually deliver on its promise, as most addicts know in their hearts.

3.6.1   The Overlap Between Emotion and Physiological Regulation

We've already discussed Damasio's idea that emotion is built on top of the brain's machinery for homoeostasis and physiological regulation (including appetites, aversions, drives). I gave the example of blood flow changes mediating both temperature control and emotions such as anxiety. Blood sugar control is another example of overlap. Sensing low blood sugar can trigger feelings of hunger. High blood sugar can trigger the *feeling* of anxiety (remember feeling is the *perception* of bodily changes triggered in the process of emotion). Actually anxiety as an emotional response can generate rises in blood sugar.

This complex interconnectedness between feeling, emotion and physiological regulation explains why it's quite easy to make mistakes and get confused. Raised blood sugar may be triggered either by eating, or by anxiety as an emotional response to threat. In either case it can *feel* like anxiety. A racing heart feels like fear, and physical fatigue may feel like sadness or depression. But they may not be.

Conversely emotions can trigger desires and cravings that would be more appropriate as responses to non-emotional cues. This is just what happens in "comfort eating". We experience a painful emotion such as loneliness, and perhaps not recognising it for what it is, we try to blot it out with the promise of future pleasant feelings (otherwise known as craving). Eating can of course give rise to pleasurable sensations, but it isn't an effective response to negative emotion – for that you need to access positive emotion.

Is Fatigue an Emotion?

We might intuitively feel that fatigue isn't an emotion but rather the feeling of a real physical state of low energy, perhaps in the muscles in the case of exercise-related fatigue. But there's evidence that the brain creates the feeling of fatigue in response to the *prediction* of low energy rather than an actual low energy. This makes fatigue more akin to an emotion.

The brain's feeling centres (which sense emotional responses in the body) also sense the body state in other ways – they're involved in allostasis. They can sense for example *falling* blood sugar levels, and even though blood sugar may not be particularly low, the brain responds by conserving energy, and by creating feelings that will get us to conserve energy[27].

As an aside, your blood sugar level is one of the most important factors in emotional regulation, as well as energy, motivation and appetite regulation. All the more reason to get it right by eating a healthy diet – but that's getting beyond the scope of this book.

3.7   The Biology of Arousal

Arousal is the process of summoning up or heightening energy or awareness. Actually there are a number of different senses of the word, which it would be useful to differentiate.

We've encountered the idea of arousal in the circumplex model of emotion (chapter two) – it's one of the two coordinate axes (the other being emotional valence) that define or differentiate emotions. The idea is that emotions can be positioned along a spectrum from low arousal (e.g. sadness, boredom, serenity) to high passion (e.g. fury, panic, rapture). In this context arousal seems to connote physical activation or energy level of the body. We also use the word to refer to degree of alertness or awakeness, or intensity of awareness – as when we are roused from sleep. Consider peak meditation states: there is physical and emotional stillness, tranquillity and serenity, at the same time as intense and vivid awareness or awakeness, perhaps also heightened positive emotions such as compassion and love.

So at a broad level it seems it would be useful to distinguish physiological or bodily arousal from what we might loosely term "brain arousal". In states of high physiological arousal the body is active, energised, or at least prepared for action. It consumes energy – even if relatively immobile – for example the heart beats strongly and rapidly.

Let's consider in more detail what these two concepts – physiological arousal and neurophysiological (brain) arousal – actually mean[28].

3.7.1   Physiological Arousal

The brain sends messages to the body via at least three channels: the Autonomic Nervous System (ANS), the somatic nervous system, and neuroendocrine (hormonal) system. In turn the body sends information back to the brain via both nerves and hormones, forming complex feedback loops (meaning that the outgoing signals are adjusted based on the incoming signals).

The Somatic Nervous System

The somatic nerves control the skeletal muscles (while the viscera are controlled by the ANS). That means movements of the arms, legs, head etc. – which are in large part volitional. Somatic nerve signals mostly originate in the outer part of the brain, the neocortex, which is considered the seat of the rational, thinking, conscious part of us. That doesn't mean that all skeletal muscle activity is voluntary or willed. The muscles of the face are obviously involved in the expression of emotion, and so are at best partially volitional. We all know the difference between a genuine smile (a Duchenne smile) and a put-on smile (sometimes called a Pan Am or Botox smile). In the former, muscles around the eyes are involved, raising the cheeks and corners of the eyes.

Emotions are expressed through the body too – we call it body language. For example, sad or depressed people tend to be slumped, heads looking downwards. Anxious people tend to be tight in the arms and shoulders.

The somatic nervous system also controls breathing. Breathing is most of the time automatic (control originates in the brainstem) yet we also have some conscious control over it. Breathing is also expressive of emotion. Breathing is such an important topic that it gets its own chapter – chapter four.

The Autonomic Nervous System

We've already encountered the ANS as one of the major effector systems in emotion. The ANS isn't exclusively an emotional system – it controls or influences many (though not all) of the automatic "visceral" functions of the body, as part of normal "house-keeping" or homoeostasis. For example it can speed up and slow down heart rate. We don't have conscious control over these functions, except perhaps indirectly, but that doesn't mean to say that all the body's automatic functions are autonomically controlled – breathing for example is mainly regulated via the somatic nervous system (though the ANS has some influence).

As we've seen, emotions piggy-back on the machinery of self-regulation – so for example anxiety can trigger increased heart rate via the ANS.

The old model of the ANS was that the two branches, sympathetic and parasympathetic, were like the two arms of a set of scales – when one goes up the other goes down. When the sympathetic arm is more dominant we are aroused, and when the parasympathetic arm is dominant we're relaxed. Furthermore, it was thought that autonomic activation was global and non-specific (i.e. more or less the same bodily effect whether you were feeling anger or fear).

In recent years a richer understanding of the ANS has emerged. Some evidence suggests that the ANS can be quite specific in its activity – for example both anger and fear involve sympathetic nervous system activity but having different specific effects – anger triggers a more significant rise in blood pressure for instance[29]. Moreover some emotions may involve both sympathetic and parasympathetic activations at the same time.

Polyvagal Theory

Polyvagal theory, proposed by Professor Stephen Porges[30], is a new view of the global organisation of the ANS. Porges's theory grew from a set of anomalies in the old arousal-balance model of the ANS. One such inconsistency was the finding that while the parasympathetic nervous system is responsible for the relaxation response, in some circumstances it seems to control a defensive reaction to threat that takes the form of outward freezing and inward slow-down of metabolism. Animals are observed to show this survival response, and it's interpreted as feigning death. It's also known that some species can shut down their metabolism to a bare minimum in times of scarcity.

Polyvagal theory proposes a threefold division of the ANS. The three branches form a hierarchy, each level having arisen separately in evolution, and the higher levels supervening over the lower. The three are anatomically distinct as well, traceable to different nuclei in the brainstem.

The name of the theory derives from the vagus nerve, which carries parasympathetic stimulation from the brain to many parts of the body. (It also carries information back the other way, but we're only concerned with the output side of the system here.) Vagal stimulation is found to originate from two different brain nuclei – thus two of the three levels are "vagal" (the third is the sympathetic nervous system). Let's look at the three levels in turn.

The Old Vagal System – the Immobilisation Response

At the bottom of the hierarchy, and phylogenetically the oldest, is the old vagal system, which effects the freeze response I alluded to earlier. It is an ancient survival response, still present in mammals and humans, and works by shutting down body systems. It may actually be quite dangerous in humans, because since the origin of the old vagal system the brain has evolved to be much more critically dependent on oxygen, and an unmitigated old vagal shut-down could deprive brain cells of oxygen to the point that they die. Professor Porges speculates that something like this may be happening in cases of cot death, now known as sudden infant death syndrome. The old vagal system may also be at play in post-traumatic stress disorder (PTSD).

Sympathetic Nervous System – the Mobilisation Response

At the intermediate level, the phylogenetically newer mobilisation response over-rides the old vagal response, and is mediated through the sympathetic nervous system. It increases arousal – as we've said before it mediates the fight-or-flight response, or puts us in a state of readiness for action, mentally and physically.

The New Vagal System

At the top level is the new vagal system – perhaps the most interesting and the most human of the three. Originating in a distinct brain nucleus called the nucleus ambiguus, its nerves differ from the old vagal system's in being myelinated (covered with an insulating layer) and so carry signals faster. It modulates the sympathetic nervous system, or in other words suppresses the hyper-vigilant wariness and defensiveness.

The new vagal system evolved to enable mammals (and humans in particular) to engage in a new way of behaving: socialising. The problem with sympathetic mode is that it is defensive, competitive, even aggressive, and gets in the way of the kind of social cooperation that is key to our success as a species. So the new vagal system suppresses sympathetic activity, while at the same time it promotes activation of our social systems. The muscles of the face come alive so that they can express all our positive social emotions like friendliness and compassion. Something similar happens with our voice – prosody or tonal expressiveness increases to enable richer social communication. Positive emotions are engaged, which as we've seen earlier, broaden our perspective both physically and psychologically, and move us towards social resource-building. Play is a good example of a new vagal activity – it develops social skills and social bonds.

So it makes sense that new vagal system engagement is reflected in activation of the prefrontal cortex (PFC)[31] which we've already met. The PFC plays a key role in our skills of socialisation, as well as focusing, decision-making, empathy, positive emotion and motivation. Psychologist Suzanne Segerstrom calls the set of changes mediated by the new vagal system the pause-and-plan response, which I think is a very apposite summary.

Heart Rate Variability

It happens that there is a way to measure new vagal system activity: via heart rate variability (HRV). HRV is a measure of how heart rate changes over time. The new vagal system drives a rhythm in heart rate, which sees heart rate increasing and decreasing in sync with the breath. This synchronisation is particularly interesting (we'll return to it in chapter four on breathing). Its technical name is respiratory sinus arrhythmia (RSA), and it's also known as heart coherence. It's possible to quantify RSA (and hence new vagal activity) from heart rate data – appendix A gives an account of the method.

In research, HRV is increasingly used as a biomarker for various different psychological constructs. For example, Dr Kelly McGonigal describes baseline HRV as a very good index of willpower, or reserve of willpower, and also of the pause-and-plan response[32]. Research shows that people with higher baseline HRV are better at resisting temptations, ignoring distractions, delaying gratification and dealing with stress.

Barbara Fredrickson (whose work on positive emotion we've already encountered) has done research showing that baseline HRV correlates with positive emotion, and that a nine-week programme of monitoring and reporting positive emotion and social connectedness led to increases in HRV in parallel with positive emotion and social connectedness[33].

Research also demonstrates that HRV correlates positively with executive function, working memory, focus and even reaction times, and negatively with anxiety, depression, loneliness, anger and weaker self-control.

Why should this be? At least part of the answer must be that HRV also correlates with activation of the PFC, the seat of executive control. A correlation is not the same as a causal link – but from a practical point of view using HRV as an index of self-control makes sense. HRV is a powerful parameter for biofeedback, as we'll see in chapter ten.

Neuroendocrine System

Everyone is familiar with the hormone adrenalin, and the so-called "adrenalin rush", which is the sudden increase in body arousal in response to things exciting, stressful or fearful. Adrenalin is produced in the adrenal glands (you have two of them) – actually in response to the sympathetic nervous system.

The adrenal glands produce numerous other hormones, many of which affect our emotional and mental functioning. One of the most important is cortisol. Cortisol is like a milder but longer-acting version of adrenalin – it stays in your system for hours rather than minutes. It helps you cope with stress and challenge, in part by making more energy available. Cortisol is secreted by the adrenals in response to another hormone, ACTH, which is produced by the pituitary gland, in turn stimulated by the hypothalamus (the brain region we've already encountered). The control system is known as HPA axis (after the three anatomical structures, hypothalamus, pituitary and adrenals). Cortisol levels are detected in the brain – high levels of it tend to dampen down the signal to produce more cortisol. (This is an example of a self-correcting feedback loop.)

The problem with cortisol is that chronically high levels cause damage. It isn't designed to be continuously high, but the constant nature of modern stressors (e.g. financial worries) can make it so. Cortisol levels can also fall too low – this seems to happen in the exhaustion or burn-out stage of stress.

With high cortisol levels you tend to feel wired, restless, perhaps energised or perhaps anxious, while with low cortisol levels you tend to feel tired, but you may feel both at the same time – tired and wired – and it's not necessarily easy to tell high and low cortisol states apart.

The adrenal glands also produce the sex hormones testosterone, progesterone and oestrogen (in both men and women) – these also influence mood.

For a much fuller account of the role that hormones play in stress and emotion see "Why Zebras Don't Get Ulcers" by Robert Sapolsky.[34]

3.7.2   Neurophysiological Arousal

As I've said it's possible for the body to be very still, quiet and relaxed at the same time as the mind is intensely alert, alive – the peak meditation state is an example. This state of relaxed focus is highly productive, and we'll return to it in the more practical parts of the book.

A different kind of aroused brain state is experienced as mental restlessness, agitation and racing thoughts. (In other words, brain activation itself is complex and multidimensional.) In contrast to the peak meditation state, agitation generally feels unpleasant and out-of-control, and is not productive.

Biologically, brain activation is likewise multidimensional. At a broad level we have:

- metabolic activation or energy consumption – measured in brain scanning technologies like fMRI
- brain rhythmicity – the pattern of electrical and magnetic oscillations, as reflected in EEG and MEG scans
- neurochemistry – especially the relative predominance of the neuromodulators, serotonin, dopamine, noradrenalin and acetylcholine but many others besides
- connectedness, or patterns of communication and information flow within the brain (complex computations based on EEG or MEG can tell us something about this).

Perhaps the key thing about optimal (useful, productive) brain activation is that it is a highly ordered state – neither rigid nor chaotic but coherent, flexible and adaptive.

3.7.3   The Biology of Flow

We introduced flow in chapter one as the experience of peak performance, characterised by heightened awareness, attention and engagement yet loss of self-consciousness and absence of struggle – in other words, effortless absorption.

In his book "The Rise of the Superman"[35], Steve Kotler investigates flow in the context of extreme sports – athletes who risk life and limb in the pursuit of excellence. You might assume these people are sensation-seekers, adrenalin junkies. In a sense they are sensation-seekers, but in fact it's not the adrenalin rush that drives them but the experience of flow in its purest, highest form – being transported out of themselves almost to a mystical level. That's a very different thing from the adrenalin rush. Extreme athletes describe adrenalin (or more generally the SNS-mediated fight-or-flight response) as the enemy of flow – an indication of imbalance, too much fear, which is a real threat to their safety.

Flow actually involves relaxation. To appreciate this you need to understand flow as a stage of a wider experience, involving a lot of preparatory work. What is it that precipitates the onset of flow? There are several factors, but one of the most important is struggle and effort – hard work. For instance a professional tennis player may experience three hours of flow in winning the final of a major competition, but a lot of desire, drive and hard work got him to that edge, from where he dropped into flow. Or a writer may pour out a whole book in a two-week creative flood, but before that she struggled with research and planning, maybe even some writer's block. So typically when we enter flow we let go of or "drop out of" SNS dominance and high cortisol, at least into the zone of "good stress".

You might expect to see increased HRV or heart coherence in flow but curiously research doesn't back this up (in fact if anything it's decreased)[36]. Researchers at the Heartmath Institute have identified a state they call "emotional quiescence"[37], characterised by very *low* HRV. Subjectively it's experienced as internal quiet (freedom from mental and emotional "chatter"), feelings of peace, serenity, love, of being "totally alive" and "fully present in the moment", a sense of greater connectedness. It sounds like a lot like a flow state (albeit a quiet, meditative one). It could be that in flow, the ANS enters an unusual state of balance, in which both sympathetic and parasympathetic systems are activated.

Flow involves peak attention and decision-making (the state of relaxed focus we touched on earlier), so you might expect that the PFC accesses a state of heightened activity, but Kotler's idea is that large parts of it actually shut down in flow. He quotes a couple of brain-imaging studies that indeed show parts of the PFC deactivating – specifically the superior frontal gyrus, which creates our sense of self, and the dorsolateral PFC which is involved in self-monitoring and impulse control[38]. It certainly makes sense that these two functions should drop out in flow, given the actual experience of flow as absorption and loss of self-consciousness. On the other hand another study showed that another area within the PFC, the medial PFC which governs creative self-expression, actually activates (this study monitored jazz musicians, so the finding makes sense too). Let's not forget there is a wide range of flow states and intensities of flow, so probably any shut down within the PFC is selective depending on the specific nature of the state – e.g. studies of meditation consistently show a general activation of the PFC. We can probably assume the attentional networks within the PFC don't shut down.

Kotler lists a set of brain chemicals that are key in flow. They include dopamine and noradrenalin which are involved in attention and alertness, also endorphins which block pain and create pleasure – so it makes sense that these neuromodulators are boosted in flow.

3.8   Psychoneuroimmunology

Another channel of communication between brain and body is offered by the immune system. The science of psychoneuroimmunology studies the interactions between psychological processes and immune system responses. The immune system communicates using signalling molecules called cytokines, which work something like hormones. It's been shown that brain cells respond to cytokines, and that immune cells also respond to signals from the brain. To add to this hormones from our glands play a significant part in what is a three-way interaction. From research in this field it's clear that stress affects our immune function and therefore plays a significant role in physical illness, and equally that illnesses once understood as purely physical can have a profound effect on the brain and emotions. This fascinating subject is getting beyond the scope of this book, so I refer you again to Robert Sapolsky's excellent book "Why Zebras Don't Get Ulcers"[39].

3.9 Putting It All Together – an Account of Addiction

The point of this whole discussion of the biology of the mind-body connection is to create a much fuller understanding of what's going on in your own self-control challenges, as a basis for seeing a way forward. An example may help you to see the personal relevance.

Suppose you've decided to give up smoking. You get up on the first day of life as a non-smoker and the first thing you do is make a cup of coffee. Normally you have a cigarette with your coffee, so by association, thoughts of smoking arise. They kindle desire by stimulating the mesolimbic dopamine pathway. Dopamine creates a buzz, the anticipation of feeling good. But this time the executive control (PFC) where your long-term plans and values reside, sends down the message 'no'. The resulting conflict of interest activates the threat-detection systems which initiate a small-scale "fight or flight" response in the body via the autonomic nervous system.

The brain's feeling centres (insula, anterior cingulate) detect this new state of affairs (stress). It doesn't feel good. The brain tries to deal with the bad feeling by looking for a something that promises a better feeling. Unfortunately it alights on the idea of smoking, which has felt good in the past. As you think about how good that first drag of a cigarette will feel (simulator mode) the dopamine effect is amplified further, and so on round the loop.

At this stage the PFC can easily engage its suppression circuits and attention is directed elsewhere. But as the day goes on, the anterior cingulate keeps sending the message to the PFC (executive) that this bad feeling requires attention. Your focus is pulled back to thoughts of cigarettes. As the day wears on the continual effort to suppress these insistent demands lead to fatigue. In the afternoon as your blood sugar drops and PFC function naturally begins to flag, you can no longer keep up the willpower, and a cigarette gets lit.

An alternative scenario: instead of dealing with the bad feelings by imagining how good smoking a cigarette will feel, you find another way. Instead of looking for a dopamine buzz you engage the brain's self-soothing or contentment systems. The resulting parasympathetic activation allows craving to be seen as it really is: just a passing urge. At other times you engage positive motivation by imagining how good it's going to feel when you're free of smoking – your clothes don't smell, your hacking cough is a distant memory, you're fit and healthy enough to take up your old hobby of badminton. This time using simulator mode creates positive emotion – hope, interest. The outcome is much more favourable this time.

3.10 Emotional Hijacks and Trauma

We'll close this chapter with a look at what happens when we "lose it" – when our emotions become so strong that they overwhelm us and we seem to act on automatic pilot, maybe even against our will or better judgement. Such experiences have been termed emotional hijacks[40].

Let's look at an everyday example: you get into a disagreement with your partner, that becomes more and more heated, you become more and more angry, until you really blow and scream something really hurtful. At that moment your mind has closed down and your only thought is to attack (in fact not really a thought but a blind impulse). Later you apologise and claim you weren't yourself, or you lost control of yourself.

What's likely to be going on in the brain? In the beginning, your amygdalas (you have two of them) are detecting emotionally salient elements in what your partner is saying, and signalling a sort of general alert. This message is conveyed to the body as an increase of arousal (a mild fight-or-flight response). With each further escalation of the argument the amygdalas become more activated, while the PFC, which is responsible for your calmer, more measured, more self-possessed responses, gets less active. Normally it keeps a brake on the amygdala but now the tables are turned, and the amygdalas suppress the PFC.

I once witnessed the reality of this see-saw effect when I serendipitously recorded my neurophysiological response to an incident. Figure 3.2 shows the recording. One Saturday at my office I was practising HEG biofeedback, in which a sensor detects changes in metabolic activation of the PFC. The trace that you see in figure 3.2 is a kind of infra-red temperature measured at the forehead – increasing signal means the PFC is activating, falling signal means the opposite.

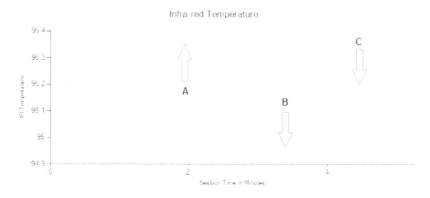

Figure 3.2 A HEG biofeedback session involving an "emotional hijack" event

On this particular occasion a group of kids were playing outside in the car park, and when one of them noticed me, they all gathered round my window, interested to know what I was up to with this strange box on my head. I decided to ignore them, even as they tapped on my window for my attention, but inside I was becoming first embarrassed and second annoyed. The biofeedback signal, which had been steadily rising (indicating my PFC was activating), began to plummet (after point A in figure 3.2) – until they got bored and moved on, at which point my signal recovered its steady rise (B). My interpretation is that my rising emotions (initiated by my amygdalas) got the better of my PFC and caused it to deactivate. (Interestingly the signal began to fall back again some minutes later (C), this time triggered by my replaying the event in my head, and thoughts about how I should have gone out and given the kids a piece of my mind!)

3.10.1 Trauma

People who have lived through traumatic events (and who could be diagnosed with Post-Traumatic Stress Disorder or PTSD can experience a particular kind of emotional hijack known as a flashback. Flashbacks are memories that are relived, as though the events were happening right now. They're not necessarily full-blown hallucinations – more commonly it's just the feelings that are relived. Here's a case vignette: Jack was involved in a road traffic accident. He wasn't badly injured and soon recovered, but at times when driving he would feel himself seized by terror – his heart would pound, his chest would feel gripped and he struggled to breathe. He didn't really know why he was feeling like that.

The amygdala can store memories – but not memories in the normal sense. When the brain processes experiences normally, our memories are contextualised – they fit into the narrative of our life. For example I remember when I climbed Ben Nevis – it was when I was in sixth form and went on school trip to Scotland for a week in the summer. I remember the friends who were with me and I tried water skiing on the same trip. I can bring the memories to mind as mental images etc. but I know it is a memory.

It seems that traumatic memories aren't processed in the same way. The amygdala's memory trace is not integrated, it doesn't fit into the life narrative. When amygdala memories are triggered, the amygdala fires off the same kind of response as it would for a current threat. The process of remembering is automatic and non-conscious, and the resulting experience doesn't feel like a memory, but like real anxiety happening here and now as a bodily response. In Jack's case, flashbacks were perhaps triggered by incidental association (e.g. seeing a red van, and there was a red van there at the time of his accident). He wasn't conscious of the connection, and the amygdala fired involuntarily.

Effective therapy for trauma is possible. It seems to involve reprocessing and re-integrating the cut off memory traces. Dan Siegel discusses the nature of trauma at greater length in his book "Mindsight"[41].

3.11   Summary of Key Points

- Emotions evolved to serve functions. They can be seen as a kind of self-regulation mechanism designed to keep us in a healthy place.
- Biologically, emotions are built on top of physiological homoeostasis mechanisms.
- Conceptually there are two parts to self-regulation systems, (i) monitoring the current state of affairs in relation to some goal state, and (ii) effecting change to reduce the gap between current state and desired state.
- Self-regulation systems are feedback systems – the current output forms the basis of the next input, and so on.
- The brain is a complex self-regulation system (or set of self-regulation systems). Emotions can be seen as self-regulation mechanisms.
- Three high-level emotion systems are (i) the threat-detection and self-protection system (ii) the incentive system (resource-seeking) and (iii) the soothing and contentment system. Most emotions can be seen as part of one or other of these systems.
- A useful distinction is to refer to feeling as the perception of the physiological changes (in brain and body) as part of an emotional response.
- Several brain structures are involved in the emotion-feeling process. The prefrontal cortex (PFC) plays a key role as a kind of executive control centre.
- The brain is able to simulate experience using the emotion-feeling circuits, and this important ability is the basis of decision-making, planning and empathy.

- Desire and pleasure are distinct, neurologically speaking. Desire is driven by the brain's dopamine system, which promises reward, but doesn't necessarily deliver. Craving involves persistent stimulation of the dopamine pathway, promising a reward that never comes.
- Emotions and physiological appetites and drives are closely related and can easily be confused.
- Arousal is a physiological process of mobilising energy in preparation for action. Arousal in the body is effected through three channels: the somatic nervous system, the autonomic nervous system and the neuroendocrine system. Only the first is under conscious control, and that only partially.
- Polyvagal theory offers a new view of the autonomic nervous system as a three-tier hierarchy.
- Heart Rate Variability (HRV) is an important biomarker for executive function, focus and attention, willpower and emotional well-being.
- It's useful to distinguish body arousal from brain activation. It's possible for the mind to be clear and alert while the body is calm. This state of relaxed focus is highly productive.
- Sometimes the locus of control in the brain flips from the PFC to the emotion-triggering limbic system. This emotional "hijacking" is experienced as "losing it" or as an emotional "melt-down". It's an important dynamic in PTSD and other emotional disorders.

4   Psychophysiology of Breathing

4.1   Introduction

This chapter is really a continuation of the last chapter which laid out the scientific groundwork for our understanding of the mind-body connection. From a practical point of view, breathing is such a significant topic within the science of optimal health and performance that it gets its own chapter.

Breathing is the process that delivers oxygen to all our cells. Brain cells in particular are oxygen-hungry – though they amount to only about 2% of body mass they use up to 25% of the oxygen we breathe. Cognitive performance (memory, focus etc.) and emotional regulation depend on optimal breathing – but what exactly is optimal breathing and why is it so important?

Put simply, breathing is optimal when it delivers optimal amounts of oxygen to our cells, and brain cells in particular. Non-optimal breathing can reduce the brain's oxygen supply by as much as 60%. That is the key reason why breathing is so important – but not the only reason.

Breathing is not some rigid, mechanical process like a clockwork, it is a highly complex and variable function. It is very much an arena in which mind-body dynamics play out – breathing is influenced by our emotions, our level of physiological arousal and alertness, even how we pay attention. Conversely good breathing is a platform for developing emotional balance and optimal cognitive performance. For these reasons breathing is central to our project of developing mind-body intelligence.

Breathing occupies a significant middle ground between two levels of the mind. On the one hand we can volitionally guide our breathing, on the other it is heavily conditioned by non-volitional influences.

4.2   Biology of Breathing

For practical purposes we can divide breathing into:
- mechanics of breathing, or ventilation – how we get air in and out of the lungs
- chemistry of breathing – how oxygen is taken up by the blood and delivered to the cells, and how carbon dioxide makes the reverse journey.

The latter is the more fundamental and important aspect (from the practical point of view) so we'll consider it first[42].

4.2.1   Chemistry of Breathing

The blood takes up oxygen from the air we've breathed into the lungs, transports it around the body and delivers it to cells that need it. In the blood oxygen attaches to a protein called haemoglobin, found in red blood cells. All our cells use oxygen to burn nutrients such as sugars and fats, releasing usable energy, and carbon dioxide as a waste product. As blood passes through tissues, it releases oxygen and picks up carbon dioxide.

Role of Carbon Dioxide

Although we think of carbon dioxide as a waste product, it actually has vital functions in the body. It dissolves in the fluid of the blood, where it exists as carbonic acid, which is the main determinant of blood pH or acidity.

Blood pH is vitally important as it governs how oxygen is taken up and released by haemoglobin. The body must regulate blood pH tightly – if it drifts out of range by much, death can result.

The most common dysregulating influence on blood pH is over-breathing.

Over-breathing or Hyperventilation

You've probably heard of hyperventilation in the context of panic attacks, which can involve an extreme degree of hyperventilation. Fundamentally, over-breathing is exchanging too much air per minute, and is a matter of degree rather than an all-or-nothing phenomenon. In normal (resting) breathing about 6 litres of air is exchanged per minute (6 litres is breathed in, and 6 out again). Over-breathing, whether chronic or only in certain contexts, mild or serious, is the most common form of non-optimal breathing, and can mean up to 15 litres of air exchanged per minute (again in the resting state – over-breathing is most likely to happen when we are sitting around rather than engaged in physical activity).

It's worth mentioning that under-breathing is largely a non-issue, for our purposes. It's almost impossible to under-breathe without a lung disorder. (By the way, asthmatics, who suffer from restricted air ways – at least during attacks – tend to be chronic over-breathers, probably because the extreme anxiety associated with an asthma attack induces a degree of defensive breathing.)

Over-breathing is a problem because it depletes the level of carbon dioxide in the blood, which has profound implications. Two principle effects are vasoconstriction in the brain and the Bohr effect. These combine to reduce oxygen delivery to brain cells – as I said by up to 60% in the worst cases.

Vasoconstriction in the Brain

You probably know that blood vessels can constrict and dilate. Low carbon dioxide levels resulting from over-breathing trigger vasoconstriction (mediated by the release of nitric oxide), particularly in the brain where vasoconstriction is controlled almost entirely by the blood carbon dioxide level (elsewhere in the body, other factors play a role too). Brain blood flow can thus be significantly reduced.

Vasoconstriction caused by over-breathing may contribute to raised blood pressure.

The Bohr Effect

In the short term, over-breathing causes the blood to become more alkaline, which means haemoglobin holds on more tightly to its oxygen (normally it's the presence of acidic carbon dioxide in the cells that triggers release of oxygen). This reduces the oxygen delivery to brain cells yet further, and depresses metabolism.

In the longer term (if over-breathing is chronic) the body corrects blood pH by a process called buffering. We don't need to go into the details of buffering, but suffice it to say that it is not an ideal solution, and predisposes us to for example fatigue. (See the table in section 4.2.1 for a full list of symptoms of over-breathing).

Serotonin

It's perhaps worth mentioning as an aside that there is some evidence that serotonin-producing neurons in the brain are sensitive to carbon dioxide[43]. Serotonin dysregulation has been linked to depression and other mental health disorders. This is a complex topic that I don't propose to go any farther into – suffice it to say that optimising breathing chemistry may possibly help to regulate serotonin in the brain.

Signs and Symptoms of Over-breathing

Because of buffering, symptoms can be divided into acute and chronic. The table below lists them[44]. (Remember, how strongly you feel these symptoms depends on the degree of over-breathing.)

Acute Symptoms	Chronic Signs, Symptoms & Effects
Chest pain, or tightness in chest	Frequent sighing, yawning with big breaths
Shortness of breath or laboured breathing	Irregular breathing & breath-holding
Feeling faint, far away or disconnected	Fatigue
Anxiety, panic, emotional meltdown	Insomnia, disturbed sleep
Poor focus and cognitive function, confusion	Depression, anxiety, mood problems
Nausea	Headaches, migraines
Sweating	Poor concentration, executive function
Palpitations	Cold, numb or tingling in hands, feet
	Gastrointestinal: bloating, IBS
	Blurred or hazy vision
	Muscle pain or spasms or stiffness
	Loss of magnesium and potassium in urine

Try sitting in front of a mirror, so that you can watch your chest and abdomen as you breathe naturally. Do you see your shoulders rising and falling? Your upper chest? If so it's likely you have a degree of habitual over-breathing.

Another test you can do on yourself: at the end of a typical out-breath, just pause before taking the next inhalation. Count the seconds till you feel air hunger. If it's just a few seconds it's again likely you're an over-breather. I don't consider this a particularly accurate test as it's dependent on what you call air hunger which is subjective. Better to measure breathing objectively.

Measuring Over-breathing: Capnometry

A capnometer is a device that measures the concentration of carbon dioxide in exhaled air. There is a peak at the end of exhalation. This measurement, known technically as end-tidal partial pressure of carbon dioxide, is known to correlate with the level of carbon dioxide in blood, which is physiologically the significant factor – so the capnometer is giving us an indirect measure of blood carbon dioxide and hence degree of over-breathing.

Capnometry can be used in biofeedback training – more on this in chapter ten.

Why Exhaled Carbon Dioxide Is Low in Hyperventilation

A lot of my clients get confused that the carbon dioxide measured in their breath is low. If they're breathing too much shouldn't it be high? I find the following metaphor is useful in explaining this. Imagine a water tank, which has a tap at the bottom where water flows out, and an in-flow of water at the top. The water in the tank represents carbon dioxide in the blood – the physiologically significant factor. Water coming in at the top represents carbon dioxide being created by energy-consuming cells, while water going out at the bottom represents carbon dioxide exiting the body through the breathing lungs. The water in the tank will find a stable level such that the in-flow and out-flow are equal and cancel each other out. Now imagine what happens when you further open the bottom tap: more water flows out, and the tank level goes down (until a new equilibrium is found). This is equivalent to over-breathing – more carbon dioxide goes out of the system. Remember what the capnometer is measuring is the equivalent to the level of water in the tank, not how much water is flowing out.

The opposite scenario (reducing the out-flow at the bottom of the tank, causing the level to rise) would be equivalent to under-breathing but in practice doesn't happen unless you have a lung disease.

Optimising Breathing Chemistry (Correcting Over-breathing)

It's unfortunate that there isn't a succinct word to sum up the opposite of over-breathing, so I'll stick with the phrase optimal breathing chemistry, meaning the optimal level of blood carbon dioxide and optimal oxygen delivery to cells. It's the most important aspect of overall optimal breathing.

Correcting over-breathing means reducing the amount of air exchanged per minute. Two parameters determine air exchanged per minute:
- breathing rate (breaths per minute)
- size of each breath (technically known as tidal volume).

Usually people think only in terms of breathing rate. Slow breathing is less likely to be over-breathing, but if you're taking great deep breaths, filling the whole lungs, you may still be over-breathing because your tidal volume is large. Rather, optimal breathing is likely to be slower but gentle.

This discussion brings us to the second aspect of breathing.

4.2.2 Mechanics of Breathing

We breathe in and out by expanding and contracting the lungs using three sets of muscles:

i. The diaphragm – a sheet muscle attached to the spine at the back and the bottom of the rib cage at the front. Figure 4.1 below shows the diaphragm. When relaxed the diaphragm is shaped like a dome or parachute. When we breathe in it pulls down, pushing the belly out.

ii. The intercostal muscles – between the ribs. These expand the rib cage outwards and upwards on the in-breath.

iii. Upper chest muscles – those around the collar bones, shoulders and even into the neck. These should be thought of as reserve capacity, for use in intense physical activity when we need to get the maximum possible air into our system. If used continually, they get fatigued and sore, unlike the diaphragm and intercostals which are built for continual use.

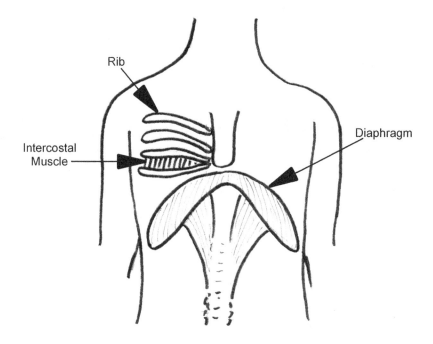

Figure 4.1 The main breathing muscles – diaphragm and intercostals. Intercostal muscles are found between all ribs, not just the ones shown.

Two Styles of Breathing

There are many styles of breathing, but I want to emphasise two common modes, which are actually two poles on a continuum rather than distinct states.

1. **Chest-Based Breathing:**
   - uses the upper chest muscles relatively more
   - is likely to be faster and shallower
   - the diaphragm is likely to be relatively immobile – the belly is relatively still
   - is typically observed as a lifting movement of the thorax – the shoulders move up and down
   - air is exchanged at the top of the lungs which is less efficient.

2. Abdominal Breathing:

- uses the diaphragm much more (giving more pronounced belly movements)
- is likely to be slower
- movement is sideways rather than lifting - it can be felt in the lower back as a sideways spreading
- air is exchanged at the bottom of the lungs which is more efficient because blood capillaries are denser.

As you can probably guess, abdominal breathing is preferable because it is more likely to create optimal breathing chemistry. It's more natural and instinctive – think of a baby sleeping, or even a pet – all the movement is seen in the belly. It feels more relaxed and comfortable.

A lot of us adults are habitual chest-breathers. Think of this as a bad habit that overlays the natural instinct.

Chest Breathing and Muscle Tension

Why do people habitually chest-breathe?

I think there are psychological (emotional) and cultural reasons (which we'll return to in section 4.3), but at a more immediate level chest-based breathing often involves tightness in the breathing muscles, particularly the diaphragm. When the diaphragm doesn't release, we can't let the breath all the way out, and since breathing regulation is linked to the diaphragm, over-breathing is more likely.

A Note on Deep Breathing

Most of us think of deep breathing as a good thing – healthy and relaxing (indeed, it's commonly taught as a stress management technique). But what is actually going on?

- We probably engage the diaphragm, so that air can get right down to the base of the lungs – in itself a good thing.
- We probably take large breaths (with high tidal volume) – which is likely to be over-breathing.

My experience in professional practice (using a capnometer) bears this out: most people, when asked to breathe deeply, actually induce a degree of over-breathing, or make it worse in the case that they're over-breathing habitually.

4.2.3 Brain Regulation of Breathing

As I've said there are different levels of breathing regulation ranging from automatic to volitional. At the most fundamental level, specialised cells in a region of the brainstem (the part of the brain controlling survival systems) detect the acidity of the fluid bathing the brain (knows as cerebrospinal fluid). Note, this is different from blood pH. This automatic brain circuit outputs to the diaphragm via the somatic nervous system (introduced in the last chapter). Energy-consuming brain cells produce carbon dioxide as a by-product. As carbon dioxide builds up, acidity increases, triggering increased ventilation, in the form of larger or faster movements of the diaphragm.

Now consider what happens in a case of over-breathing, such a classic panic attack. Blood flow is reduced, which means that carbon dioxide isn't removed effectively from the brain. The cerebrospinal carbon dioxide level rises. If it rises high enough, we feel this as air hunger, and we breathe even more. The normal feedback control mechanism is broken – in fact it has flipped from a self-correcting feedback loop to an unhelpful self-reinforcing feedback loop. This happened because carbon dioxide levels in the brain and in the blood have diverged – the former high, the latter low. This triggers a vicious cycle: even more hyperventilation, even further reduction of blood flow to the brain, even more air hunger and panic. There's plenty of oxygen in the blood, but it can't reach brain cells.

At the other end of the brain hierarchy, we do have a degree of conscious or volitional influence over breathing. We can blow a candle out, or hold our breath – for a time. I find it interesting to reflect on the experience of breath-holding – the instinct to breathe builds to an unstoppable force, making our conscious control look puny by comparison.

At an intermediate level is emotional regulation of breathing, covered in the section 4.3 below.

Breathing and the Autonomic Nervous System

The Autonomic Nervous System (ANS) was introduced in the last chapter. A brief recap:

- The ANS controls (or at least influences) many of the body's automatic or non-volitional functions such as heart rate and blood sugar levels.
- Overall, it sets the body's physiological arousal level.
- The two main divisions of the ANS are the sympathetic and parasympathetic nervous systems (SNS and PSNS), which broadly speaking work like accelerator and brake.
- In the new understanding based on the polyvagal theory, the parasympathetic is sub-divided into old and new vagal systems.

The basic movements of the breath (even automatic breathing) are mediated through the somatic nervous system, not the ANS, but even so the ANS does have a bearing on breathing. The parasympathetic nervous system can constrict the airways, while sympathetic nervous system can do the opposite. More importantly for us, breathing can affect the ANS, and these effects show up in Heart Rate Variability.

Breathing and Heart Rate Variability

Heart Rate Variability (HRV) was also introduced in the last chapter as an important biomarker. High HRV seems to reflect optimal and efficient functioning – physically, cognitively and emotionally – while low HRV correlates with anxiety, brain fog and poor physical health. All this makes HRV a powerful biofeedback parameter – more on this in chapter ten.)

The ANS has a significant influence over HRV, since the SNS speeds up the heart while the new vagal branch of the PSNS slows it. There's a physiological mechanism in breathing that "gates" this ANS influence on heart rate – essentially, the new vagal brake is applied only during exhalation, and is blocked during inhalation. The result is that the heart speeds up and slows down in sync with the breath. It's this pattern, known as Heart coherence, that is particularly associated with optimal performance.

There seems to be a sort of "resonant frequency" of breathing that maximises coherence – about 6 breaths per minute (bpm) which is quite a slow rate (one breath every 10 seconds). In this sense, slow breathing (at around 6bpm) represents an important aspect of optimal breathing. It creates a favourable balance in the ANS. However, the ANS connection to breathing is more or less independent of the chemistry of breathing (oxygen and carbon dioxide balance) and I would say the latter is more important. In other words, if I had to choose between good breathing chemistry and good HRV I would opt for the former, though of course it's possible to have both. You wouldn't expect to breathe at 6 bpm all or even most of the time, but you can have good breathing chemistry most of the time.

4.2.4   Effect of Breathing on the Brain

We've looked at how the brain regulates breathing, but what we have is a complex feedback loop: how we breathe has a strong influence on the brain. Evidence demonstrates a link between HRV and PFC activation[45], and suggests that heart coherence training may activate the PFC and boost executive function[46].

James Austin M.D. is a neurologist who has written extensively on the neuroscience of meditation and spiritual practice. His particular focus is the Zen school of Buddhism. He believes that breathing out quietens the brain – literally, in the sense that it dampens the firing of neurons. In his book "Zen and the Brain"[47] he reports his own experimental findings on animals and quotes research findings that exhalation inhibits the amygdala (remember this is the region that triggers the alarm response).

Over-breathing increases cortical excitability, meaning that neurons are more easily stimulated into firing. What this means in practical terms is not entirely clear, but it is known that sleep deprivation also increases cortical excitability.

4.3   Breathing and Emotions

I've already mentioned that emotions affect breathing, and vice versa. What is the nature of this connection?

Think about the following examples of emotionally-laden breathing:

- gasping – short, sharp inhalation, typically followed by a breath-hold, reflecting surprise, startle, shock, fear or even horror
- sighing – long, drawn out exhalation, which could be an expression of:
  - feeling fed-up or exasperated
  - feeling sad, resigned, disappointed or even hopeless
  - relief or satisfaction or pleasure.

Other long drawn-out exhalations can express anger or annoyance (perhaps more a snort than a sigh). Think of the sound a bull makes as it paws the ground, about to charge a matador.

A more general pattern is that agitated, aroused states are likely to be reflected in fast, chest-based breathing, while calm, peaceful states are reflected in slower abdominal breathing.

4.3.1   Stress, Threat and Safety

When we sense danger (not necessarily literal but more likely emotional threat) we tend to shift towards upper chest-based breathing, and we don't tend to let our breath all the way out – a more subtle version of the gasp.

Earlier I mentioned muscle tension as an aspect of chest-based breathing. Tightening up is an almost instinctive response to threat. We're literally bracing ourselves against something – even if the stress is psychological not physical. Imagine your boss giving you some critical feedback. Pay attention to how your body feels – chances are there's at least a subtle tightening. This can transmit to the breathing muscles too, and the diaphragm in particular. When the diaphragm gets locked up, we can't really let our breath out, so we're pushed into a shallow upper chest-based mode of breathing. For many people stress is of the constant nagging variety (e.g. financial worries) so chest breathing can easily become a habit.

To shift back into the abdominal breathing pattern, letting the breath right out, we need to feel safe enough that we can. Not feeling safe is an obstacle to optimal breathing.

Conversely if we want to access the feeling of safety and security (and what a valuable psychological resource that is!) then letting the breath sink right out is going to help. In other words, the relationship between breathing and emotions is rather chicken-and-egg.

4.3.2 Confidence

Lots of people suffer from lack of confidence. Like any psychological resource, confidence needs to be embodied to be felt. An important part of it is feeling safe and secure. So abdominal breathing helps to create the conditions for confidence.

Belly breathing helps us feel stable, grounded and centred – physically and psychologically. I'm talking about confidence as an inner felt sense of strength and capability rather than outward bluster and bravado.

4.4 Breathing and Meditation

The breath is commonly used as an object of focus in mindfulness meditation. Indeed it makes an excellent choice because:
- it offers a rich, engaging and constantly changing sensory experience
- it reflects our mental and emotional state
- while being subject to non-volitional influences we do have some control over how we breathe.

Most (but not all) meditation teachers, especially in the west, instruct their students merely to observe the breath without trying to change it. But that begs a question: is there a way of breathing that is more *effective* for the purposes of meditation? That depends on what you consider the purpose of meditation is; in my view, at a basic level it is to stabilise the attention and to develop positive mental qualities such as tranquillity, openness, clarity, sensitivity and contentment.

My answer is that there is indeed a more effective way of breathing. Based on our discussion of the biology of breathing earlier in the chapter, key points are:

- to minimise ventilation as a means of maximising oxygen delivery to the brain
- to breathe diaphragmatically as a means of supporting the brain's automatic regulation of breathing and also to calm agitating emotions
- to breathe slowly and regularly as a means of developing heart coherence and its associated benefits
- to draw out the exhalation phase and shorten the inhalation phase, as a means of quieting the brain.

There is some evidence that this is what at least some experienced meditators actually do. James Austin reports research findings[48] that during meditation, Japanese Rinzai Zen monks breathed a volume of 3.2 to 4.4 litres of air per minute – substantially less than the average 6.0 litres of normal controls – and at a rate of only 4 to 6 breaths per minute. Their inhalation time was only 25% of the whole breath cycle, again much less than the average 43%. Austin further reports that during meditation, breathing shifts towards an abdominal (diaphragmatic) pattern.

Researchers in Thailand investigated HRV changes seen in meditation. They found that experienced practitioners developed a much stronger degree of heart coherence during periods of "samadhi" or meditative absorption, compared to when they were sitting quietly, and also compared to inexperienced controls[49].

The question of whether one should deliberately breathe in this way is more debatable. Even if you don't deliberately try to change breathing, that doesn't mean it won't change – indeed I would expect breathing to naturally develop in this direction as you become more deeply absorbed. My personal view is that can be helpful to consciously try to guide breathing in this way, but there is danger in it too. At the least it may go against the open spirit of enquiry that is a part of mindfulness, and at worst you can over-control and end up taking your breathing in the wrong direction (further away from optimal). This is a theme we'll return to in chapter five. At this point suffice it to say, better to use biofeedback to guide you.

4.5   Practical Considerations

Such is the significance of breathing physiology that optimal breathing is right at the heart of the self-regulation skill-set.

You can't learn to ride a bike by reading a book about it; you've got to get on and do it. It's the same with breathing – you learn by doing. The rest of the book will develop a framework that will be helpful basis for beginning breathing training.

Biofeedback is a powerful tool for learning optimal breathing. Several biofeedback parameters have a bearing, including muscle tension and HRV, but in my view the most potent is capnometry, which can detect (degree of) over-breathing. We'll cover breathing biofeedback in more detail in chapter ten.

Optimal breathing is in the first place avoiding over-breathing, and thus maximising oxygen delivery to the brain. That's most likely when breathing is abdominal and gentle – gentle in the sense of a relatively low tidal volume. It's generally easier when the breathing is slower – that way you have a chance to notice the breathing reflex at the end of a breath, which causes you to take the next inhalation. Over-breathers tend to grasp after the next breath too soon. Having said that, I don't think pace is critical. It's possible to breathe optimally over a wide range of paces. In other words, there isn't one single way of breathing that is optimal but it depends on your context. Different breathing styles support different mental states. If you're lying in bed trying to get to sleep, your breathing is going to be different than when you're concentrating intently while sitting an exam. We're back to a point I've made before and will make again: flexibility or adaptability is the over-arching goal.

Optimal breathing chemistry feels above all, clear-headed and self-possessed. You have your wits about you – resources available – like you're driving the bus rather than the bus driving you. At the same time as feeling great clarity, alertness, perhaps mental spaciousness, it's possible to feel extremely relaxed. (Relaxation doesn't have to feel sleepy.)

Over-breathing can feel "spaced-out", even foggy headed. For a lot of people it's associated with feeling anxious but it doesn't have to be. I suspect that for a lot of people, deep breathing as a relaxation technique works because it induces a degree of hyperventilation which takes the edge off their awareness, makes them feel a little disconnected, separate, further away from the world, which is not an optimal state of mind.

Physically the most common sign I would say is a little tight-chestedness, but not necessarily – a lot of people are chronically over-breathing and have no idea they are doing so. Air hunger only tends to be experienced in acute hyperventilation or rather extreme chronic hyperventilation.

For most people, with the help of capnometry biofeedback it is relatively easy to learn to access optimal breathing chemistry. It's much harder for the optimal to become your baseline or habitual pattern. That tends to take a lot of practice and a lot of remembering to check in on your breathing – but I believe it's well worth the effort.

4.6 Summary of Key Points

- For practical purposes, breathing can be divided into two areas: mechanics and chemistry the latter being the more important.

- Carbon dioxide is key in breathing chemistry, principally because it determines oxygen delivery to brain cells. The brain actually monitors carbon dioxide not oxygen.
- Over-breathing or hyperventilation is common, and a significant factor for brain function because it reduces blood flow and thence oxygen delivery to the brain. It can be a cause of emotional dysregulation and poor concentration.
- A capnometer detects the degree of over-breathing by measuring carbon dioxide in exhaled air. End-tidal carbon dioxide correlates with the blood level of carbon dioxide.
- The volume of air breathed per minute is a product of breathing rate (breaths per minute) and tidal volume (size of each breath). We need to be aware of both.
- Breathing style ranges between chest-based breathing and abdominal breathing. The former is associated with stress and muscle tightness, and is more likely to dispose you to over-breathing.
- Another (more or less independent) aspect of optimal breathing is heart coherence, where the heart speeds up and slows down again in sync with the breath. Heart coherence tends to be optimal with a slow regular breath at about 6 breaths per minute.
- Emotions affect how we breathe, as does stress. Conversely, optimal breathing is a powerful method of regulating stress and emotions.
- Arguably, optimal breathing can make mindfulness meditation more effective – it can help to stabilise focus and create mental clarity and tranquillity.

Part 2

Practical Implications of the Mind-Body Connection

5 The Nature of Self-control

5.1 Introduction

Our project is to develop mind-body intelligence: emotional, attentional, cognitive, motivational control. In chapter one we started to explore the nature of self-control. Now, with a fuller understanding of the mind and its relationship to physiology, we are in a position to develop these ideas further. We'll start by revisiting the dynamics of self-control challenges: resistance, and inability to access inner resources.

5.2 Resistance, Avoidance and Acceptance

Resistance is the mental dynamic of struggling against some unwanted aspect of your experience, not wanting it in your mind. Resistance is the opposite of acceptance, and could also be termed experiential avoidance. It's a part of everyday life – I consider it a kind of psychological reflex.

Some examples of commonly resisted experiences:
- physical pain
- anxious feelings
- other unpleasant feelings such as embarrassment, shame
- worries or anxious thoughts, such as "what-ifs" (actually closer inspection suggests that it is the feelings such thoughts trigger that are the real objects of resistance)

- desires that conflict with your higher values (e.g. you're attracted to your best friend's partner)
- pop-up memories of any of the above.

In keeping with the mind-body principle, inner resistance has a bodily expression. When we're resisting we literally brace ourselves, as if against a coming blow – even when the threat is psychological not physical. Or it's as if we tried to hold something at arm's length, even when the thing is part of our own mind. So the bodily manifestation of resistance is muscle tightening – most typically in the face and mouth, also in the shoulders, arms and hands, and often holding on to the breath.

I remember once being in the dentist's chair, and as my mouth was drilled, prodded and poked I realised my legs were stuck out in the air – an example of body-wide tension. I'm sure you can think of your own examples.

If you're sensitive you can recognise even subtle examples of resistance in yourself, and see it in other people. You can even measure such resistance with a biofeedback device. Muscle tension biofeedback is a valuable tool for learning to recognise resistance (the first step), and then releasing it.

5.2.1 Avoidance

Inner resistance has its behavioural counterpart in avoidance. Avoidance is a coping strategy. Suppose one day you had a panic attack in a crowded shopping mall. Thereafter you decide that to avoid it happening again you're going to keep away from malls.

As a strategy it sort or works – you won't indeed have any more panic attacks in shopping malls. But it does make life rather awkward, and more importantly it preserves the belief that if you went to a mall you'd be in danger. Such a belief has a tendency to generalise – what about going to the supermarket? In this way inner resistance can become an ingrained mindset. You can imagine how people become agoraphobic and housebound.

Avoidant Coping Strategies

Some coping strategies are related to avoidance, or have experiential avoidance (inner resistance) at their heart. Again they can sort of work in the short term so aren't necessarily altogether bad if you're dealing with relatively trivial feelings. Here are some examples:

- distraction and procrastination
- fantasy – using imagination to create new feelings that swamp the ones you don't want (the film "Billy Liar" showcases this strategy in the extreme)
- positive self-talk – e.g. telling yourself everything is fine
- dissociation – withdrawing awareness or attention, especially from your body
- denial – for example, of your responsibility, or of the importance of something.

5.3   Inaccessible Resources and Abilities

The second of our dynamics at play in self-control challenges is failure to access resources and abilities that we know we have within us. Some examples:

- Sleep – this is one we've probably all experienced. We sleep every night. On some level we know how to do it but we can't just press a mental button and turn sleep on – much as we'd like to.
- Relaxation – again we've all experienced it at some point in our lives, to a greater or lesser degree. But when the pressure is on we don't necessarily know how to get back there.
- Focus – in my professional practice this is one of the most common complaints – clients notice they can't quite concentrate like they used to.
- Motivation and energy – it's one thing to commit to a project (like getting fit for example), but all that enthusiasm can so easily go missing when you're faced with the hard graft needed to make it a reality.

5.3.1 Self-awareness

One reason resources can be inaccessible is that they operate at an unconscious level, or in other words outside of awareness. Self-awareness is the very foundation of mind-body intelligence, and it too can be trained and developed. It has several aspects:

- body awareness, or awareness of sensations and feelings and their hedonic tone (painful or pleasant)
- awareness of thoughts
- awareness of impulses, desires and motivation
- ability to name emotions
- awareness of and understanding of the mind-body connection.

5.4 The "Quicksand Effect"

As if these two problems of inner conflict and inaccessible resources weren't enough, something more seems to be going on. At times, when faced with our self-control challenges our efforts seem to actually make things worse. I call this the quicksand effect. Stated in general terms, it's this: there are contexts where the willed effort to control has the very opposite effect to what is intended. Quicksand is an apt metaphor: it doesn't have a magic power to suck you down, but if you struggle you sink deeper.

Sleep is perhaps the clearest example. Doubtless we've all had the experience of a sleepless night. Perhaps you've got a big day tomorrow and it's important to get a good night's sleep so you can wake early and refreshed. But as soon as your head hits the pillow your mind feels as bright as a button. The harder you try to get to sleep the further away it seems to be.

The quicksand effect crops up again and again in self-control challenges. Here are some more examples:

- I'm playing tennis and having a bad day. I tell myself to focus harder, watch the ball, think about my foot work, etc. My performance only gets worse.

- I'm playing a tennis match and I'm match point up – all I need to do is win one more point. My knees suddenly feel wobbly and I serve a double fault.
- I'm trying to lose weight, and resolve not to eat any chocolate. I try not to think about the bar in the fridge, but the more I try to forget about it the more the thought keeps popping up.
- I'm nervous about my forthcoming exam. I tell myself to calm down but it seems to make me ever more agitated.
- I'm in trouble with my boss and being given a dressing down. I just can't take it seriously, yet I know I should at least look contrite. The more I try to wipe the smirk off my face, the more I want to burst out laughing.
- I've started having a problem in the bedroom with my girlfriend – impotence. I'm worried that it will happen again – I desperately don't want it to, but my worry seems to be a self-fulfilling prophecy.

Is the solution to give up trying? Should we just accept that we can't control sleep, etc.?

That would clearly be going too far. Most of us do exercise some level of choice and control around sleep. We choose what time we go to bed. We make sure it's quiet, turn out the lights and lie down in bed where it's comfortable. We create the conditions for sleep to come. (Then we let it happen.)

5.5   The Serenity Prayer

Reinhold Niebuhr's "serenity prayer"[50] was made famous by Alcoholics Anonymous. It's a prayer for three things, which I'll paraphrase, leaving out theological references:
- the courage to change the things I can change
- the serenity to accept the things I cannot
- the wisdom to know the difference.

A moment's thought will reveal this as an apt formula, not just for alcoholics but for anyone facing any self-control challenge. Get this right, and you've pretty much got life sorted.

Unfortunately it's rather easier said than done. In a sense this book is just an elaboration on these themes, and this chapter looks at the third element in particular, exploring the difference between what can and can't be controlled. A lot of self-control challenges involve at least an element of not knowing the difference, which can mean you end up either trying too hard, or being overly passive.

5.6   The Limits of Control

Let's consider the limits of self-control in relation to the aspects of mind we've been looking at.

5.6.1   Sensations

Sensations are perceptions of bodily processes and responses, and can be pleasant, painful or neutral. The body (fortunately for us) does a lot of things automatically. If you're too hot it tries to cool down (e.g. by sweating). If you cut yourself it generates an inflammatory response that hurts. You might not like it but you've got it.

On the other hand, the body also responds to internally generated triggers – in other words to imagination. Imagine biting a lemon and your mouth waters. Imagine lying on a beach in the warm sunshine and your skin temperature may actually rise. Furthermore, your experience of bodily changes depends on how you pay attention, and the further progression of bodily change depends on how you think about (judge) what's going on.

In summary, we do have a level of indirect control over bodily responses via faculties such as attention and imagination.

5.6.2   Desires and Cravings

Desires and cravings are generally given us, we don't choose to have them. Desires aren't in themselves a problem – they aren't a threat to our self-control and life would be pretty dull without them. But they are a problem when they conflict. In a typical willpower challenge, one part of the mind wants X – offering immediate or short-term reward – while another part wants Y, which is in keeping with out higher level longer term goals and values. For example the short-term reward is the pleasure of eating chocolate while the long-term goal is being slim, looking good. Another example is, you find someone attractive but you value the committed relationship you're already in.

Insofar as desires are embodied in physiology they are like bodily responses and can be indirectly influenced (i.e. in ways other than willpower).

5.6.3   Motivation and Energy

If resisting desires and cravings is one kind of willpower, another is to maintain energy in the pursuit of long-term outcomes. We don't always manage this; we can lapse into procrastination and distraction.

Again control is a matter of degree, and again motivation is conditioned by for example focus (attention) and physical energy (or lack of it – fatigue).

5.6.4   Thoughts

Thinking can be directed, purposeful, and creative. Probably most of the time it isn't, but is more like repetitive and unproductive mind-chatter. Thoughts can just pop into the mind, unbidden. As we drift towards sleep, thoughts wander, free-flowing, autonomous and random. At times mind-chatter is "loud" enough or emotionally-charged enough to stop us getting to sleep when we want to. But when focus is sharp and intense and the mind is "peeled", and particularly when it is externally directed, mind-chatter quietens.

In summary, though we have perhaps rather more control over thinking than we do over bodily sensations, it is certainly limited, and the control that we do have is mediated by attention and brain arousal.

5.6.5 Beliefs

Beliefs are like thoughts that keep recurring, or that are relatively stable. When we think them we *feel* some kind of sense of trueness. Many of them are leaps of faith beyond the available evidence - for example I may believe that I'm no good at my job or that salesmen are all out to rip me off – which raises the question of why we actually believe them.

It's important to realise that such beliefs are conditioned by the context in which they come up – I believe I'm no good at my job, whenever I have to give a presentation (and I'm in a state of anxious physiology). Later when I've calmed down I have a clearer, wider perspective and can see it's not true.

It doesn't seem right to say we choose our beliefs, rather we believe them because they're objectively true. We'd like to think our beliefs are rational and evidence-based but research shows we're more likely to believe something simply because we've thought it lots of times before (e.g. I'm rubbish at presentations.) Repetition seems to create the feeling of trueness.[51]

Beliefs also have some kind of emotional appeal, depending on our sense of identity. Just think of racists and bigots, who believe that such-and-such a group of people are the root of all evil, not because it's true but because they find the idea somehow appealing in the sense that it meets their emotional needs.

5.6.6 Behaviours

We've got relatively more control over what we do and say outwardly, compared to inwardly (within the mind). You may occasionally feel like slapping your boss or telling them what you really think, but most of us can manage not to. But we've all had times when we've said something or done something we've later regretted. We do this when our emotions are running high. Or perhaps we fail to act when our emotions are running high. Later we claim we weren't ourselves, we don't know what came over us.

Our control over our outward behaviour is conditional on our physiological state. I'm reminded of the scene in the film "Saving Private Ryan" where the young translator witnesses the death of his fellow American at the hands of a German soldier – something he could have easily prevented had he not been frozen with fear. No-one would choose to do as he did. Who among us knows for sure that we wouldn't have done the same?

5.6.7   Emotions and Feelings

As we saw in chapter three, emotions are complex things – responses to triggers, or sets of responses, which direct us to act in certain ways and prepare our bodies for acting thus. Feelings are our perception of those responses. Emotions are composites of sensations, thoughts etc. which we've already looked at. To sum up, our control over emotion and feeling is incomplete and indirect.

5.6.8   Attention and Focus

Generally speaking, at least over the short term, most of us do have relatively good control over where and how we direct our attention, certainly compared to our control over sensations. However physiological constraints place some limits on attention. Our most intense, rapt focus can only last seconds to minutes – it demands such a high level of brain resource.

As we saw in chapter three, the prefrontal cortex (PFC) plays a key role in quieting other brain regions (such as the emotion-triggering centres of the limbic system) which might otherwise generate distracting influences. Stress and emotional arousal makes focusing harder. So while attentional control gives us indirect influence over emotions and desires, optimal focus is founded on emotional balance and positivity. Fatigue can also impact attention – a well-functioning PFC is energy and oxygen hungry.

Problems with focus and concentration are common. ADHD (Attention Deficit Hyperactivity Disorder) is an extreme form.

5.6.9 Summary of the Limits of Control

In this discussion recurring themes are:
- Control is not black and white, all-or-nothing, but a matter of degree.
- That degree is conditioned by physiology. For example if we're fatigued (low energy) we're more likely to flip out emotionally, give in to temptations, procrastinate, and leap to irrational conclusions.
- Control is often indirect – not a matter of what we might think of as willpower but via faculties such as imagination and attention.
- We have relatively little control over our inner life, but more control over outward expressions.

5.7   Control Strategies

5.7.1   Expectations of Control

As the serenity prayer hints, one major factor in self-control failures is unrealistic assumptions about what you ought to be able to control. If you think you should be able to control something, you will try. If the reality is that you can't, you're into mental quicksand.

A lot of emotional self-control failures are in this category. Volatile and short-tempered people often think they ought to be able to keep a lid on their irritation and as a result they feed the energy of the irritation until it blows. Anxious people often go to lengths to avoid anxiety and in the long run reinforce the pattern.

Why do we over-estimate the extent of our emotional control? Probably the culture we live in plays a part. Some people are good at not expressing emotion, and we mistakenly assume they are in perfect possession of their feelings. Especially as children, we make this assumption of adults, and expect that when we grow up we'll be able to do the same. Again as children we may have been told what our emotions should be (e.g. 'Stop crying!' Or, 'you don't hate your sister!' Or my favourite, 'you should be grateful!')

Of course such behests are almost always ineffectual, save in creating some guilt. Nonetheless as we grow up we internalise the process, and learn to tell ourselves what we should and shouldn't feel. We make quasi-moral judgements about our own feelings. We can be harshly self-critical and feel guilty for what we feel. Actually much the same applies to thoughts as well.

5.7.2 Over-Control Versus Under-Control

So a lot of self-control challenges are turned from difficulties into problems by our attempts to cope, either by exerting too much effort or by being overly passive. For instance the examples that I gave earlier in section 5.4, or "quicksand" scenarios, can be seen in terms of trying too hard.

Conversely, if you think there's nothing you can do about a certain state of affairs, when in fact there is, then your problem is under-control. You're being overly passive. This situation seems to be quite common in depression. Martin Seligman highlighted this in his work on "learned helplessness"[52]. Depressed people are overly pessimistic in their assessment of their own capabilities, or of the possibility of feeling better, and as a result don't help themselves.

5.7.3 Responsibility

Related to our "control strategy" is our sense of responsibility. Depressed people often compound their under-control with a sense of over-responsibility – a tendency to blame themselves for things they couldn't help[53]. I remember an incident with a depressed client that illustrates this pattern. On this occasion she attempted to hang her coat on a peg, only to see it fall to the floor – twice in a row. I asked her what thoughts went through her mind and she replied that she was so useless she couldn't even hang her coat up. The reality was that the peg was a very short, rounded, horizontal stump, quite dysfunctional as a coat peg. My own coat fell on the floor nearly every day I went in there.

If you give it some thought, you can probably think of people who are under-controlling but don't take responsibility. These people just come across as immature. Others are over-controlling and over-responsible. Perfectionists are often this way. Clinical psychologist Dr Michael Yapko covers these themes in depth in his books, such as "Breaking the Patterns of Depression" – which I recommend not only if you're depressed.

5.7.4   The Human Performance Curve

Performance in any task depends on how much effort you put in. But if we were to plot the relationship as a graph, it wouldn't be a straight line as you might naively think but rather would look like figure 5.1 – the well-known human performance curve[54].

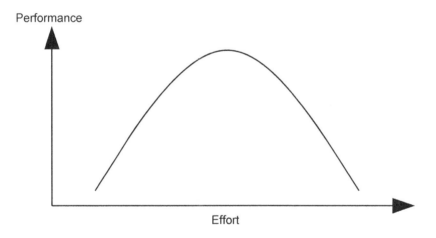

Figure 5.1   The Human Performance Curve depicting the relationship between effort (or arousal) and performance

Bringing to the mind-body perspective, we might equally well replace the horizontal axis label of "effort" with "physiological arousal". An example: your performance in a maths exam would be the worse for being tired or uninterested on the one hand, and on the other for being anxious and over-hyped.

From this perspective, the art of self-regulation is a matter of first, knowing where you are on the performance curve, and then either moving yourself left or right, depending on which side of the peak you find yourself.

The human performance curve gives us a useful way of thinking about control strategies and the quicksand trap. If your strength is in working hard to solve problems, if you're one of life's "doers", then in your self-control challenges you're likely to be right of the peak and applying effort in such a way that you inadvertently head down the slope not up (this is the quicksand trap). If your problem in life is that you're a little too laid back, your challenges are about finding yourself to the left of the peak and unwilling to climb.

Even so the performance curve doesn't explain everything – something is left out. In a sense, quicksand situations involve not simply too much effort but the wrong sort of effort. We are applying the mind in the wrong sort of way.

The performance curve suggests two opposite and complementary skills: firstly being able to increase effort, activation, arousal, and secondly being able to let go, relax, lower arousal. This latter is not simply a passive non-doing but a different way of applying the mind. Together these two abilities are integral to mind-body intelligence, and we'll return to them repeatedly in the remainder of the book.

5.8   Conscious Control Versus Automatic Pilot

The sleep example is complex. We could say that a part of the mind knows how to sleep, it's just not the conscious part.

Much of our lives are spent on "auto-pilot" – we don't have to make conscious choices about life's minor details, for example, which shoe to put on first, or which teeth to brush first. Rather we can trust a more automatic part of the mind to look after them. Although sometimes our auto-pilot is portrayed as the villain and can get us into trouble – for example you put down your car keys somewhere then can't find them later on – on the whole it serves us well. Life would be quite unmanageable if we had to make conscious decisions about everything. Moreover, the auto-pilot can't be blamed for most self-control challenges, such as those I described at the beginning of the book. If anything, these problems are characterised by the conscious mind attempting to over-appropriate control at the expense of the auto-pilot. For example when I'm trying to get to sleep the conscious will is attempting something that only the non-conscious mind knows how to do.

Again the point is that being in control is not simply a matter of exercising conscious choice. In fact, in some peak performance states we can experience a rather paradoxical combination of a sense of control on the one hand, and loss of self-consciousness on the other. These are flow states.

5.9　Flow States

We first encountered flow states in chapter one, where I described them as in a sense the archetype of self-control.

The term flow was first used in this sense by Mihaly Csikszentmihalyi[55]. A Hungarian-born psychologist, Csikszentmihalyi spent years researching and investigating happiness – not as a state of pleasure or positive emotion (which tend to be fleeting) but as a state of engaged living. This is what a flow state is: an experience of being engaged to the point of absorption. Also termed being "in the zone", I think most of us know intuitively what is meant. Flow states are times when we feel at our best, or fully our selves, though we might only realise it retrospectively. They are deeply rewarding, gratifying experiences.

Of course it's possible to experience flow in many different contexts, from playing sport to creating art to writing computer code. (Interestingly, research shows most people experience most flow at work, where it is a highly productive state[56].) Csikszentmihalyi wanted to discover the common characteristics of flow, so he travelled the world interviewing people from all sorts of cultures, and asking them to describe how they felt when at their best, doing the thing that they lived for. Csikszentmihalyi discerned eight core characteristics:

1. Challenge – the activity has the right level of difficulty – not so easy as to be boring and not so hard as to be stressful. There is the possibility of learning to do better.
2. Clear goals – we know what we're trying to do.
3. Immediate, direct feedback – we know when we're doing the activity well and we know when we're going off-beam.
4. Absorption – attention is fully and intensely engaged in the activity; we have no mental space for distractions. Flow is a state of integration – all the different parts of ourselves are engaged, our energies are unified.
5. Effortless – there is no sense of trying, striving or struggling in the mind.
6. Control – we have a feeling of control, of personal autonomy – we're actively engaged rather than being the passive recipient of the experience. (This may at first seem rather paradoxical in light of the simultaneous quality of effortlessness.)
7. Loss of self-consciousness – we lose awareness of ourselves doing this activity. There is no separation between the doer and the task – there is just the doing of it. At the same time there is great clarity of awareness.
8. Altered sense of time – subjectively time seems to speed up or slow down or both at different times.

The first three features are in a sense the most important: they are preconditions for flow. Some of the others are merely descriptive and are not going to be present in all flow experiences.

It's interesting to note what's absent from the list:

- Pleasure – though there is usually a retrospective sense of enjoyment.
- Emotion – even positive emotion. Often flow experiences are emotionally neutral – arguably there is a background positivity (at least interest) but it seems you don't need to overtly feel it, and your attention is fully engaged anyway.

- Thinking – inner dialogue is usually absent or minimal, though there is decision-making (Steve Kotler, co-founder of the Flow Genome Project, defines flow as "near perfect decision-making"[57]).

The ability to readily enter the state of flow is key in mind-body intelligence – in fact in some ways the holy grail – how do you consciously and deliberately enter a state of selfless absorption? It's a question we'll return to later in the book.

5.10   Primary Versus Secondary Suffering

We've seen how we can actively compound our difficulties by either over-controlling or under-controlling, and that it's useful to be able to accurately assess our level of control and therefore responsibility. It's important that we can make the distinction between things we do and things that just happen to us – though not easy because the two categories blur into each other. The concepts of primary and secondary suffering relate to this[58]. It's vital we understand them in order not to fall into over-controlling or under-controlling.

Suppose I stub my toe. There is a sensation of pain. This is primary suffering. It's just the fact of the matter. Secondary suffering is my mental proliferation around and beyond the fact of the matter. For example I might berate myself for being so careless, I might intensely regret having done it. I might reflect that I do this kind of thing a lot these days, and that it must be a sign of getting older, and that I can expect more and more of it as I degenerate towards dementia.

Emotional suffering usually involves a large degree of secondary suffering. A major part of depression is the enhanced capacity to remember all the previous times we felt low, together with the expectation that the future will be similarly bleak, and the (false) belief that no attempt at therapy is going to be successful in our case.

Summarising, secondary suffering typically involves:
- projection of present moment pain into past and / or future

- being judgemental either towards self or others, e.g. blaming.

With emotional pain people sometimes get caught in secondary suffering in attempting to understand their pain better – another case of mental quicksand.

If we wish to reduce suffering, we should mainly target secondary suffering.

5.11   Conclusion: The Serenity Prayer Revisited

The serenity prayer says we need three things to meet self-control challenges:
- the courage to change the things you can change
- the serenity to accept the things you can't
- the wisdom to know the difference.

Actually changing things needs more than courage – you need energy, motivation and commitment for one thing. You also need ability and knowledge (i.e. knowing what to do and how to do it).

Whilst acceptance is important, if you find yourself unable to change things maybe you need to set about developing the skills and abilities so that in future you can change the things you can't.

Knowing the limits of control is itself easier said than done, especially as they aren't fixed in stone.

This book aims to provide you with the understanding of mind-body processes as a basis for developing the skills and abilities to put the serenity prayer into effect.

5.12   Summary of Key Points

- Resistance is struggling against some aspect of your experience (e.g. pain), not wanting it in your mind. Resistance has its behavioural counterpart in avoidance. Resistance and avoidance tend to perpetuate problems in the longer term.
- Another important dynamic of self-control challenges is not being able to access resources and abilities that you know you have within you.

- When problems are internal to the mind, our attempts to solve them and get rid of them can actually make things worse, as in the sleeplessness example. I've called this the "quicksand effect".
- A useful formula for living life is (i) change the things you can control, (ii) accept the things you can't, and (iii) know the difference.
- Our control over the mind is always going to be limited, not least because we are conditioned by our physiology, and what control we have is often indirect.
- When we don't accurately assess the bounds of our control and responsibility, we can compound our troubles either by over-controlling or under-controlling.
- The human performance curve captures the idea that optimal performance is a matter of balanced effort – neither over-controlling or under-controlling.
- Self-regulation calls for two complementary faculties: firstly being able to increase effort, activation, arousal (this moves us right on the performance curve), and secondly being able to let go, relax, lower arousal (this moves us left on the performance curve).
- Optimal performance is not simply about amount of effort, but a matter of applying the mind in the right way. There are other ways of achieving things besides effort.
- Flow states are peak performance experiences characterised by effortless absorption and absence of self-consciousness. They are states of *integration*, in which energy and information flow coherently and harmoniously within the mind. The ability to access flow is at the heart of mind-body intelligence.
- Primary suffering is that part of our painful experience that is given us, as a fact of the matter, while secondary suffering is a mental proliferation of the primary pain. In secondary suffering the mind tends to project pain into past and future. Another form is blaming either self or other. Secondary suffering can be changed – this is where we need to apply ourselves.

6   Useful Models

6.1   Introduction

So far we've explored in some depth the nature of self-control challenges, particularly in their mind-body aspect. How we frame a problem shapes how we frame solutions – and it is to this that we're now ready to turn. In this chapter I'll present some practical models that give us ways of thinking about how to apply ourselves to self-regulation.

In part 1 we highlighted two dynamics of self-control challenges: (i) inner-conflict or resistance, and (ii) failure to access inner resources and abilities. Framing these as questions we need to answer, we have:

i.   How do we resolve inner conflicts? Or how do we apply ourselves so that they don't arise?

ii. How do we access hidden or out-of-reach resources?

The models we'll look at in this chapter help us think about what is involved in resolving inner conflict and accessing out-of-reach resources.

6.2   The Relationship Between Thoughts and Feelings

6.2.1   CBT: Thoughts Condition Feelings

Cognitive-Behavioural Therapy (CBT) is a widely used and successful form of psychotherapy founded on the idea that our thoughts and beliefs condition our emotions and feelings[59]. A moment's reflection will confirm the truth of this. For example, I'm giving a presentation at the office, and as I stand up to speak, I think to myself that I'm not going to be able to do a good job of this, and my audience knows it. They're expecting me to fail. I feel anxious – my heart pounds and my chest and throat feel tight. My thoughts of impending failure create my anxiety – anyone who believed that would be anxious.

CBT focuses on this connection between thoughts and feelings, and teaches us to challenge the beliefs that give rise to difficult emotions. It tries to change how we feel by changing how we think. (Actually that's a rather simplistic understanding, but it'll suffice for now and we'll return to the topic in chapter fourteen on thinking.)

6.2.2   Feelings Condition Thoughts and Beliefs

Whilst it's undeniable that our feelings are affected by our thoughts, it's not the whole story. In my example, I'm likely already to be anxious as I stand up, before the thought pops into my head. In fact my anxiety is a big part of why I believed my audience expected me to fail. Hours later, when I've calmed down again, I know it isn't true, but in the heat of the moment I believed it. So my feelings conditioned my thinking, just as my thoughts conditioned my feelings: a classic chicken-and-egg scenario. We have a loop of causation. Figure 6.1 expresses this graphically. (Note that I use the terms feeling and sensation here rather than emotion in line with the definitions I presented in part 1 – emotion is a general concept that includes thinking patterns while feeling refs to the (perception of) bodily responses associated with emotion.)

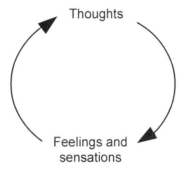

Figure 6.1 The relationship between (i) thoughts and (ii) feelings & sensations

What we're looking at here is an important aspect of the mind-body connection: thoughts are experienced in the mind but they have measurable effects on the body (and in the case of biofeedback we do measure them).

CBT focuses on the right hand side of the loop, but it clearly doesn't exhaust the possibilities for creating change. The mind-body strategy I'm advocating in this book emphasises the left side. Of course both are important.

The model is not yet complete, because we haven't included triggers that set up the loop. The environment is an external conditioning factor (in my example, the context of the meeting). My previous experience of giving presentations is an important internal factor (e.g. I've had bad experiences of presentations before, so I'm predisposed to expect this one to be the same). The Human Givens school of psychotherapy refers to this as pattern matching[60]. The mind recognises specific experiences as examples of a general category, and says "this is just another case of such-and-such". We do this all the time of course, and usually to our benefit – but pattern matching can be unhelpful, if the pattern that's being recognised (e.g. presentations) are associated with destructive emotions such as anxiety.

A more complete model is shown in figure 6.2 below.

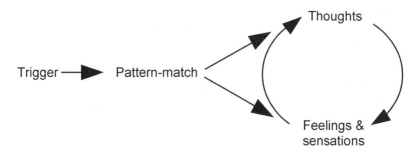

Figure 6.2 Complete model of the relationship between (i) thoughts and (ii) feelings & sensations

You can probably readily accept that the model describes my presentation example quite well, but it's important to see that it applies all the time in our experience, even down to subtle passing thoughts. Imagine the following everyday thoughts flitting through your mind:

- I left a message for my friend and she hasn't called back.
- I forgot to call my friend back.
- It's nearly lunch time.
- I really should do some gardening.
- Next week it's my performance appraisal.
- I've eaten too many biscuits.
- The price of petrol has gone up again.

Can you sense the subtle emotional responses? Does it seem right that feelings are something to do with the body? Notice what further thoughts might be triggered by the feelings.

Chain Reactions

Typically we go round the loop several times in quick succession, creating a sort of feedback loop. The process can rapidly get out of control. Figure 6.3 shows an example.

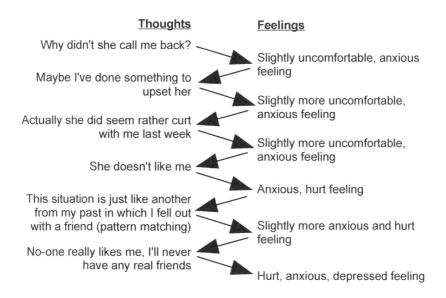

Figure 6.3 Example thoughts and feelings feedback loop

6.2.3   Mind as Simulator

Recall from chapter three Antonio Damasio's idea that the brain can in a sense simulate experience: it uses its emotional systems as a sort of sounding board, so that we can predict our emotional responses to imagined scenarios, and use the results to inform decision-making. It's as though there is an automatic part of the mind which, for whatever thought or image comes to mind, asks "what would that feel like?", and then the body (or at least the body-sensing regions of the brain) gives us the answer. The simulator hypothesis explains how it is that thoughts give rise to feelings. I see it as fundamental, and as having considerable practical importance. Simulator mode is operating all the time. It can work for you or against you.

Impact Bias

We're continually imagining how we *would* feel, but how accurate are our predictions?

Impact bias is a construct of cognitive psychology and refers to our tendency to overestimate the intensity or duration of our predicted feeling responses. Research from positive psychology suggests a rather surprising finding that in time we tend to return to a sort of happiness set-point, after significant events (such as winning the lottery or becoming disabled after a road traffic accident).

Impact bias is well evidenced in psychological research. It's an example of a cognitive bias, which in psychology is a thinking pattern that tends to lead to flawed or distorted beliefs and assumptions.

Why does impact bias happen? I would speculate that it's a result of inner resistance, which leads us to stop our mental simulations at the worst point. We imagine something bad happening, we *feel* bad (here and now) and we want to push that feeling away by stopping thinking about it. No doubt it would be awful to lose your job or if your partner left you, but in reality we would eventually find a new job or partner, or discover unexpected up-sides to the loss. Only we tend not to simulate that part of the story.

When I'm working with clients I find it's important and useful to draw attention to this mental dynamic.

6.3   The Dual Intelligence Model

We've seen in early chapters that the mind has skills and resources available which aren't under the control of the conscious mind. Have you ever grappled with a problem, perhaps something as trivial as a crossword clue, only to have the solution spontaneously appear in your mind some time later after you've been otherwise occupied? Clearly an unconscious process has carried on under its own steam.

There are many things we can do but we can't necessarily consciously decide to do them whenever we feel like it. Examples are the ability to fall asleep, creative and artistic abilities, and to some extent sporting abilities. Many practical self-control challenges fit this pattern. The conscious mind's attempts to draw on these capacities can back-fire, having the opposite of the desired effect – this is what I've termed the quicksand effect.

The dual intelligence model is a way of making sense of these rather anomalous tendencies. It's a model of the mind as consisting of two intelligences: firstly the thinking mind or cognitive intelligence, and secondly the body or somatic intelligence[61]. Figure 6.4 represents the model graphically.

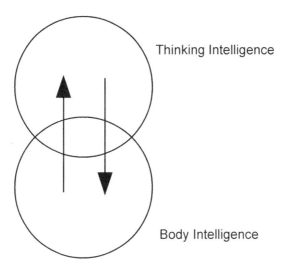

Thinking Intelligence

Body Intelligence

Figure 6.4 The Dual Intelligence model

The two intelligences are different and complementary ways of knowing and understanding, and also doing. Let's take eating as a context for explaining how they work. All of us make decisions every day about what to eat and when. The thinking mind contributes to the process, for example by knowing that fresh vegetables are good for you since they contain vitamins and minerals etc., and that too much sugar is unhealthy. The body intelligence by contrast, knows when you're hungry, and when you've eaten just enough that you don't need any more. That's a qualitatively different way of knowing.

The body intelligence communicates messages to us in the form of feelings and sensations. (Words and language are the purview of the thinking mind.) Actually, putting it like this makes it sound like *we* are separate and distinct from the two intelligences, which is is probably where the model starts to break down (let's remember it is just a model). However it does seem that the conscious mind is more related to (or closer to) the thinking intelligence, while the body intelligence is more about subconscious processing.

The body intelligence can also receive messages. Sometimes it seems the body isn't very intelligent at all, even rather pig-headed, but we need to appreciate it doesn't understand words – instead it picks up on the emotional tone of messages. If you're a dog owner you've probably noticed something like this going on with your pet. You might be telling a friend a story, about something that made you angry, and the dog starts getting edgy. The dog is picking up on the emotional edge in the sound of your voice, but of course doesn't understand that there is no threat right now. It's like this with the body: if I'm feeling nervous and tell myself with gritted teeth "come on, relax damn it!" then the body will pick up a sense of threat and will more likely respond defensively (in other words the opposite of what I wanted).

As I've said, each intelligence represents not just a way of understanding but also doing. The thinking mind does things deliberately, consciously and volitionally – it's faculties are willpower and problem-solving. The body intelligence does things instinctively, intuitively, automatically. We can think of the ability to sleep as residing at the level of body intelligence. (We can't think our way to sleep.) Likewise with sporting performance, artistic and creative performance, and other types of flow state.

6.3.1 Resistance Revisited

Ideally the two intelligences work together. Making healthy eating choices, for example, requires both. That's why I've drawn the two circles overlapping in figure 6.4. But they don't always work in harmony. Many of our self-control challenges can be seen in terms of conflicts between the two – they don't always share a common purpose.

We can think of resistance as the thinking intelligence's response to messages coming from the body (in the form of feelings, sensations) that it doesn't like. It tries to block them, reject them, or at least hold them at arms length. Doing so may actually feed the process that's generating these feelings, resulting in a quicksand effect.

6.3.2   Unavailable Resources

In other self-control challenges, there is a breakdown in communication between the two intelligences. If the thinking mind pays no heed to the messages being offered by the body intelligence, problems are likely to result. It may then over-extend itself, trying to take on tasks that are best left to the body intelligence. Or messages may be misinterpreted by the thinking intelligence, leading to similar problems. In chapter five I portrayed these situations as cases of over-control, and as applying the wrong sort of effort. Now we can see this in terms of disharmony or lack of integration between parts of the mind.

Or perhaps it is simply that the thinking intelligence never learned how to access the resources that lie at the level of the body intelligence. An analogy: we often complain that computers are stupid and get things wrong. In reality computers do exactly as they are instructed, it's just that we gave the wrong instruction and don't know how to give the right instruction.

6.3.3   Weight Management as an Illustration

Let's consider how these processes manifest in the challenge of weight control:
- Not heeding messages – overweight people often eat in a state of stress and guilt – they don't savour the pleasurable feelings of eating and don't notice when they've had enough.

- Misinterpreting messages – unpleasant feelings are taken as triggers to eat, when they might be emotional messages rather than hunger. The result is comfort eating.
- Thinking mind over-extending – you decide you know what's best for the body and over-rule hunger, but the urge to eat doesn't necessarily go quietly ...
- Negative attitude to the body - I remember one client who described her body as something she dragged round with her all day. With a negative attitude such as this, you're not going to access all the resourcefulness of the body, not least because it's getting the wrong messages.

6.3.4   Timothy Gallwey's Inner Game

Some years ago I read the book, "The Inner Game of Tennis" by Timothy Gallwey[62]. Gallwey was a coach who taught his clients about the mental side of playing tennis (and it's a very considerable side). His way of thinking about the mind is very similar to the dual intelligence model. He calls the two agencies self 1 and self 2.

Self 1 is the judger, the teller, the trier (similar to my "thinking intelligence"). It judges our performance as good or bad, acceptable or not acceptable (and furthermore seeks approval from others and wants to avoid disapproval). Self 1 has a tendency to generalise (e.g. I played a bad shot → I'm a bad tennis player) and to go off into the past and future (I've never been a good tennis player, I never will be a good tennis player).

Self 2 is the non-verbal, present-moment centred and sensory-based self. It's not concerned with judging but just doing. It already knows how to do lots of things, like play a good tennis shot (or substitute your own example) and where it doesn't already know, it has the capacity to learn spontaneously, naturally and effortlessly. It learns by seeing, sensing, doing, not by talking.

People get into problems when self 1 interferes with self 2 and gets in the way. Self 1 tells us what we should be doing instead of trusting self 2 to learn naturally. This is equivalent to what I've called the quicksand trap.

Whether you're a tennis fan or not, I'd certainly recommend reading the Inner Game of Tennis. Gallwey has lots of practical advice about how to access self 2's considerable resourcefulness, which is of course a central theme of our mind-body intelligence project. (In the next chapter we'll take a detailed look at the topic of accessing resources.)

6.3.5   More Inner Splits

My thinking and body intelligences, and Gallwey's self 1 and self 2, are two examples of ways of dividing up the mind. There are several other ways, each one drawing out some particular aspect of multifaceted nature of mind. Of course none is a real hard-and-fast split, but each offers a useful insight.

- **Conscious / unconscious**
  The conscious part is the known, volitional side of ourselves while the unconscious is the hidden, inaccessible part. To an extent, the conscious mind is associated with my "thinking intelligence" while the "body intelligence" is more unconscious.

- **Left-brain / right-brain**
  The left hemisphere is popularly held to be logical, rational, analytical, linear, literal and language-based while the right hemisphere is holistic, imaginative and imagery-based, non-verbal, metaphorical, intuitive and emotional. Probably we shouldn't overstate the neurological basis of this split (any complex mental task involves both hemispheres) but it seems that people can be "one-sided" in this sense (see Daniel Siegel's book "Mindsight" for more on this[63]).

- **New brain / old brain**
  The brain is anatomically divided into the outer cortex (the wrinkled part) which is evolutionarily newer and responsible for our higher functions such as thought, creativity and morality, then the old brain consisting of the old mammalian

brain (which includes limbic structures such as the amygdala) and the reptilian brain (the brainstem). These latter two between them are responsible for our more automatic and instinctual behaviours, our more "primitive" drives and emotions. Self-control challenges result when the new and old brains don't connect or work together or get into conflict.

- **Ego / id**
  This is the Freudian version of the split. The id is the instinctual and largely unconscious side and the ego is the rational, moral side.

- **Thinking / feeling**
  Thinking and feeling are often used in personality typing systems such as Myers-Briggs. We all know people who seem to live in their heads, not aware of what's going on neck-down. Other people are dominated by their feelings and are prone to irrationality. As is the case with all the others, this split points to the value of integration (two sides of the split working together).

- **Head / heart**
  Sometimes we say things like "my head says one thing and my heart says another". The head represents the cool, rational self while the heart represents the emotional self. Actually it's rather misleading to think that the cool rational self is independent of feelings – as we saw in chapter three decision-making relies on at least some feeling. It's just a question of whether the feelings are accessible to awareness. Head versus heart conflicts usually boil down to wanting different things at the same time, such as stable finances and extravagant purchases.

- **Elephant / rider**
  This more metaphorical version of the head / heart split is from positive psychologist Jonathan Haidt[64]. The rider is the conscious, rational mind: the thinker, the planner, the controller. The elephant is the doer, and also the automatic mind, or even unconscious mind, and of course it's the emotional mind. The key point is that to some extent the

elephant has a will of its own. The rider has some influence but isn't in complete control. The image of the elephant conveys the great strength of emotions: if your rational mind is at odds with your emotional mind, there's no doubt who'll win out in the longer term.

Animal imagery works well for conveying the different levels of mind, and is popular. Sports psychologist Steve Peters uses the idea of the "chimp brain" in his book "The Chimp Paradox"[65], and biohacking aficionado Dave Asprey speaks of the "Labrador brain"[66]. They're both essentially referring to the limbic system of the brain, which, as we saw in chapter three, plays a role in triggering emotions. (The rider is more like the prefrontal cortex.)

- **Conceptual self / true self**
This split draws together elements of several others. The conceptual self is the idea we have of ourselves, who we *think* we are, our "story", the parts of ourselves that we identify with. The true self is the totality of ourselves, including all those capabilities we don't realise we have – of course we're all capable of so much more than we think. The true self contains the contradictory bits, the "shadow" or the parts we wish we didn't have[67].

- **Top-down / bottom-up processing**
Cognitive psychology looks at the mind in terms of computational processes. In top-down processing the locus of control is at the higher levels. Suppose you're looking around at the sea-side. Two ways of doing this are, first, you're looking for fossils, and second, you're just generally curious, and you're letting your attention be grabbed by whatever interesting things you come across. The former is an example of top-down processing, while the latter is bottom-up[68].

- **System 1 / system 2**
These are terms used by Nobel prize-winning psychologist Daniel Kahneman to refer to two different modes of cognitive processing (thinking)[69]. System 1 is fast, instinctive, automatic (sub-conscious) and emotional while system 2 is slower, more

effortful and more logical – our stereotypical notion of thinking.

Kahneman has spent much of his career studying decision-making, and especially how we get things wrong. We make thousands of decisions every day, most of them sub-consciously using system 1. The trouble is, system 1's speed and effortlessness sacrifices some accuracy – Kahneman and others have found it to be riddled with cognitive biases, such as impact bias referred to earlier.

6.3.6   Value of Splits

What these splits offer us is a way of thinking about self-control challenges: they are breakdowns of communication and integration between the two parts. At times the two have divergent purposes, e.g. one part wants to look slim, look good, the other part wants to eat. Another kind of problem is that one part tries to appropriate the role of the other (over-control). Loss of integration can mean that resources (e.g. ability to reduce arousal) become unavailable to us. The models reframe the project as one of integration: how to get the parts effectively communicating and working together.

6.4   The Human Performance Curve Revisited

In chapter five I introduced the human performance curve, which represents the relationship between performance and effort, and draws out the idea that optimal performance is a matter of *balanced* effort. The human performance curve is reproduced in figure 6.5 below.

Technically known as the Yerkes-Dodson law, the graph is not just a theoretical construct but has been borne out in experimental data. It applies to performance in a range of contexts – sport, music and artistic performance, cognitive and attention tasks, and job performance. It even applies to organisations, as well as individuals.

The horizontal axis can be labelled in different ways – more abstractly, effort, arousal, stress level or even intensity of awareness or focus. More concretely, it could be level of the stress hormone cortisol, or activation of the sympathetic nervous system.

Daniel Goleman, in his book "The Brain and Emotional Intelligence"[70], divides the graph into three regions, as figure 6.5 shows.

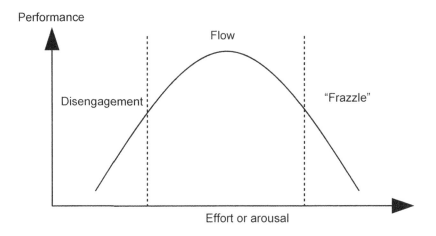

Figure 6.5 The Human Performance Curve

At the left hand end of the curve is the zone of disengagement. Here, we feel bored and distracted, perhaps because the activity doesn't offer enough interest or challenge to fully engage the attention. In a sense, there is not enough stress (there is a view that a certain amount of stress is a good thing).

At the other end of the curve is the zone of "frazzle". Here, the stress tends to be overwhelming, we become reactive rather than responsive, rigid rather than creatively flexible and adaptable. Attention is distracted by over-aroused emotions.

The middle region is the zone of optimal performance, or optimal self-control, or as Goleman labels it, flow. (We looked at flow in chapter five.) Here's how Goleman describes it:

"Flow represents a peak of self-regulation, the maximal harnessing of emotions in the service of performance or learning. In flow we channel positive emotions in an energized pursuit of the task at hand. Our focus is undistracted, and we feel a spontaneous joy, even rapture."

If disengagement is too little stress and frazzle too much, flow is the region of good stress. Attention is fully engaged.

It's interesting to note what brain imaging reveals of the three states. In disengagement, random areas of the brain are activated, reflecting distracted attention. In frazzle, the emotion centres of the brain are overly activated, compared to flow where they are less aroused and only those brain regions actively needed for the task are activated, reflecting an economy of action.

6.4.1 Accessing and Staying in Flow

Having a means of reliably accessing flow is something of a holy grail in the world of personal development. But there's an obvious paradox here: how can you deliberately and consciously achieve a state of mind which by definition lacks willed effort and even self-consciousness? This is an important topic, which we'll return to later in the book. Here I'll confine myself to making a few points in connection with the human performance curve.

Firstly, we need an awareness of which side of the peak we're on at any point in time. In a sense it's like balancing a ball on top of a hill – we will always tend to fall one side or the other, and we must work continually to return to balance. Our awareness must be likewise on-going.

Secondly, depending on which side of the peak we find ourselves, we need to bring to bear one of two complementary faculties or skills:

- Increasing arousal level or energy level or intensity of focus; activating; at the psychological level, engaging motivation, intention, will. (This faculty moves us to the right in the graph.)

- Decreasing arousal level or intensity of focus, disengagement, letting go; or in psychological terms, acceptance. (Note this is a positive resource in itself, not just an absence of the opposite. It moves us to the left in the graph.)

Note that these two are best conceived of as *mind-body* skills.

Goleman makes the point that key to maintaining flow is focus or attentional control. Focus is a skill that needs to honed through practice and exercise, and – like effort – also needs to be balanced. We'll go into this in more detail in chapter twelve on attention.

6.4.2   Mindfulness as a Balance Point

Mindfulness, introduced briefly in chapter one, is the practice of present-moment, non-reactive focused attention. We'll cover it in much more depth in chapter nine, but I want to touch on it again here because I think it's useful to see mindfulness as a balance point or "middle way" between extremes, just as we have seen with flow. We could recast the human performance curve as the "human attention curve", as in figure 6.6.

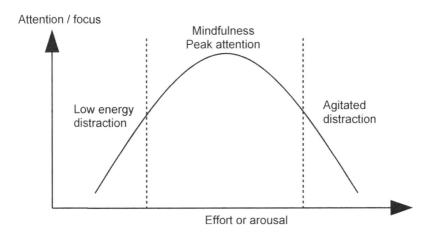

Figure 6.6 The "Human Attention Curve"

As a state of awareness, disengagement is dullness, low intensity awareness, "day-dreamy" distraction, slothfulness or even sleepiness, while frazzle is a kind of over-excited, agitated distraction or overly wilful focus.

There's another sense in which mindfulness is a balance. It's to do with the way the mind engages with the object of focus. At one pole, the mind loses its sense of spaciousness and perspective and becomes "sucked in" to its experience, too much involved with experience. At the other extreme, the mind is overly separate from the object of experience, perhaps alienated from it. This may sound rather obscure at this stage in the book but I hope it will become clearer when we discuss mindfulness in more depth (in chapter nine).

6.5   Summary of Key Points

- An important aspect of the mind-body connection is the relationship between thoughts and feelings. Thoughts affect how we feel and feelings condition how we think.
- In "simulator mode" the mind simulates how we would feel in response to hypothetical circumstances. These simulations help us make decisions. This dynamic is going on all the time and is a fundamental aspect of inner life.
- The dual intelligence model frames self-regulation as split between two parts of the mind: thinking intelligence and body intelligence. These two represent useful sets of resources – different ways of understanding but also doing.
- Problems result from breakdowns of communication and integration between the two. For example they may have divergent purposes, or resources may become unavailable. Our project of self-regulation involves creating better integration between the parts of the mind.
- The human performance curve frames optimal performance as a matter of balance. To stay in flow we need to balance two opposite and complementary skills: firstly being able to increase effort, activation, arousal, and secondly being able to let go, relax, lower arousal.
- Attention also needs to be balanced.

7   Accessing Mind-Body Resources

7.1   Introduction

Our project is to develop the skills needed to manage the mind, which at a fundamental level is the skill-set of mind-body regulation. But we're faced with a difficulty: many of our inner resources and abilities aren't always responsive to conscious choice or willpower. Indeed applying effort in the wrong sort of way can make things worse (get us into mental quicksand). So how then do we access these resources when we need them? Or, to put it another way, how do we bring them into the purview of conscious control? Or again, framing the question in mind-body terms, how do we access the positive and adaptive physiology that is the basis of constructive, positive, focused states of mind?

In the last chapter we looked at the dual-intelligence model of the mind, which posits that the body intelligence has capabilities and resources beyond direct conscious control. Often it already knows how to create adaptive physiology – but how do we as conscious minds call upon these resources – if not by willpower which we know doesn't work?

A related question is, how do we deliberately and consciously access flow, when almost by definition flow states aren't deliberate?

This chapter builds on the models presented in the last chapter, but moves further into the territory of solutions rather than problems.

7.2   How We Learn

In chapter six I referred to Timothy Gallwey's outstanding book "The Inner Game of Tennis" in which he expresses thinking along similar lines to my dual intelligence model. Gallwey was a tennis coach. He was concerned with helping people play better tennis – but more than this, he wanted his clients to *enjoy* playing. Though he didn't use Csikszentmihalyi's language of flow states, we can say he wanted to help people access flow. What he was talking about went way beyond tennis.

Tennis is a *doing* thing. Gallwey was interested in how we *learn to do*. He realised the learning process had little to do with instruction, but rather happened easily and spontaneously in response to *seeing* and *feeling*. (In my terms, the body intelligence learns rapidly and naturally through direct perception.) Gallwey had his students watch themselves in a mirror, and his emphasis was very much on paying attention to sensory experience rather than thinking.

Brains are "designed" for learning and have been doing it well for many millions of years. Learning doesn't require effort, or conscious thought. The human capacity for conscious language-based thinking is no doubt a wonderful evolutionary invention, but it isn't necessary for learning to do. Our capacity to form judgements about how well we did, and especially how good or bad we are, adds little if anything. Indeed it can get in the way (create mental quicksand). Neither does making effort, trying hard. The key is simply *interest* (which, remember, is one of Barbara Fredrickson's ten positive emotions.)

Most of us learned to walk before we could speak and understand language in any meaningful way – probably just as well since the complexity of the task is way beyond what the conscious mind can take on through instruction. We saw others around us doing it. We didn't have to make effort because we naturally wanted to do it too.

So in self-control challenges we just need to let go of effort or the involvement of the thinking, conscious mind, and trust in our natural capacity to learn. Now I'm aware this is a rather trite thing to say, far easier said than done. In practice our self-control challenges are the times when the conscious mind feels the most need to do something. The conscious mind needs occupation – it's not a realistic option just to let go. Part of the answer to this question is that we channel our conscious energy into focus on direct sensory perception (more on this in section 7.5 below).

7.3   Attitude of Trust

The dual intelligence model emphasises that we're capable of so much more than we realise, and that there's more to who we are than our limited conscious idea of ourselves. We can count on support and help from this wider self, but we need an attitude or mindset of trust and respect. Such a mindset opens us to a quite different "relationship" to ourselves and in particular to the body – more of a partnership where we invite our inner resources to express themselves, in a spirit of freedom, openness and even play.

The opposite of this is a harsh, demanding, master-and-slave-like attitude, that creates more possibility of inner conflict and "quicksand". As a therapist I'm constantly surprised by how harsh and critical people can be with themselves – an attitude which if expressed towards others would be abusive.

7.3.1 Asking for Results

Body intelligence is not just an abstract or theoretical idea. We can actually ask it for help. We can ask the unconscious mind for help – or the other part of the mind, conceived in any way you prefer. We can ask for results, or as Gallwey puts it, ask for form. And if the request is made in the right spirit, we'll get a response.

Asking is very different to telling. Just think about your own experience – when we're asked for help we usually respond positively because we like helping. When your boss tells you what to do, well you might respond less willingly, perhaps even resentfully.

I'm reminded of the well-known parable of the sun and the wind. Originally one of Aesop's fables, this story became part of our culture because it points to a fundamental psychological truth. In case you've forgotten it: the sun and the north wind were disputing who was the stronger, when they see a man walking by wearing a cloak. The sun challenges the wind to part the man from his cloak, so the wind blows and blusters, with the sole effect of making the man hold on ever more tightly. Then the sun comes out, and the man willing de-cloaks so he can better enjoy the sun's gift.

Another apposite metaphor: imagine you're trying to coax a rather shy animal like a kitten to come to you so you can feed it or stroke it. You have to encourage but wait – if you move towards it, it'll likely take off. Animals don't understand words as language but they do pick up on the emotional undertones. The body intelligence is the same. It can react defensively to harshness and force.

Appreciation

A quality that goes hand in hand with trust is appreciation. We're naturally appreciative when others help us, and if we're not we're less likely to get more help in the future. When we start relating to our own mind as in some sense "other" then again we naturally appreciate its "help". When we get a good response from ourselves, a warm attitude of appreciation will encourage more.

7.4   Imagination

So Gallwey advises us to ask for results, then he suggests we *visualise the results.*

Visualisation is a technique widely used by coaches and therapists – because it works. In fact neuroscience research suggests that mental rehearsal is reflected in brain processes that are almost equivalent to the real thing, and results in genuine learning (embodied in neuroplastic change) likewise similar to real training. The brain is that good as a simulator.

Actually visualisation doesn't have to be conscious and deliberate. Remember "simulator mode" – my label for the mind's capacity to automatically simulate experience, such that for any thought or image that pops into our head, we get a sense of what it would feel like were it to become true. We're using simulator mode all the time. Would you like tea or coffee? Would you like to take a day off work? Would you like to give a presentation? We use simulator mode to make decisions, and it is fundamentally a somatic and emotional process rather than a logical, reasoned one (which is not not to say it's irrational).

This automatic operation of the imagination faculty can work for us or against us.

7.4.1 Worrying

When things go wrong in life, we feel bad. If you imagine them going wrong, you don't have to wait for the bad feeling, you can have at least some of it here and now. If you are worrying, and your worries take the form of 'what if …', then your mind is automatically giving you the answer to that 'what if', and yes, it's a bad feeling. People adopt this strategy (of thinking of all the things that could go wrong) in order to avoid bad things happening, and indeed it *can* help you avoid mistakes. It can work for you especially if you then imagine things working out well, having avoided the pitfalls you foresaw (this will leave you with a good feeling). But so often worry is not like this, rather it's a repetitive loop of worry and bad feeling without any positive thoughts to counter-balance.

We can get stuck in loops of worry in part because of resistance. It starts with a thought along the lines of, what if something bad happens... ? We don't like the feeling that the thought engenders, and then we're into subtle inner resistance, which is the mind saying "let's not even go there". We distract ourselves, but because we haven't really dealt with the thought we're left in the physiology of resistance, even anxiety, and that makes the same thought much more likely to arise again a short while later.

Remember our chapter one case vignette of Barbara who was anxious about giving presentations at work. Her anticipatory anxiety would start with the thought, what if she blushed. A train of mental images followed, ending in Barbara becoming so flustered that she ran out of the room. That prospect was so awful as to be unthinkable, so her imagining ended at that point (the worst point). Later the thought would recur and the sequence would repeat. She never got to the other side of that worst point, she never imagined her recovery. This is a common pattern in anxiety – our imagination stops at the worst point.

7.4.2 Constructive Imagination

Imagining positive outcomes also gives rise to feelings, but this time good feelings. Imagining getting promotion, winning the match, going on holiday, people treating you kindly, yourself treating others kindly, etc. triggers positive emotions such as (anticipatory) enthusiasm and hope. The associated physiological states are pleasurable, rewarding. Of course this is what successful athletes and others are doing when they practice mental rehearsal.

When we imagine things going wrong, we need to counter-balance that with imagining something positive. That might be finding a solution to the problem, or recovering from the bad thing that might happen (nothing lasts forever, including problems), or just imagining an alternative possible scenario. We need to inculcate this as a habit through repeated practice, just as many of us have done with worrying and "catastrophising".

Using "The Force"

When George Lucas conceived the Star Wars film saga, he created a modern day mythology by tapping into psychological truth. (If you haven't seen the films, this section probably won't work for you so by all means skip to the next.) In Star Wars, the mythical force represents a part of us outside of our normal everyday selves, and using the force is a metaphor for accessing flow. When a Jedi uses the force, he allows something to flow through him, by inculcating a calm receptive attitude – the Jedi masters speak the language of trust, summed up in Master Yoda's words, "Try not. Do... or do not. There is no try."[71] Trying is the way of the limited conscious mind, not of the force. I remember one day when I was a (rather star wars obsessed) child, playing tennis and becoming pretty frustrated at my inability to live up to my expectations. So I decided to pretend to use the force. I let go of judgements about whether I was doing it right, etc. I imagined something working through me. I knew the force wasn't "real", but I did it whole-heartedly in the spirit of play and imagination – a rather enviable talent that children have – and I got results.

In fact the Star Wars films are replete with relevant metaphors. Another example: Anakin Skywalker's turning to the dark side is born of inner conflict ...

Play

Play isn't about success or failure, or performing well or badly. When children play they have nothing of the judgemental mindset we adults are so familiar with. They're not asking themselves whether they're doing it right when they're playing, they just *are* a cowboy or a princess, or whatever role they're playing. They are imaginatively exploring what it is like to be that person. Of course play isn't just idle diversion, it's a highly effective way of learning.

We can all benefit from something of the spirit of play (we had it once). If you lack confidence, you can start wondering what it's like to feel confidence – perhaps by recalling some area of your life where you are confident, or by bringing to mind someone you know who embodies confidence – what would it feel like to be them?

Method Acting

Whilst I'm no drama student, still less teacher, I think the concept of method acting points to the same idea. Method actors use imagination to create the thoughts and feelings of their characters. They imagine what it is like to *be* that person, to the extent that they feel their character's emotions etc. If the character is angry, they don't try to feign angry looks, they actually are angry. They don't think about how well they are doing in portraying their character, they just *are* that character.

Using Imagination in Biofeedback Practice

When I'm working with clients I like to use biofeedback to demonstrate the reality of the mind-body connection, and in particular that the body responds to imagination. Either directly or indirectly I suggest things to imagine, and observe the response. Here are some of my stock images:

- Imagine getting into a hot bath.
- Imagine feeling completely safe. You're in a place that's completely safe, and with people you fully trust, or perhaps on your own if you prefer.
- You've been on your feet all day, perhaps a long shopping trip (with bags to carry) or perhaps doing some physical work. You finally get to sit down in a comfortable chair, taking the weight off your feet, and maybe with a cup of tea.
- Can you remember a time when you were feeling constant stress, perhaps low level but just there all day, and then it finally came to an end. Maybe you were doing exams at school or college. Maybe you went through a divorce. Maybe you were in a job that you hated and then got a new one. What did the relief feel like?

There are many other possibilities. You get the idea.

7.5 Attention

Flow states are about active engagement, they are not just passive letting-go. They are not the same as operating on auto-pilot where a part of you does something (like driving) while another part of you thinks about what you're going to do later on.

It's all very well to let go of resistance, trust in deeper resources or the wider self, etc. but what does the conscious mind actually do? As I said back in section 7.2 above, in self-control challenges we need something to engage the will – passivity is not a realistic option. Well, that something you can do is *focus*. But focus in a certain way.

There's a lot to say about this topic of focus or attention, so much that it gets its own chapter. Here I'll summarise a few main points that we'll cover in depth in chapter twelve.

- Attention acts like a filter on your reality. To an extent, what you perceive depends upon what you're looking for, or perhaps are (unconsciously) pre-conditioned to look for. What you pay attention *to* is important.
- Attention acts like an experiential amplifier. What you give attention to, tends to grow, in the sense that your awareness of it becomes richer and more refined. Again, what you pay attention to is important.
- *How* you pay attention is equally important. Different styles of attention are possible, and having flexibility of attentional style is a key skill.
- The mind-body principle applies to attention too. The different styles of attention are supported by different physiological states. This is perhaps the most important point I want to make in this section: shifting our mode of attention is a way of indirectly shifting physiology and thus is a means of accessing body-intelligence-level skills. But it cuts the other way too: developing physiological adaptability can improve focus.
- Attention is very much an arena for training. Attention skills can be honed through practice and exercise. Training attention

builds the "muscle" of the pre-frontal cortex, so you can expect that as attention improves so do many other things. Of course, attention training and mind-body training go together.

7.5.1 Sensory Experience

Gallwey advised his students to watch, listen and feel, to become absorbed in sensory experience rather than in thinking – at least self-oriented thinking. Remember flow is in a sense the opposite of self-conscious thinking. To the extent that you're absorbed in present-moment sensory-based awareness you aren't thinking (in the sense of self-oriented inner dialogue) because you can't really do both at the same time. Within the prefrontal cortex, there are regions involved in external sensory focus on the one hand, and self-oriented mind chatter on the other, that mutually inhibit each other. (we touched on this in chapter three).

7.5.2 Interest

Attention doesn't stay still for long. It follows interest. To stay absorbed in sensory-based awareness you need to find some interest in it.

Interest is wanting to know about something or someone. It's an emotion – it kindles physical and mental energy, expresses itself, for example in our facial expression. It moves us to find out – it's vital for learning.

We all know what it feels like, or at least we've all experienced interest at some time in our lives. Whilst as individuals we have our own particular interests, one thing we all share is interest in stories – films and books for instance. The best ones are the ones where we really want to know what happens next, how things turn out, and all the better if we're kept guessing.

Interest and curiosity lead us towards flow – we lose our sense of self-consciousness and become absorbed.

Like all positive emotions, interest can't be switched on and off on demand. The judging mind tends to kill interest (e.g. thinking you *should* be interested). Instead we've got to notice what naturally kindles interest. It helps to start with an open, spacious, receptive awareness, free of expectations and preconceptions. The first stirrings may be subtle and hard to perceive, but with refined attention we can notice them, and then just give our attention. What we give attention to tends to grow.

Competitiveness

I think it's natural to be interested in and curious about how well you can do at something. Especially as children, we see things that attract us and we would like to learn how to do them, and how to do them better. It's part of the natural drive towards growth.

For some people this manifests as competitiveness. Competitiveness can be a positive thing, if it embodies the spirit of interest, curiosity and playfulness. But taken too far, you can lose this spirit, and end up with ego-driven obsession, that's really driven more by the judgemental and approval-seeking mind.

If you're not the competitive type, that's fine too. Certainly none of the ideas and methods I'm writing about in this book are anything to do with being better than other people. But watch out for going too far the other way – it may be this is just an expression of avoidance, or the decision that it's better not to try than to try and fail. This kind of "anti-competitiveness" is just the judging, approval-seeking mind again, adopting a different tactic.

7.5.3   The Importance of Pleasure

Interest and pleasure are linked – it feels good to be interested and engaged, at the same time pleasurable feelings spark interest. Pleasure is something that it pays to be aware of.

Pleasure is very largely given us – it's nothing to do with effort or will. All we can do is savour it, appreciate it – while it lasts, because pleasure tends to be fleeting. Not only that but pleasure tends to habituate. For most people, it's pleasurable to eat a piece of chocolate, and as the pleasure fades you're moved to take a second piece, but the real truth is that second piece is not quite as good. If you're not convinced, imagine eating the whole bar – how does it feel to eat the last piece? How would it feel at the end of the second bar or even the fifth?

Pleasure seems to be fundamentally to do with the physical senses, and especially the body. Mental activities (e.g. doing a crossword) can be enjoyable too but it's important to distinguish pleasure from what Martin Seligman (founder of positive psychology movement) calls gratification[72]. Unlike pleasure, gratification requires application of the mind and is not subject to habituation. In Seligman's understanding gratification is the enjoyment we experience in flow states.

Recall that in the dual-intelligence model, we're looking for a constructive "dialogue" with the body intelligence, which communicates not in words but in feelings and sensations. When the body intelligence gets things right, we are rewarded with pleasurable feelings. Whether you're dancing or playing sport or playing music, if you're doing it well it feels good, it feels comfortable.

From a practical point of view the key points are:

- It's important to pay attention to pleasurable feelings because they are *feedback*. In a large class of mind-body activities, they tell us when we are getting it right.
- We need a mind-set of openness and receptivity to pleasure, savouring it but not grasping after it. In life, think of pleasure as *only* feedback, not the goal, not the purpose.

Even in mental rehearsal (imagination), the same applies. Pleasure is a key aspect of the learning process.

7.6   Accessing Flow

In chapter six we touched on the paradox of deliberately and consciously accessing flow. We clearly can't will ourselves into flow, so how do we access it? There's no simple answer to this question but there are a number of things we can say.

- Flow is rather like sleep insofar as it's in the ambit of the body intelligence more than the willpower or thinking mind.

Therefore we need all the indirect methods of accessing body intelligence resources that we've discussed in this chapter.

- We should work to set up the preconditions of flow, or triggers for flow. I discuss these in section 7.6.1 below.
- We have to recognise and accept that we can't be in flow all the time. As we saw in chapter three, flow is a stage of a broader experience, and it's often necessarily preceded by hard work and struggle. At other times we need down-time where we don't have any particular purpose.
- Another way to think of flow is as the region around the peak of the human performance curve (as we saw in chapter six). We need sufficient self-awareness to know which side of the peak we are on, and then either increase effort, arousal, intensity etc. or let go and relax.

7.6.1 Preconditions for Flow

We've already touched on the most important preconditions for flow in chapter five. They are:

- The right level of challenge or difficulty (in relation to current ability). We need to be pushing the envelope of our comfort zone. Steve Kotler tells us[73] the generally accepted view (in the world of elite athletes and the like) is that the optimal is 4% greater than your current skill level. It's going to be hard to quantify that in everyday activities like playing the guitar, but the point is, don't push it by much. Play pieces that a just a little difficult.
- Clear goals – makes paying attention much easier. To be clear, the goal most be fairly immediate. If your goal is to perform at the Albert Hall that's a little too far off. Your immediate doesn't need to be anything glorious, it could be simply to play the next tennis shot into the court, or play the current piece of music.
- Feedback – meaning that you can clearly perceive the effects of what you do, in as short a time-frame as possible. In guitar playing, the feedback is the sound of the music. In tennis, it is

seeing where your shot goes and feeling how your body feels as you hit the ball. In other words, feedback is sensory in nature, and it helps if your sensory experience is as rich as possible, involving as many sense channels as possible.

These three help to create interest and the sense of enjoyment. External factors contribute to interest too: novelty, unpredictability, complexity, even a little risk helps. Another important factor for accessing flow is a growth mindset: openness to learning and development. But ultimately you have to allow flow to happen.

7.7   Summary of Key Points

- The dual-intelligence model frames the challenge as how to consciously and deliberately access the resources and abilities of the non-conscious mind, if not by willpower which doesn't work and can create more problems.
- Learning, at the level of the non-conscious mind or body intelligence, happens easily and spontaneously (without effort) in response to seeing and feeling, not (language-mediated) instruction.
- We need an attitude of trust and appreciation towards the "other" part of the mind.
- Imagination is an important faculty that can achieve results as an alternative to effort and willpower. It taps into "simulator mode" - the mind's automatic capacity to simulate emotional experience.
- Worrying and catastrophising are ways that imagination can work against us, but it can be applied constructively too – we can imagine positive and favourable outcomes.
- How we pay attention is another important factor in creating responses from the non-conscious mind / body intelligence. Focusing (in the right way) engages our conscious mind, freeing the non-conscious part to do its thing without interference.

- Interest is a positive emotion that is naturally conducive to learning, and so should be valued and cultivated.
- Pleasurable feelings can be considered as useful feedback from the body intelligence – they should be appreciated and savoured but not grasped-after – they are *only* feedback not the goal.
- To give yourself the best chance of experiencing flow, work to set up triggers and preconditions for flow – but ultimately you have to wait and allow it to happen.

8 Arousal, Stress and Relaxation

8.1 Introduction

Chapter three presented a scientific understanding of the biological basis of arousal. In this chapter I want to expand on the practical implications, particularly in the context of managing stress.

You'll recall the human performance curve introduced earlier in the book and reproduced in figure 8.1 below.

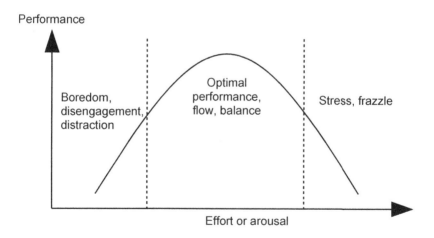

Figure 8.1 The Human Performance Curve

The human performance curve is a useful construct because it draws out some key ideas:

- Peak performance is about balance – balance of effort, balance of arousal.
- To function well we need two complementary mind-body skills:
  – activation or increasing arousal – mobilising energy
  – decreasing arousal – relaxing, calming down, letting go.
- Peak performance is founded on self-awareness – seeing where you are right now in order to see which way you need to go.

Like all models the HPC also has a weakness – it's overly simplistic and glosses over a lot of complexity. Arousal isn't a simple undifferentiated state but rather is a manifold concept. In this chapter we'll look at what this means in practical terms.

8.2   What Is Stress?

In physics and engineering stress is a force acting through and within a body that tends to pull it out of shape. In biology stress is any challenge to an organism that tends to pull it away from its physiological norm, and thus requires a response from the organism so that it can maintain its well-being or allostasis. An example of mild physical stress: skipping a meal – blood sugar tends to fall so the body responds by mobilising stores to maintain available energy. In broad terms stress increases physiological arousal.

In common parlance we use the word stress in its psychological sense: the feeling of being challenged, to a point that's close to the edge of our comfort zone, perhaps beyond. Dr Kelly McGonigal describes stress as what arises when something you care about is at stake[74]. There's some question mark over our ability to successfully meet the challenge – in other words, the challenge is in some sense a threat. Though skipping a meal is a physical stressor, many people wouldn't think of it as stress because they don't doubt their ability to handle it. (It would be significantly more stressful if you didn't know where the next meal was coming from.)

Often the source of stress is purely psychological or emotional (e.g. your boss gives you critical feedback on a piece of work you've done). But there's still a physiological adaptation, one that's similar to that for a physical challenge.

If you can adapt easily and comfortably to stressors, you're said to have high stress tolerance or stress resilience. When you have low stress tolerance, even little things cause a lot of upset. If your body can't easily mobilise energy stores, skipping a meal will make you feel bad. So stress tolerance is founded on mind-body adaptability or flexibility.

8.2.1 Stress and Resistance

Stress tends to give rise to inner resistance, or the desire to rid yourself of the experience of stress. Inner resistance is itself a source of stress. This is a key point here: it augments the physiological response, potentially creating a spiral of worsening stress. We have an example of a self-reinforcing feedback loop (first described in chapter three). It's the reason why the notion of resistance is such an important one to be aware of.

I've seen this many times while doing biofeedback training with clients. Their inappropriate efforts to control the physiological signal create a worsening spiral – it's reflective of a lot of real-world self-control challenges where the real problem is that inappropriate attempts to control tend to amplify the issue into a major difficulty.

8.2.2 Arousal Is Not Stress

As I've said stress tends to increase arousal or mobilise energy. But not all arousal is stress (in the sense of threat). If you take a roller coaster ride, your hair may stand on end and your heart may pound, but we call this thrill rather than genuine fear. (The differences are firstly your cognitive appraisal: you know you aren't really in danger and secondly willingness. Of course for some people it can easily tip into fear – there is no hard and fast boundary.)

Arousal is not a bad thing in itself – think of it as the mobilisation of energy. Stress management is not the avoidance of arousal, rather it is the art of keeping it within bounds, and rapidly recovering. This is important because if you see arousal as a problem to be avoided, then any experience of it becomes a potential threat, automatically triggering resistance – even experiences that would otherwise be enjoyable. A stress management strategy of avoidance of arousal doesn't tend to work very well, because of the danger of mental quicksand, and leaves you with a rigid inflexible mindset and a rather restricted lifestyle.

8.2.3 Stress and Mindset

It's clear from this discussion that how you view stress, or how you interpret what's happening (and in particular your assessment of how well you'll be able to cope) is a significant factor in determining how much of a problem stress is.

This is the subject of Kelly McGonigal's excellent book, "The Upside of Stress: Why Stress Is Good For you and How To Get Good At It". She discusses the common perception that stress is harmful, both to your health and to your performance – and asks, is it really so? Her answer is interesting and surprising: stress is harmful but only when you believe it to be. And that's because responding with resistance and avoidance makes it so.

The physiological stress response is your body's attempt to meet a challenge, or to up your game so that you can perform better. A research study showed that for people sitting an exam, those who showed the biggest rise in the stress hormone cortisol (i.e. had the greater stress response) actually performed better in the exam[75]. This and other studies show that the stress response really does help – and not just for minor stress.

But for stress to be helpful we need what we can term a positive stress mindset, which is the view that stress is a challenge to be embraced, and the stress response is your body's stepping up to the challenge and boosting your performance – as opposed to a negative stress mindset which sees stress as a threat to be avoided because it can harm your performance and even your health.

When I'm working with clients I emphasise the importance of adopting a positive stress mindset at the outset. Without it, any stress reduction technique is likely to fail because it will tend to be used as an avoidance strategy.

(I should say for completeness that another way stress can be harmful rather than helpful is when it is persistent, even if minor, so that your system doesn't have a chance to calm down again, as we shall see later in the book.)

8.3   What Does Stress Actually Feel Like?

Being *aware* of stress responses in the body is a key foundation of mind-body regulation, but what exactly are the physiological changes that make up stress, and what do they feel like?

Recall from chapter three that physiological changes are mediated through three channels: (i) the autonomic nervous system (ANS) which is divided into sympathetic and parasympathetic nervous systems (SNS and PSNS), (ii) the somatic nervous system which controls skeletal muscles, and (iii) hormones.

The table below lists the specific effects of the autonomic and somatic nervous systems. Hormonally-induced changes, which generally take place over a longer time-scale, are discussed in section 8.5 below. Not all changes are directly perceivable (e.g. blood pressure changes). I've tried to focus on actual experience.

Body System	Physical change and mediator	What It Feels Like
Heart	SNS – speeds up heart rate, and increases force of contraction, and reduces HRV (variability).	Acute stress – heart races and pounds. Maybe palpitations. HRV changes are harder to perceive.
	PSNS – slows down heart and increases variability.	Though heart rate can't really be felt directly by most people, with practice you can get a sense of heart coherence (see chapter ten).
Gut	SNS – diverts blood away from the gut, and reduces motility (movements) in upper part of gut while increasing it lower down. Digestive secretions (e.g. stomach acid, pancreatic juice) suppressed. (PSNS does the opposite.)	Acute stress can trigger butterflies, loose bowels. Chronic stress can cause indigestion, bloating, pain, IBS, due to the suppression of digestive function.
Muscles	SNS can divert blood towards the main skeletal muscles	This may contribute to feeling strong and powerful (in anger). In anxiety the legs and arms are more likely to feel like jelly.
Breathing	SNS can increase blood flow and dilate the air passages, increasing the efficiency of respiration. Somatic NS can change respiration rate and shift towards chest breathing.	Acute stress can trigger need to fill the lungs right up – the diaphragm tightens and doesn't easily relax again. Breathing can speed up and shift to a chest-based pattern. In chronic stress this pattern can become habitual. See chapter four for an extended discussion of breathing.

Face	Somatic nervous system triggers facial expressions of emotion – e.g. smile for happiness, frown for frustration.	In persistent stress, tight jaw and brow can become set. You may not necessarily notice it. Teeth grinding at night is also associated with stress.
	SNS can adjust blood flow in face.	Blushing and blanching.
Hands, feet, skin	SNS diverts blood away from peripheral parts of the body.	Low blood flow can leave the hands and feet feeling cold.
	Another branch of the SNS triggers sweating in the hands.	The hands can feel clammy.
	The SNS also triggers piloerection.	Goose pimples – hairs standing on end.
Sex drive	Too much SNS activity can suppress libido	Stress can cause loss of interest in sex.
Energy	SNS activity generally increases metabolic rate (cells' energy consumption) while PSNS decreases it	Acute stress can increase your sense of energy (which can feel good). In chronic stress (burn-out) you can get stuck in parasympathetic dominance and feel flat and listless.

8.3.1 Global Feelings

We can't necessarily consciously feel all the details of the stress response. Most of us aren't aware of our heart beat most of the time, still less how it's changing from beat to beat. Often what we get at the conscious level is a vague, generalised feeling of the body or the "viscera", that would be hard to put into words. Stress has also been shown to affect the immune system, but we can't directly sense this change, except perhaps as a global change in our feeling of well-being and energy.

We need to take this into account as we learn to be more aware of stress in the body – sometimes we may not see the forest for the trees. It's a good idea to see both the forest and the trees.

8.3.2 Stress and the Brain

In the above table we've focused on bodily changes and their associated feelings, but of course the brain is affected too. In general terms it's fair to say that short-term mild to moderate stress heightens performance, while chronic stress degrades functioning – in other words the human performance curve (first introduced in chapter five) very much applies.

Acute stress boosts alertness. Reaction times are reduced. Levels of the neuromodulators noradrenalin (associated with alertness, vigilance) and dopamine (associated with drive and energy, also reward) are increased, but chronically elevated levels may lead to a down-regulation of the receptors for noradrenalin and dopamine, leading to reduced attentional performance. Certainly chronic stress impairs PFC functioning, weakening focus and concentration.

Memory is also heightened by short-term mild to moderate stress – both memory retrieval and memory formation. (You've probably noticed you have a much clearer memory of emotionally significant events like your wedding day.) Chronic stress again impairs memory, especially retrieval. Extreme stress can do strange things to memory – it can lead to PTSD (which was considered briefly in chapter three).

As you may have noticed, stress affects sleep, triggering a reduction in the overall amount of sleep but also a change in sleep quality – you spend relatively more time in shallow sleep at the expense of deep sleep (also called slow-wave sleep) and in consequence you tend to wake up feeling unrefreshed. This pattern is prominent in depression. It's bad news because deep sleep is physically restorative.

Sleep changes are mediated by the hormones such as cortisol, and also by the sympathetic nervous system. Normally the SNS deactivates as you enter sleep (only to rev up again during REM sleep which is associated with dreaming) so it's no surprise that excess SNS activation hinders sleep access. A pattern of insomnia characterised by early morning waking (3 or 4 am) is associated with adrenal dysregulation – see section 8.5.1 below on the "burn-out" stage of stress.

Sleep deficit is itself a source of stress so there is potentially a vicious cycle that's hard to break out of.

Pain perception may be altered by stress too – in acute stress pain sensation may be heightened (hyperalgesia) or inhibited (analgesia) – as when a soldier in battle doesn't notice he's been seriously wounded. Stress-induced analgesia is probably mediated by the release of substances known as endogenous opioids (endorphins and enkephalins) but it doesn't last. Chronic stress is associated with chronic pain.

8.4   Stress and Polyvagal Theory

In the old model of the ANS, stress tilts the arms of the scales in favour of the sympathetic arm and away from the parasympathetic. Stress was typically seen as the short sharp shock that punctuates the equilibrium of parasympathetic dominance. In the classic stress scenario, cave-man ancestor meets sabre-toothed tiger – a real case of fight-or-flight. A modern version might be, you realise you need to run for the bus or you'll miss it. Once you've caught the bus or seen off the tiger, panic over, the parasympathetic brake goes back on again and you calm down. (Again we're reminded arousal in itself is no bad thing – it helps you catch that bus.)

In chapter three we met the polyvagal theory: a view of the ANS as a three-level hierarchy:

- At the lowest level, the old vagal system triggers rarely-if-ever-helpful shut down.
- At the intermediate level, the sympathetic system triggers fight-or-flight activation.

- At the highest level, the new vagal system inhibits the sympathetic and enables social engagement and higher level cognitive functioning.

In modern life sudden shocks are much less the norm. More likely are more enduring stressors, such as worrying about whether you'll be able to pay the mortgage, or knowing that your husband drinks too much, or not knowing what sort of mood your wife will be in when you get home. Not necessarily traumatic by any means, and not necessarily enough to trigger sympathetic activation in any major way, but perhaps enough to cause withdrawal of the new vagal brake. That may be all that's needed to send you into sympathetic dominance. You may not be pouring sweat but your social engagement systems are deactivated, you're hyper-vigilant and thinking of all the things that might go wrong.

The new vagal system is activated by perception of physical, and crucially *social and psychological* safety – while detection of social and psychological threat triggers withdrawal of the new vagal control, sympathetic dominance and social withdrawal.

Again the old view of the ANS was that its actions were global and non-specific (much the same whatever the particular emotion was) but more recent findings dispute this – it seems the ANS can mount quite specific responses, differentiating the various emotions.

8.5   Loss of Regulation

The body's stress systems are connected through various feedback loops. For example recall the "HPA axis", the hormonal branch of the fight-or-flight response: perception of stress in the brain triggers the hypothalamus (remember, it's the brain's interface to the body) to signal the pituitary gland to release a hormone (ACTH) to trigger the adrenal glands to secrete cortisol. The brain then detects higher cortisol levels which suppresses the hypothalamus's demand for more cortisol.

The system is designed for brief stressors that punctuate the norm of benign safety and comfort.

What happens to the feedback loop when stress is chronic or persistent? Well, there is evidence that it breaks, and regulation is lost or at least weakened. In other words, chronic stress can cause you to lose adaptability and flexibility.

8.5.1   Stages of Maladaption

Evidence suggests there is a discernible pattern or progression of stress, culminating in exhaustion. Our modern understanding of the stages of stress owes a lot to Hungarian endocrinologist Hans Selye who developed a theory of the stress response which he called the General Adaptation Syndrome[76].

Early Stage

At first you get stuck in a stage of high arousal – "chronic acute" stress if you'll forgive the oxymoron. It may feel like you literally can't switch the brain off – thoughts race, you're stuck in constant busyness, driven from task to task, feeling restless, wired, perhaps anxious, unable to transition into sleep. You may notice blood pressure drifting upwards, and a craving for sugar and carbohydrates.

Adrenal Dysregulation

It seems that in particular the HPA axis regulation is prone to breaking down. In stage 1 stress ("chronic acute") cortisol levels become chronically high. Remember cortisol is a key energy currency in the body, so you're likely to still have energy at this stage (it might even feel quite good) but the problem is cortisol starts to do damage when chronically elevated. It can kill brain cells and also suppress the immune system. Some people feel a strange combination of tired plus wired at the same time.

Burn-out

Eventually you hit the exhaustion stage[77], when cortisol levels drop low. Your energy and drive tend to drop with it – especially mid to late afternoon. (Actually in the classic pattern you may get a second wind in the evening, then struggle to get to sleep, then you are wakeful in the early hours again (3 or 4am) only to feel dog tired again when it's actually time to get up.) You may be especially dependent on regular intake of food, because lacking cortisol your body is unable to adequately maintain your blood sugar levels. Mentally you tend to feel foggy and flat. Because cortisol helps you meet the challenge of stress, your stress tolerance likewise drops off and any little thing feels like a crisis. You struggle to calm down again but eventually you crash in a heap, feeling tired for perhaps days afterwards.

The adrenals also produce several other key hormones which also become dysregulated including:

- Testosterone – in both men and women – it's also linked to motivation and energy.
- Oestrogen and progesterone – PMS often accompanies adrenal dysregulation in women.
- DHEA – the most abundant hormone in the body, DHEA is associated with general well-being. Dubbed the "youth hormone" because it's at its highest levels in the 20's before dropping off as we age, DHEA can drop low in exhaustion-stage stress.
- Aldosterone – this hormone regulates blood pressure. Blood pressure usually drops low in exhaustion-stage stress, and often fails to respond in the normal way, which is why you may notice dizziness on standing.

Adrenal regulation can be assessed using laboratory testing. Probably the most commonly used test looks at levels of cortisol in saliva. Besides the actual level of free or active cortisol, the diurnal rhythm is also important, and this test gives an sense of this based on four samples taken over the course of the day. Most commercially available adrenal profiles also include DHEA. I emphasise these tests are stress assessments rather than medical assessments, just as adrenal dysregulation is a stress condition rather than a medical condition. As such they are not commonly used in mainstream health services, at least in the UK.

8.6   Varieties of Arousal

I've described arousal as the mobilisation of energy. But energy can take many forms and flow down many pathways, and thus arousal is a complex manifold process. In chapter three we looked at the biological basis of arousal and I began to make the case that it's useful to distinguish brain arousal from bodily arousal. I used the example of a peak meditation state, combining bodily stillness and tranquillity with intense awareness. In more everyday terms we can call this state of calm body and active brain simply relaxed focus or relaxed concentration. It's a supremely useful state, relevant to so many contexts in life – indeed I considered sub-titling the book "the art of relaxed concentration".

In figure 8.2 below I've developed the idea further by using the two notions of brain and body arousal as axes of a map of mental states. Note, this chart is purely speculative, and is based on my own subjective estimates rather than on any sort of scientific data.

I've put "emotional meltdowns" in the bottom right quadrant. I'm referring to times when emotions take over and we lose our self-possession – what I termed in chapter three "emotional hijacks". I placed this one low on the brain arousal graph because according to the neuroscience understanding the brain's executive control centre (the prefrontal cortex) would be inhibited. But at the same time the emotion-triggering centres (in the limbic system) are probably highly activated – so we see even the notion of brain arousal is an over-simplification.

I've put "effortful concentration" as spanning the division between high and low body arousal. Sometimes we put quite a bit of "huff and puff" into concentration, tightening the brow and maybe the shoulders, hands and more.

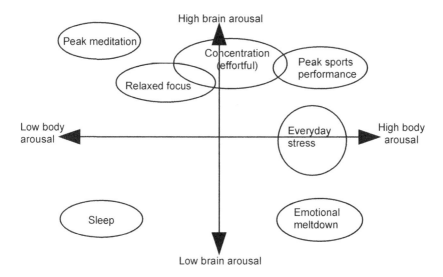

Figure 8.2 Speculative map of various arousal states

8.6.1 Brain Arousal

What does brain arousal mean in practical terms? Again it is not a simple concept. Keeping things simple I think it's useful to distinguish four senses.

1. Alertness or intensity of awareness. When we focus or concentrate we ramp up arousal in this sense. When we dose off it ramps down again.
2. Cognitive activity – at times the mind can generate high volume thoughts, ideas, images – either creatively and constructively, or unhelpfully as when we're distracted from whatever it is we'd rather be focusing on (e.g. sleeping).
3. Desire, drive and motivation – when we are intensely determined or craving, for example.
4. Emotional arousal – emotions can be more or less intense.

The latter two overlap significantly with bodily arousal. Negative emotions usually have a much stronger body arousal component than positive emotions.

In the brain the key player is the prefrontal cortex, as we saw in chapter three. Strengthening its function is key to developing the ability to consciously intensify alertness and quieten the less helpful forms of brain arousal such as racing thoughts, cravings and negative emotions.

8.7   Relaxation

Relaxation is the art of reducing arousal, especially bodily arousal. It means moving leftwards on the human performance curve – a useful ability when you find yourself to the right of the peak.

In this section I'll review some of the key concepts we've developed so far in the book and we'll see how they apply to the question of how to relax.

In terms of the dual intelligence model, the ability to relax resides at the level of body intelligence. The thinking mind doesn't know how to do it, and when it tries (by exerting willpower) it tends to create mental quicksand, making things worse, all the more so if there is a sense of urgency. Remember the body intelligence doesn't understand words, it just responds to emotional undertones. If your mindset is along the lines of, "I need to relax or else ...", then the body reacts as if to threat. Another way to create mental quicksand is to do a kind of performance anxiety. If you're thinking "what if I can't relax" or even more overtly "I'm no good at relaxing, this is not going to work", that will exaggerate the threat response.

On the other hand, your body already knows how to relax. We just have to let it happen. We use the phrase "letting go" synonymously with relaxation, and I think it's very apposite. When you let go of an object you release muscle tension so that your grip relaxes. When you let go of stress, emotions etc. you're likewise releasing muscle tension.

In chapter seven we reviewed some of the principles involved in accessing body intelligence resources. To recap:

- An attitude of trust that your body knows how, together with appreciation when it does. Of course it's easier to have that faith as you build up more experience of actually feeling relaxed.
- Attention to the senses – especially looking for comfortable, even pleasurable feelings, which are feedback from your body when it actually gets things right. Pay attention with an open, curious mindset rather than a "grasping" one. When you're in a relatively comfortable context, take in sensations in the body, but if you find yourself in a stressful situation this may be unhelpful and counter-productive, and it may be better to attend to what's going on externally – what you see and hear around you.
- Imagination – with a small "i" – within the context of sensory-based attention, wondering what it would feel like to feel relaxed, or to be even more relaxed. Imagine sensory details – the shoulders feeling heavier, droopier, the hands softer, floppier, the breathing slower and gentler. Or imagine different settings – lying on a beach, walking in the mountains, whatever is your thing.

8.7.1   Physical Relaxation

At the physical level the process of relaxation involves these key elements:

- muscles go loose
- breathing shifts (for more details see chapter four)
- the ANS shifts away from sympathetic dominance towards parasympathetic dominance.

The former two changes are mediated by the somatic nervous system which is more amenable to conscious influence, while autonomic changes are less so, and can only be guided indirectly. In part 3 we'll cover our tool-set for mind-body regulation (biofeedback and mindfulness) and we'll see how these key changes can be achieved.

8.7.2 Acceptance

Acceptance is letting go at the psychological level. Here are some examples of contexts where acceptance is needed:

- Self-critical thoughts: you didn't perform well at X (fill in your own example – driving test, job interview, presentation, etc.).
- Self-view: you're not the world's greatest X (tennis player, lawyer, mother, husband).
- Ethical appraisal: your behaviour in situation X was morally culpable (e.g. road rage, food binge, unfaithfulness)
- Self-restraint: you can't afford that particular X you've been wanting (e.g. new car, new dress). (Here I'm referring to the need to let go of desire rather than the inhibition of reckless spending.)
- Disappointment: e.g. you lost the tennis match, didn't get the job, failed the exam.
- Anxiety: situation X is scary but it's in your long-term interest to go through with it, e.g. driving test, flight before your holiday, job interview.
- Uncertainty: not knowing can be frustrating or anxiety-inducing – e.g. you're working on a short-term contract or a zero hours contract and you're not sure if you'll still be able to pay your mortgage in six months' time.

The opposite of acceptance is resistance or experiential avoidance – the mindset of fighting against unwanted experiences, such as anxiety or physical pain. The examples I've listed are likely to involve an element of inner resistance. As we've seen, resistance is a mind-body phenomenon. The physiological expression of resistance is:

- muscle tension – we tighten up as though bracing ourselves against a threat, or holding something at arms length
- breathing changes
- sympathetic activation.

In other words, the opposite of the physical aspects of relaxation (not surprisingly).

Throughout the book I've been emphasising the importance of the mind-body principle. In order to feel the "heat" of stress, anxiety, etc. (i.e. the unpleasantness of it) we have to *embody* stress. Shifting out of the physiology is like letting the air out of a balloon. For example, self-critical thoughts such as "you made a mess of the interview" have the power to hurt to the extent that they trigger a physiological response (tightening up muscles, etc.) but if you block that physiological response or weaken it or reverse it, it becomes just another thought – you shrug your shoulders and think "so what", and move on.

So acceptance as a psychological skill is *founded* on letting go as a physiological skill.

Practical Considerations

The ability to let go (of resistance) is one of the most important components of mind-body intelligence. As a professional working with clients I almost always start with the skill of letting go of muscle tension. Later in the process we cover breathing training and autonomic rebalancing, and then it's a matter of making sure these general skills are transferable to real-life contexts. Muscle tension control is a good place to start because it's relatively easy for clients to learn, and to grasp the relevance.

Letting go of muscle tension sounds easy, and for some people it is, but in my experience, for a lot of people it isn't. It's easy to not notice a certain amount of tension, especially if it's habitual. Of course you need to be aware of something before you can consciously change it. That's why biofeedback is the ideal tool for working with muscle tension. You can increase your sensitivity and learn to fully release tension. Biofeedback is covered in part 3 so I'll defer further discussion till then.

Forgiveness

What should you do after a self-control failure? A lot of people are hard on themselves, believing that so doing will help them avoid repeated slips. You may be surprised to learn that research suggests the opposite is true. Being hard on yourself makes it more likely that you'll repeat your mistake, while a self-forgiving attitude makes it less likely. (It's also good to learn from your mistakes. Thinking about what you did wrong – but without any blaming – and how you can do things differently in future, will serve you well. But that's a very different thing from guilt and self-recrimination.)

In life it's inevitable that sooner or later other people will not do right by us, and we need to be able to let go of resentment. Living with resentment is like holding a burning coal in your hand with the intention of throwing it at your enemy – we're the ones who get burnt.

Forgiveness is another form of letting-go, or acceptance – extended to the social and ethical level. It isn't just a moral capacity that you're born with, you have to know how to do it. It is a skill, that can be developed. The same principles apply: forgiveness needs to be embodied in physiological change.

8.8   Summary of Key Points

- Peak performance is a matter of balanced effort and balanced arousal.
- Speaking biologically, stress is any challenge that pulls you away from physiological balance (allostasis) or psychological balance. In everyday usage stress means the feeling of being pushed to the edge of or beyond your comfort zone. Generally the stress response involves arousal or the mobilisation of energy.
- Inner resistance (struggling against your experience) itself provokes a stress response, potentially creating a worsening spiral.
- Arousal is a response to stress, but not necessarily experienced as stressful if you're confident of your ability to cope.

- The stress response involves numerous bodily changes, some of which can be sensed directly, others of which contribute to a sort of global visceral feeling.
- Classically stress is thought of as a short sharp shock punctuating equilibrium but modern stress is often low-level and persistent. It doesn't necessarily trigger the classic "fight or flight" response so much as a withdrawal of the parasympathetic brake, leaving you feeling hyper-vigilant and on-edge.
- Persistent low-level stress can lead to a breakdown in the normal feedback loops regulating the stress response.
- Over the longer term this loss of regulation follows phases: firstly "chronic acute" stress and later an exhaustion stage or burn-out. Adrenal hormones such as cortisol are affected.
- Arousal can be divided into brain activation and bodily arousal. In relaxed concentration the body is calm but the brain alert and engaged.
- Relaxation is the art of reducing arousal, especially bodily arousal. It's an ability that resides largely at the level of body intelligence, and keys to accessing it include a mental attitude of trust and appreciation, paying attention in a certain way, and using imagination constructively.
- Acceptance is letting go at a psychological level. It includes forgiveness. It is founded on the skills of letting go at a physical level, or reversing the physiological expression of resistance, notably muscle tightening, breathing changes and sympathetic nervous system activation.

Part 3

Tools for Training the Mind

9 Mindfulness and Meditation

9.1 Introduction

In chapter one I framed the solution to various problems such as out-of-control emotions and wandering focus as a process of learning, training and development. Mindfulness fits that framework – it's a centuries-old form of mind training, a way of applying the mind aimed at gradually transforming the mind. Mindfulness has its origins in the ancient spiritual traditions of the East, most notably Buddhism. In more recent times Mindfulness-Based Therapy (MBT) has emerged as an evidence-based approach to mental health issues such as depression and anxiety[78] – though mindfulness isn't a therapy in itself but a tool or faculty that anyone can use and benefit from.

In this chapter I'll make several references to Buddhism because I think it's important to understand mindfulness in its own context. You don't have to be a Buddhist or even interested in Buddhism to practise mindfulness, and I don't think anything I say will conflict with any religious beliefs you may have.

9.2 What Is Mindfulness?

Mindfulness is the practice of being actively aware in the present moment, with a sense of openness and interest, kindness and non-reactivity. This simple sentence carries within it a lot of meaning, so let's unpack the elements.

- **Actively aware** – in mindfulness we pay attention with conscious intent. The intent is to maintain awareness, and to keep on gently returning to present-moment awareness whenever the mind wanders into distraction, as it almost inevitably does.
- **Present moment** – whatever we are attending to (whether a specific focus or otherwise) the focus is in the here and now. By contrast distraction tends to take us off into the past or the future.
- **Openness and interest** – we are receptive to whatever is, without preconceived notions of how things should be, and with a spirit of curiosity and possibility, even hope and optimism. We are open to uncertainty, to newness and change.
- **Kindness** – awareness is coloured with a background emotional warmth or good-will.
- **Non-reactive** – we accept our experience just as it is, on the one hand not resisting or struggling against what we don't like, and on the other hand not getting sucked into or swept away by or over-identifying with thoughts and feelings that we do like, but maintaining a sense of spacious self-possession. We're also accepting of ourselves, without need to judge our attempts as good or bad, worthy or unworthy, success or failure. (Often mindfulness is described as non-judgemental[79], but I prefer the term non-reactive or even objective – more on this later.)

The opposite of mindfulness is mindlessness. If we're honest we spend much of our lives running on "auto-pilot", in a semi-conscious state, not making conscious choices and decisions but engaging automated patterns of thinking and behaving. This happens when we decide we already know what's going on, what we need to do, and what to expect. We fail to appreciate the newness and uncertainty of each moment[80].

The Purpose of Mindfulness

Why would you want to spend time in the practice of being actively aware in the present moment, with a sense of openness and non-reactivity?

I've described mindfulness as a kind of mind training, and the purpose of training is to develop skills, abilities, qualities or knowledge. In Buddhism mindfulness practice aims to develop selfless love and compassion, plus direct knowledge of (insight into) the true nature of reality beyond words and concepts – in fact the complete transformation of the mind. You don't necessarily have to aim that high – in a sense the purpose of meditation is whatever you want it to be. Most people come to mindfulness wanting a bit more of qualities like stillness, calmness, clarity, openness, peace and contentment, emotional positivity, compassion – all of these are worthy aims.

Yet there is an incongruity here: we want these qualities, yet the practice is to simply observe the mind, neither grasping after particular experiences nor rejecting them. We want the mind to be calm, yet we are to hold it as a matter of indifference whether it actually is calm. How are we to resolve this apparent paradox? We'll return to this question in section 9.4 below.

Mindfulness and Insight

Mindfulness is about training awareness, but this awareness goes beyond concrete awareness of the immediate moment to include awareness of the mind's patterns and tendencies: how it tends to behave. We might call this meta-awareness. For example you might notice that today you are tired and sleepy, or that irritability is persistently coming to mind, or that you habitually respond to boredom by thinking about what you're going to do later on.

At a deeper level, and in its original Buddhist context, mindfulness aims at what we might call spiritual insight, or insight into the true nature of reality, perceiving the qualities of impermanence, insubstantiality and unsatisfactoriness – but this line is taking us beyond the scope of this book.

9.2.1   The Spirit of Mindfulness

We can add to the somewhat bare and simple definition I gave earlier with more figurative descriptions of mindfulness. Buddhist scriptures give us several metaphors for mindfulness, which communicate something of the spirit. Here are just a few[81].

- Being mindful is like walking with a bowl filled to the brim with oil balanced on your head. Moving with smoothness, grace and precision, not a drop is spilt. In other words this metaphor emphasises the *balancing* influence of mindfulness.
- Mindfulness practice is like climbing a tower, enabling you to see a long way. With mindfulness we gain *perspective, clear-sightedness*, and perhaps *detachment*.
- Mindfulness is like a strong post to which a wild animal is chained. The wild animal is the unruly mind. This metaphor emphasises the stabilising influence of mindfulness. A variation of this metaphor from the Tibetan tradition says that it is best to tether a wild horse with a long rope. Then the animal still has some freedom, plenty of space to move about it, and thus does not struggle and strain. As it gets used to captivity, the rope can be shortened – a metaphor for balanced effort (not too wilful, not too lax)[82].
- Mindfulness is like a city gate keeper, who allows the good citizens to pass, but keeps out undesirable elements. Mindfulness *protects* the mind. (This metaphor emphasises that in Buddhism mindfulness is not separate from ethical awareness and practice.)
- Mindfulness is like a surgeon's probe. It is incisive and can uncover the truth of what is really going on. This metaphor emphasises the *insight* element of mindfulness.

9.2.2 Mindfulness as Balance

In chapter six we touched on the idea of mindfulness as a balanced attention, a middle way between dull, low-energy distraction, and over-active, agitated distraction. The following table summarises different aspects of mindfulness as balance.

Aspect of mindfulness	Pole 1	Pole 2
Arousal level	Low-arousal mind, dullness, sleepiness	Agitated, restless, over-aroused mind
Nature of effort applied	Laziness, passivity	Wilfulness
Nature or style of focus, awareness	Lacking self-consciousness	Overly self-conscious (lack of flow), perhaps even alienated from the body
Relationship to mental contents	Overly passive, overwhelmed, sucked-in, too close to experience or too involved	Struggling, resisting, over-controlling, too far away from or alienated from experience

9.3 Mindfulness as Meditation Practice

Mindfulness can (in theory) be practised any time, whatever we are doing, or even all the time. In this sense it's a mindset more than a practice. But it's practised more formally in meditation.

One of the most common meditation practices is the mindfulness of breathing. Traditionally (in the Buddhist world) it's taught to people in the early stages of their training. It's an incredibly simple practice (though not necessarily easy to do) and at the same time an incredibly rich practice – don't expect to out-grow it. The instruction is simply to keep the attention on the breathing – observing and feeling it, without trying to change it, judge it or analyse it. When the mind wanders off, simply return your focus to the breath, gently and without reacting emotionally. (More detailed instruction involves counting and stages within the practice, but the essence is simply observing the breath.)

Another mindfulness practice is "just sitting", also called "open awareness" or "pure awareness". Here there is no object of focus at all. The practice is to remain aware of whatever comes to mind, neither resisting or rejecting any content, nor becoming so drawn in and involved with it that you lose your self-awareness. Of course the mind won't remain blank, contents will appear. It helps to be able to identify what is happening – aspects of experience, or domains of mindfulness include:

- the body – sensations and feelings (another common form of mindfulness practice is the "body scan" meditation)
- pleasure and pain – strong, weak or pretty neutral
- emotions, in all their aspects (which we listed in chapter two)
- thoughts, images, memories and other internally-generated mental goings-on.

9.3.1 Systematic Meditation

In my experience this just sitting form of mindfulness is a much more challenging practice than the mindfulness of breathing, and really quite a different practice. To fully understand the difference, we need to consider meditation as a *system* of training. In Buddhism, meditation practices are classed as either *samatha* (in the original Pali language, meaning tranquillity or calm abiding) or *vipassana* (meaning insight). In truth the practices themselves have elements of both, so perhaps it's better to say a practice can be done as either samatha or vipassana. Traditionally, in the early stages of training, samatha practice predominates, though the insight element is never totally absent.

Samatha meditation aims to calm, still, clarify, stabilise, compose, unify and concentrate the mind. It aims to strengthen volitional control, so that the mind can be directed, and also to strengthen what we might call positivity. In other words samatha develops *integration* – gathering the mind's energies into a unified flow. The opposite of samatha is restlessness, agitation, confusion, different parts of the mind pulling in different directions ("dis-integration"), and inconsistency. Mindfulness of breathing is a classic samatha practice.

Vipassana or insight meditation aims to reveal to the meditator the true nature of reality and experience. Gaining insight is not simply passive seeing but is radically transformative. This is a truly spiritual level of practice, which I alluded to earlier, and is largely beyond the scope of this book, so I'm not going to attempt to say what the true nature of reality is! I'll confine myself to saying that pure objectless mindfulness practice is much more of an insight practice, compared to mindfulness of breathing, though of course it has a strong tranquillity component too. Again, I think it's much more challenging to practice objectless mindfulness effectively. Traditionally samatha practice is done first because it creates a platform for much more effective vipassana.

Many people find it difficult to keep their mind stable and focused for any length of time at all, and they spend much of their meditation time in distraction, which isn't very gratifying. (Modern society seems to be conducive to over-stimulation, leaving us with agitated, restless minds.) If this is the case for you, I recommend mindfulness of breathing rather than objectless mindfulness, at least to begin with.

The notion of a system of meditation is a way of understanding different forms of practice and how they relate to each other. The idea is developed much more fully in the book "Buddhist Meditation: Tranquillity, Imagination and Insight" by Kamalashila[83].

9.3.2 Progression in Meditation

Implicit in the Buddhist conception of a system of meditation is the idea of progression within meditation practice. There is a skill in practising meditation, and over time, with consistent practice, you should become in some sense more accomplished or more adept – just as you would with any other skilled activity. (There is research evidence that attentional control does indeed improve.)

In Buddhist terms, samatha practice leads to *dhyana*, or absorption. Dhyana is the point at which meditation becomes easy or effortless. The mind becomes very stable – distracting influences drop away, or at least lose their power to pull you away from your focus. The experience is quite blissful.

The essence of dhyana is integration – the energies of the mind are unified and flowing in the same direction. Your attention is fully taken up with the present moment focus – nothing is left over. The Buddha gave a metaphor: a skilful bath attendant mixes soap powder with water and kneads them into a ball of lather, so that the water fully pervades and permeates the soap, and yet no water is left over and wasted. In dhyana the mind is likewise fully suffused with present-moment awareness.

You might be thinking that dhyana is starting to sound like a flow state, and indeed I think in large part it is, but I think there are differences; in meditation you don't lose self-awareness, though you do lose the "separateness" of self-awareness.

In the course of a meditation session, you can progress from an everyday mind towards dhyana, gradually stabilising attention and deepening absorption. And as your practice develops over months and years, hopefully this absorption will become easier to access. That doesn't mean that dhyana will inevitably happen, and it certainly doesn't mean the practice was a failure or waste of time if it didn't happen. Nor does it mean that after ten or twenty years of daily practice you'll be able to slip into dhyana as easy as changing clothes. (You can learn to drive a car and eventually you can do it automatically, without needing to pay much attention. Meditation is the one thing where this never happens – it always calls for your whole attention.) I would guess that most practitioners don't experience dhyana in most of their sessions. Nonetheless I think it's useful to think in terms of developing skill in meditating. Dhyana is not the goal of meditation but you can think of it as helpful *feedback* in developing your skill.

Mindfulness as Skill and as Fitness

In summary, mindfulness is a form of training, and with training you develop your skill – you get better at holding the mind steady in its focus. As time goes on your experience of contentment, tranquillity, love, freedom, etc. becomes fuller and richer and deeper. You learn from your experience. You learn what works and what doesn't work.

Yet any experienced practitioner could tell you it doesn't always appear so! I've practised mindfulness meditation consistently for over twenty years, and yet I still have days where I struggle to hold my focus for two consecutive breaths.

Another way to view training is that it increases your fitness – mind fitness and / or brain fitness. Stop training, and your fitness level soon starts to drop. Even a couple of weeks break from practising, you can find your concentration loses its edge. Neuroplasticity works both ways. Of course you can quickly regain your edge, but however many years you've practised for, *consistent* practice matters.

9.3.3   Summary of Forms of Mindfulness Practice

The following table summarises the differences between the two forms of mindfulness practice.

Mindfulness of breathing	Just sitting / open awareness
Active, concentrative, one-pointed focus	Receptive, open focus
More effortful	Relaxed effort
Predominantly samatha (tranquillity)	Elements of vipassana (insight)
Narrow attentional style (see chapter twelve)	Broad attentional style
"Top-down" attention	"Bottom-up" attention

Leads to absorption, stability of focus	May lead to insight
Done earlier in one's training as it builds stability, which is to some extent prerequisite for open focus practice	Tends to be much more effective if practised from a platform of stability / samatha practice

9.4 Mindfulness and Purpose

Let's return to the apparent incongruity I pointed out earlier: we come to mindfulness with the aim of developing certain qualities (even if only stable focus), yet we're to practise as though it didn't matter whether we succeed or not. I think virtually all of us come to meditation because we want to experience the mind in a certain way: tranquil, clear, bright, still, loving, open, expansive, sharp, content, free, creative, steady, relaxed (or whatever else you might want to add). And we don't want (or we want to move away from) agitation, disturbance, restlessness, craving, negative emotions such as anger and ill-will, states of awareness that are dull, foggy, narrow and confined, rigid, chaotic, constrained. I don't think there is anything wrong with this. Yet the practice is merely to observe impartially.

One part of the answer is that the purpose of the practice is distinct from the actual intention we hold in mind. You might cycle to work every day, and as a result you get fit. But on any given day, your intent is only to get to work. Nonetheless, you appreciate being fit. Likewise, if you stick to the intention of simply being aware, returning to the focus, then the mind will naturally become calm, clear, still, etc. by itself as it were, without trying.

Another part of the answer has to do with levels of the mind. Remember the dual intelligence model introduced in part 2. The intent to only observe without partiality is the instruction for the thinking mind, or the conscious mind, while the purpose is like an intent at a deeper level of mind. We can in a sense delegate the intent of developing tranquillity, warmth, serenity, etc. to this other part of the mind, we can put our trust and faith in it. Sleep is perhaps a helpful metaphor: we can't try to do it, we have to just let it happen – though at the same time we need to deliberately set up favourable conditions. Indeed when the conscious, thinking mind tries to over-extend itself and starts to grasp after particular experiences, it tends to create more trouble of the mental quicksand variety.

A third part of the answer has to do with the Buddhist view of the true nature of reality. In this view all experience is marked with three characteristics: impermanence, unsatisfactoriness and insubstantiality. When you truly see these marks, you see that in a sense nothing really does matter – and yet you act wholeheartedly as if it did. Living life takes on the character of play.

So in mindfulness we embrace this rather paradoxical mindset of holding to goals and purposes but not attaching any importance to whether or not you are successful. It's as though we're playing a game, or acting a part in a play. You aim to keep your focus on the breath, but it doesn't matter if you get distracted. You are open to positive qualities such as peace, stillness, stability etc. but you don't grasp after such experience, since nothing lasts forever anyway. You wait for such qualities to emerge naturally, in their own time, as a gift from your deeper self. Mindfulness is about travelling more than it is about arriving at any particular destination.

9.4.1   Is Mindfulness Judgemental?

As we've said, mindfulness is commonly described as non-judgemental. This is worthy of closer inspection as there's some potential for misunderstanding.

The gist of the idea is that we need to watch out for an everyday sort of attitude we can call "doing mode"[84], because it's effective for getting things done, getting things finished. In doing mode, our awareness is wrapped up with our progress towards some end-state, rather than actual experience of the present moment, as though constantly asking the questions, "am I doing it right?" or "am I finished yet?". This is useful if you've got a deadline for a project, but antithetical to the open, even playful spirit of mindfulness, which is not about achieving anything in particular, not about arriving at any particular destination. (That's not to say mindfulness doesn't have a purpose or a direction of travel.)

There's a danger of throwing the baby out with the bathwater here, because there's another sense in which mindfulness *is* judgemental.

You may be surprised to learn that in Pali, the language of the ancient Buddhist scriptures, there isn't a single world for mindfulness. Rather the meaning is conveyed in two words, which are sometimes compounded together, expressing two component concepts[85]:

- Sati – meaning bare attention, in the present moment. It's awareness of what is going on right now. It includes an ability to describe experience (e.g. naming your emotions, which research shows is very useful).
- Sampajanna – usually translated as "clear comprehension", it means an awareness that is more extended in time, to include an awareness of where you've come from and where you are going – in other words it includes awareness of purpose.

I find the latter aspect is not often emphasised in western expositions of mindfulness (i.e. in the MBT tradition). Mindfulness is discerning. Let's consider a couple of examples: suppose you're practising meditation and you notice some rather pleasurable sensations of strong relaxation in the belly. You find this peeks your interest, and you can "go with it", not grasping after it but savouring it, while it lasts. Suppose some time later, thoughts related to sexual desire arise, perhaps out of a sense of boredom. Though such thoughts are alluring, you decide not to "go with it", since your sampajanna tells you going there is not consistent with your purpose of developing calm contentment etc. So in this sense mindfulness is "lightly" judgemental: you decide to either subtly embrace or gently turn away from particular experiences depending on how they will affect you.

Mindfulness is not judgemental in the "heavier" sense of judging sexual thoughts as bad, unworthy etc., still less judging yourself as bad and unworthy for having such thoughts, or as morally culpable and deserving of punishment. Equally mindfulness isn't about judging yourself as good and worthy for not having such thoughts or for keeping focused on the breath.

As intensely social creatures we humans naturally seek the approval of our fellow humans, and we want to avoid their disapproval. We've learned to internalise this process by imagining what others would think, even about our innermost thoughts and feelings if they were made public, and thus we approve or disapprove our own inner contents. It's judgement in this sense that is no part of mindfulness.

Mindfulness involves the recognition that we have little control over what happens to appear in the mind, but we do have some control about feeding such contents with the energy of our attention.

Again we need this paradoxical mindset: you recognise "negative" (or "unskilful" as Buddhists say) qualities when they arise, but you accept them without resistance or struggle. You're looking for clarity, contentment, etc. without grasping, without trying to achieve any particular end-point.

9.5   Mindfulness and the Mind-Body Connection

Many of the mental qualities we've talked about are actually mind-body phenomena. Tranquillity involves a stillness and relaxation in the body, as well as the mind. Agitation is a physical restlessness as well as over-activity of the mind. Thus awareness of the mind-body connection is a key aspect of mindfulness.

In his book "Touching Enlightenment: Finding Realization in the Body" Reginald Ray[86] suggests we need to "meditate with the body". He means we need to be intimately aware of what's going on in the body and how it intimately connects to the mind. But further, to fully experience the positive qualities of "enlightenment" we need to embody them.

In chapter eleven I advance the notion that biofeedback can support mindfulness practice, and make it more effective in achieving its purpose of developing qualities of mind such as stillness, clarity and compassion. Biofeedback guides you towards physiological states that are more conducive to the qualities you aim to develop.

Working with biofeedback calls for something of the same paradoxical mindset of holding a purpose yet without any attachment to success or failure. There is a "goal" state or at least a direction you want your physiology to move in, yet you must allow it to happen, rather than grasping after it (which tends to be counter-productive). In chapter five we looked at several everyday examples where this dynamic applies, sleep being probably the clearest example.

9.6   Loving-Kindness Meditation

Another of the core Buddhist meditation practices is *metta bhavana*, which translates as development or cultivation (bhavana) of loving-kindness or good will or friendliness (metta). Technically speaking it is not a mindfulness practice, but of course focus and awareness are an indispensable basis for the practice. As with mindfulness you can practice metta bhavana without being a Buddhist. Metta bhavana complements and balances mindfulness training – without it the mind can become overly cool and maybe even alienated.

Metta could be described as positive emotion. As I've said earlier in the book, emotion is a complex concept with several components. With metta, the emphasis is firmly on the volitional or intentional aspect rather than the feeling aspect. In other words, metta is good will. It is wishing others (and ourselves) happiness and well-being. Metta practice is intimately connected to one's ethical stance in life, rather than being a hedonic pursuit. Metta is perhaps more like a *value* than a positive emotion (remember I made this distinction in chapter two). You can focus on good will even when you don't *feel* very emotionally positive yourself. It's a common mistake to put too much emphasis on positive feelings – don't judge the practice by what you feel, especially within the time frame of the practice.

As with mindfulness we need to embrace the paradoxical mindset of holding the purpose of developing positive emotion without being at all attached to success. Positive emotion can't be forced or grasped after. Rather, we need to invite it into the mind – with an open, playful, imaginative and trusting mind-set. I like the word cultivation. When we cultivate plants we focus on setting up the conditions in which plants will thrive – then the plants will naturally grow themselves. It's like that with metta, and with positive emotions generally (more on this in chapter fifteen).

Barbara Fredrickson researched the effects of loving-kindness meditation and found that it "produced increases over time in daily experiences of positive emotions, which, in turn, produced increases in a wide range of personal resources (e.g., increased mindfulness, purpose in life, social support, decreased illness symptoms)"[87].

For a fuller account of metta bhavana practice, see "Loving-kindness: the Revolutionary Art of Happiness" by Sharon Salzberg[88], or "Metta: the Practice of Loving Kindness" by Nagabodhi[89].

9.7   How Mindfulness Creates Change

If you practise mindfulness and meditation regularly and consistently you can expect positive qualities such as contentment and stability to gradually develop.

Mindfulness strengthens your faculty of **attention** – it exercises the brain's "attention muscle" (the PFC or prefrontal cortex, introduced in chapter three). Research confirms mindfulness enhances attentional performance[90]. Brain imaging research shows the PFC is more active during mindfulness meditation[91,92] and that mindfulness genuinely stimulates enduring neuroplastic change –

parts of the PFC have been found to be thicker in regular meditators[93].

Mindfulness builds **emotional resilience**. Recall from chapter three that Professor Richard Davidson showed that emotional resilience is reflected in a small but measurable predominance of activity in the left side of the PFC relative to the right. He found that mindfulness practice shifts this balance favourably towards the left. Other research shows mindfulness favourably shifts the balance between the PFC and the (anxiety-invoking) amygdala[94].

Mindfulness builds greater **self-awareness**, particularly of the body. Self-awareness is an indispensable foundation of mind-body intelligence. Again research shows that the brain area associated with mapping body states (the insula – introduced in chapter three) is thicker in regular meditators. Mindfulness builds a meta-cognitive awareness of your mental habits, patterns and tendencies.

In terms of the skill-set of self-regulation, mindfulness especially develops **acceptance** and **letting-go** (the faculties we need to counter resistance). Mindfulness creates a sense of spacious awareness that allows us to see thoughts *as* thoughts, rather than as reality. For example, let's say you're about to sit an exam, and, feeling rather anxious, the thought comes into your head, "I can't do this". When you're drowning in anxiety you can't see beyond this thought, but with a little mental space you can stand a little apart from it, you can see it as just a thought that entered your head. It's not that you suddenly see through it and no longer believe it, it's more that you know it's not the full picture, not the whole story. You don't have to act on the basis of it. You've been able to separate yourself a little from the thought. This ability has been termed *cognitive defusion* in Acceptance and Commitment Therapy, which is one of the better known versions of mindfulness-based therapy. Cognitive defusion is very much related to acceptance – it is acceptance of thoughts. (And of course it is facilitated by letting go at the physical level.) Ultimately mindfulness can help you move to a broader and more flexible self-view[95].

9.8   The Nature of Distraction

If you've ever tried mindfulness or meditation you'll know that it's only a matter of time before the mind wanders off into distraction. You start thinking about what you're going to do later on, or replaying the conversation you had earlier, etc. The practice is simply to return to awareness, non-reactively, again and again. But first you need to recognise when you've "gone off". This ability to catch distractions as early as possible is a key part of the skill of stabilising the focus.

To improve at recognising distraction, it helps to know something of its nature and the forms it takes. Being able to characterise different ways in which we can become distracted enables us to devise counteracting strategies appropriate to each form of distraction. Each of us as individuals tends to have habitual styles of distraction (these are traditionally known as hindrances)[96].

9.8.1   Dimensions of Distraction

I find it helpful to think in terms of a series of distinctions or dimensions – these aren't a set of mutually exclusive categories, rather they define the axes on a sort of multi-dimension map. Any particular distraction could be characterised as a set of "coordinates", or points on each of the dimensions. (Note, this is not a traditional way of thinking about distraction.)

Some of the dimensions range between two opposite poles (they are bipolar) with the optimum state being in the middle, while others have only one pole and vary between zero and high (zero being the optimum).

Energy or Arousal

You can have too little energy or too much.

Low energy distractions are sleepiness, mental tiredness, slothfulness, laziness, boredom, daydreaming.

High energy distractions include restlessness, agitation, anxiety, fretting and worrying, and craving.

Another way to describe this distinction would be high arousal versus low arousal (both physiological and psychological).

A related distinction is between chaotic and rigid functioning. When we are over-aroused we tend towards chaotic mental states, while under-arousal often goes with repetitive and inflexible thinking, and feeling stuck.

Emotional Valence

I borrowed this distinction from the circumplex model of emotion (chapter two). The emotional quality of a distraction can be negative or unpleasant or positive (pleasant).

Negative emotional distractions include anger, resentment, ill-will, anxiety, gloominess and misery. First we need to let go of and be accepting of our negative emotions (not the same as suppressing them), then we need to allow positive emotions to grow.

Positive emotions are less clearly distractions, but they can be if they lead us away from the object of concentration into excitable frothy mental activity.

Thinking or Self-talk

Probably one of the more common manifestations of distraction is being swept away by inner mind-chatter. Thinking activities of the mind include planning, speculating, worrying, ruminating, reminiscing, doubting.

This is a mono-polar dimension (varying from zero to too much).

Sensing and Feeling

Sometimes we are overloaded with mental imagery – including non-visual "imagery" such as a tune playing in your head. Fantasising and craving are mental processes high on this dimension (which is another mono-polar dimension).

Resistance or Inner Conflict or Dis-integration

Resistance is the fundamental dynamic of the mind that I've referred to throughout this text. It can arise in meditation practice, particularly when different parts of the mind are pulling in different directions. At its most basic, a part of us doesn't want to be meditating, wants to be doing something else. We are not integrated, we are far from flow.

Control

This is a way of characterising not so much the distraction as our way of working with it. Sometimes we can be wilful to the point of being counter-productive – we end up in the quicksand trap. At the opposite pole, under-controlling means being overly passive, not making much effort.

This dimension is dependent upon our beliefs about what is possible. If I believe that I should be able to stay focused on my breath all the time, then I'm likely to become wilful. If I believe my mind is never going to change, I'll be overly passive. Both positions are unhelpful.

9.8.2   Countering Distraction

A model of different forms of distraction is useful to the extent that it can help us in countering distractions. For each pole of distraction we need an antidote or strategy to reduce it. As you gain experience of meditation practice you'll develop a sense of your individual propensities for distraction. In any practice session you'll see patterns arising and you'll see how to adjust your mental application in response.

In high-level terms here are some strategies for particular forms of distraction.

- High energy or high arousal distraction needs to be countered by calming and stilling the mind.
- Low energy distraction calls for interest-kindling and energy-rousing mental application.

- For negative emotions we need first acceptance and then we need to access positive emotions.
- Frothy and over-excitable positive emotion needs to be calmed and deepened.
- Excessive mind-chatter can be countered by attending to sensory experience (body and outward senses, hearing and vision).
- Craving and fantasising can be balanced by reducing arousal, cultivating stillness and contentment.
- The antidote to resistance is letting-go and acceptance.

9.8.3 Distraction and Biofeedback

In the next chapter, we'll cover biofeedback in some detail, looking at the different physiological parameters that can be used. Later (in chapter eleven) we'll see how biofeedback can support mindfulness practice, in part by functioning as a distraction detector. We'll return to the different forms and dimensions of distraction, and consider the strengths and weaknesses of different biofeedback parameters in countering distraction.

9.9 Summary of Key Points

- Mindfulness is a form of mind training first developed in the ancient spiritual traditions of the East, and now supported as a therapeutic intervention by a growing body of research. It is the practice of being actively aware in the present moment, with a sense of openness and non-reactivity.
- The purpose of mindfulness is to develop qualities of mind such as stillness, calmness, clarity, stability of focus, contentment, emotional positivity and insight. The intent of the practice is to maintain awareness in the present-moment, neither grasping after nor rejecting any experience.
- Mindfulness can be practised at any time, but more formally it's practised in a context of meditation.
- Samatha (tranquillity) meditation aims to stabilise attention while vipassana (insight) meditation aims to see into the true

nature of reality and experience. Different forms of mindfulness emphasise one or the other. Traditionally, samatha practice is done first as it builds a platform for more effective vipassana.

- With consistent practice you can develop your skills in mindfulness – e.g. your attentional control is enhanced. Mindfulness is also a matter of fitness – stop practising and you soon start to lose your edge. Consistent practice counts.
- Mindfulness calls for a rather paradoxical mind-set of holding goals and purposes, but with complete impartiality – as if it didn't matter whether we achieve our purpose or not.
- Mindfulness is "lightly" judgemental – in the sense that we are discerning of whether our attention is leading us in a fruitful direction or not. We need to exercise a kind of ethical judgement – but not in the "heavier" sense of judging things (or ourselves) as good or bad in any absolute or enduring sense.
- Mindfulness is a mind-body practice: we need to *embody* the qualities of mind we seek to develop.
- Metta bhavana meditation aims to develop loving kindness, or good will towards all beings. It is an important complement to mindfulness practice.
- Mindfulness creates change by (i) strengthening the attention faculty (strengthening PFC function), (ii) developing self-awareness, particularly body awareness, and (iii) improving emotional self-regulation and resilience.
- Distraction can be (non-traditionally) characterised in terms of several dimensions. Thinking in these terms, and getting to know your personal habitual tendencies, helps you systematically counter distraction.

10 Biofeedback

10.1 Introduction

Biofeedback was introduced in chapter one as a tool for developing self-regulation skills, by exploiting the possibilities inherent in the mind-body connection.

In earlier chapters we've explored the science behind the mind-body link, and seen how subjective experiences are reflected in quite specific physiological processes. Though science has no doubt yet to plumb the full depth and richness of the mind-body link, what matters here is that there are a few key aspects that we can measure easily and cheaply. In biofeedback we feed these measurements back in real time via computer, either visually or through sound. As the feedback varies in conjunction with passing thoughts, feelings and other inner experiences, we get a clear demonstration of the reality and practical relevance of the mind-body link. Thus the feedback provides opportunity for developing a more sensitive and refined mind-body awareness, which in turn is the platform for learning to influence or guide our physiology towards a state more supportive of calm, focused and emotionally positive mental states.

What is the specific nature of this "positive" physiology, and how do we measure it? In this chapter we explore some of the most useful biofeedback parameters in some depth.

Of most interest are parameters that correlate with emotions or emotionally-laden thoughts. Emotions are complex phenomena and we can't hope to measure every aspect or even most. The most expedient biofeedback parameters will meet the following criteria:

- easy to measure
- clearly recognisable relationship to subjective experience (meaning that the parameter is responsive to everyday mental life – it changes with passing thoughts and feelings etc.)
- relatively easy to influence.

We'll consider EMG (a measure of muscle tension), Heart Rate Variability (HRV), Electrodermal Activity (EDA), skin temperature, capnometry and other breathing measures, and Hemoencephalography (HEG). HEG is a neurofeedback parameter, meaning it is based on a direct measure of brain activity.

10.2   How Biofeedback Creates Change

There are three main ways that biofeedback can create change. Each biofeedback parameter tends to exemplify one of the three more than the other two.

10.2.1 Insight into the Nature of Mind-Body Dynamics

In the first place biofeedback opens up awareness of the mind-body connection. This is the foundation of training in mind-body regulation skills.

Mind-body intelligence is the awareness of how the mind-body connection works in practice – how thoughts condition physiological responses and vice versa, and what works and what doesn't work in terms of influencing the process.

I remember a client, a lawyer who was seeking help for her explosive rages. A couple of years earlier her marriage had been strained by the husband having an affair. She had decided to work at repairing the relationship, but every few weeks something would trigger an emotional outburst in which all the old anger would come back to the fore. She wanted to keep a lid on these emotions so that she could move on.

We worked with EDA (described later). I asked her to attempt to control the signal, knowing she wouldn't be able to, since variations in EDA are largely involuntary. The result was extreme volatility – the signal would go shooting up, followed by a precipitous drop, followed by another lurch upwards. My client realised that her attempts to control her rage were having an exactly parallel effect – extreme emotional instability and volatility. It was a classic example of the quicksand effect. This was a key insight for my client, and though we did a few more sessions after that, I think we probably didn't need to. She stopped having the emotional meltdowns.

So biofeedback offers a hands-on demonstration of the ideas (such as the quicksand effect) that I've been discussing, which is always so much more convincing than reading about it.

10.2.2 Mind-Body Skills Development

Suppose you want to learn to play violin, or to play tennis. You need only a minimal amount of verbal instruction, to get you started. The rest is practice. In the context of practice, the brain learns naturally and spontaneously through sensory feedback. Take tennis: visual feedback is seeing whether the ball goes where you want it to go, or into the net or out the back of the court. You also *feel* the shot – when you time the ball well and catch it in the middle of your raquet it feels good; if you mistime it, it doesn't. There is also sound feedback – the well-timed shot makes a pleasing sound. For the violin the feedback is much more auditory and kinaesthetic rather than visual.

In either case, change gradually happens – you get better, your ability or skill-level improves. Within the nervous system, neurons are adapting themselves – perhaps by growing new connections or synapses, or perhaps by recruiting more cells for the task. (This process, known as neuroplasticity, is the subject of much interest in neuroscience.) Muscles are likewise developing and strengthening too but the key is the brain's control of them, which is becoming more refined. Another way to think of the change process is as creating new habits, or new conditioning, embodied in new brain pathways.

With biofeedback and neurofeedback, a similar gradual enhancement of ability happens. We can assume there's an accompanying neuroplastic process. In psychological terms you get better at quickly and easily accessing your desired mind-body state. Your focus improves, or your emotional stability and positivity improves, or your executive function improves. You can expect that these core skills will generalise to wider contexts, so that you function better at work, or in social situations.

10.2.3 Exercise and Fitness

If you go to the gym every day and lift weight, then over a timescale of weeks, months and years, your muscles will bulk up. The change doesn't happen during the exercise periods – in fact you're causing some mild damage to the muscle tissue (and in the early stages at least, you feel it the next day). But that mild damage is the cue for the body to begin a regenerative process, which doesn't stop at mere repair but actually enhances muscle strength.

Biofeedback is like weight training for the brain and nervous system. Regular practice is the cue for neuroplastic change, again over a timescale of weeks and months. The result is improved brain fitness.

Does it mean that if you stop exercising then you regress? Perhaps to some extent, but though we may stop doing biofeedback sessions we never stop using our brains – we never stop emoting, focusing, concentrating, planning etc. Certainly the experience of biofeedback practitioners is that change is lasting.

The exercise mode of change might not sound very different from skills development described in the previous section. I think the difference is that skills give you real conscious choices in the context of your life. When you find yourself in a stressful situation, there is something you can now do that you weren't doing before.

Exercise improves your fitness. If you're late for the train you can run and catch it, if you've been in regular training recently. Similarly, biofeedback is fitness training for the brain and nervous system so that in life you naturally cope better with stress.

Another way to think of the distinction is that skills-biofeedback is training for the mind while exercise-biofeedback is training for the brain. (In practice, neurofeedback tends to be more in the latter category while other forms of biofeedback are more mind training.)

10.3   EMG or Muscle Tension Biofeedback

EMG or electromyography (also known as surface EMG or SEMG) is a way of measuring muscle tension by attaching sensors to the skin. The placement of the sensors decides which muscles are measured – either a single muscle or a group of muscles.

EMG is a good starting point for biofeedback because:

- the correlation between the measured signal and subjective experience is very apparent (usually)
- it's relevant – everyday thoughts and feelings produce non-volitional changes in EMG
- it's relatively easy to change
- it produces benefits quickly (although the benefits aren't necessarily dramatic).

10.3.1 Muscle Tension and the Mind-Body Connection

Working with muscle tension takes us right into the fascinating and propitious middle ground between the conscious and unconscious minds - in terms of the dual intelligence model, we're right in the overlap between thinking intelligence and body intelligence (figure 6.4) - they both can effect muscle tightening.

On the non-volitional side, the basic idea is that we tighten up when we feel stressed, threatened, anxious, frustrated or angry. Few would dispute this – it's part of most people's experience. It's not something we have to think about it – it just happens in a reflex-like way.

More fundamentally, it's the experience of what I've called resistance that triggers muscle tightening. Resistance is not liking, not wanting or not accepting the experience that you've got. I remember once being at the dentist, and as she poked and scraped and drilled etc., I realised my legs were sticking up in the air. When we don't like what we're experiencing, we literally brace ourselves, as if against a physical threat. The interesting thing is, we do the same (albeit not to the same degree) to a psychological threat. Imagine sitting down with your boss for your performance appraisal, or telling your partner you want to end the relationship. Even inner emotions can trigger tightening.

Recall "simulator mode" first introduced in chapter three: a thought comes to you, usually about a future scenario or a memory of a past event, and the mind automatically creates the feeling of what it would be like – here and now. Thinking about what might go wrong in the future can hurt you right now. Memories of past hurts can replay themselves again and again. This is the basis of so much everyday human suffering. Of course simulator mode can trigger muscle tightening too – the same bracing against a threat.

It's not just emotions that affect our muscles – thinking and focusing style do too. Imagine focusing narrowly and intensely, perhaps on a problem you need to solve. It could be that your brow furrows or your jaw tightens. These are more non-volitional, reflex-like responses.

Conscious Awareness and Control

Volitional control over muscles is of course possible as well – if you notice your shoulders are tight, you can release them, or if your brow is furrowed, you can soften it. That's *if* you notice it. When you're not aware of something, you're not in control of it, at least not consciously. In my experience as a therapist, this awareness is an individual thing. Some people are only too aware of the feelings in their body, including muscle tension, while others live in a world of thoughts and ideas and for them body and feelings etc. are the undiscovered country – we say they are "in their head", perhaps even stuck there. These two types are poles on a spectrum rather than distinct groups.

If you're in the former group, you may feel you're too much at the mercy of unconscious influences and your conscious control of muscle tension is deficient. For you, EMG biofeedback will be useful especially in learning how indirect methods (such as attentional techniques) can help.

If you're more of a head type, EMG biofeedback is probably even more relevant to you because it can help you expand self-awareness, the prerequisite of control. Just because you're not aware of something, doesn't mean it isn't having a profound effect on you. Perhaps for you anxiety takes the form of worry – excessive thinking, especially about what might go wrong, or perhaps racing thoughts that you can't switch off, or even obsessive thinking. The point is, style of thinking is very much influenced by physiological state in general and muscle tension in particular.

Of course muscle tension is not on or off but a matter of degree. Often there is a level of background tension that's a bit like the sound of the fridge in the kitchen. Your mind filters it out so you're not aware of it – until it switches off and then you notice. It's easy to maintain a background tension that you're not aware of, especially if you spend a lot of time in a sort of emotionally defensive state.

Even with conscious awareness, relaxing muscle tension, and *keeping it relaxed*, isn't necessarily straight-forward. It isn't quite the willpower that does letting go – you have to allow it to happen, and you have to avoid an inner conflict with the emotional forces that may have created the tension in the first place.

Which Muscles Are We Talking About?

Stress tends to manifest as tightness in the shoulders and upper chest and neck, also facial muscles and brow, also hands.

Internal Dialogue

For most of us, thinking takes the form of inner dialogue, where we inwardly talk to ourselves. This can be productive – if we are reasoning or problem-solving for example – but more often it's a rather useless chatter that the brain seems to automatically generate when it's got nothing better to do. We can replay old conversations, or have imaginary conversations, or give a running commentary on our own performance (sometimes harshly judgemental). Often when this is happening we're using the speech muscles (in the tongue, lips, etc.) in a subliminal way.

We've probably all encountered people in the street, perhaps homeless or apparently mentally ill, who talk out loud to themselves. It seems like a shocking and highly aberrant thing to do, but those people aren't so very different from us – the difference is their inner stream of thought is being fully verbalised rather than subliminally verbalised.

For some people this internal dialogue is a real problem – it's tiresome, annoying, distracting, and they can't shut it up, much as they'd like to. It can even keep them awake at night.

An EMG device can actually detect some of this subliminal inner speech as muscle activity. Learning to fully relax muscles in the head is an excellent way of strengthening the skill of quietening the mind. This is useful for getting to sleep and also in focusing intensely and clearly.

10.3.2 Summary of Applications of EMG

EMG biofeedback is most relevant to learning the skills of emotional self-regulation – learning to handle anxiety, worry, frustration, volatility, etc. It's especially useful in letting go of resistance, which manifests as muscle tightening. In my professional practice I almost always use EMG biofeedback as a lead-in for breathing training – I'll say more about this in section 10.4.3.

In terms of the three change modalities I listed in section 10.2, EMG biofeedback fits most closely to skills development. For some people it offers insight in the sense that they gain conscious awareness of muscle holding, and particularly its relationship to inner resistance.

Most people can learn to let go of muscle tension very easily, and once you know how, you can do it whenever you want. However for some people the problem is a rather unconscious habit – though they can drop tension, it pops back up as soon as your attention is drawn elsewhere. Changing this "baseline" tension can be much harder. That's where regular mindfulness practice can be very helpful. Mindfulness is an exercise of repeatedly bringing the mind back to a certain focus.

10.3.3 Measuring EMG

EMG is an electrical correlate of muscle tension, measured by attaching three sensors to the skin. The signal is actually a rapidly oscillating voltage, that derives from the nerves that stimulate the muscle to contract. The more nerve cells that are firing to signal the muscles, the bigger the amplitude of the voltage oscillations, and the stronger the muscle fibres contract.

Two of the sensors are known as the *actives* – the third being the ground. The way to think of it is that you're measuring activity in muscle(s) between the two actives. (Voltage is always a difference between two points.) The ground is necessary to filter out background electrical noise, such as that coming from mains electricity. (The mains generates an invisible electromagnetic field that extends well beyond wires etc. – this can be picked up by the sensors.) The placement of the ground is less important – it generally goes somewhere near one or other of the actives.

For practical purposes we aren't really interested in the oscillations as such. Just as a light bulb turns the rapidly oscillating current of the mains electricity into a constant glow, it is the job of the biofeedback software to convert the raw EMG signal into something more practical – e.g. a relatively smoothly varying graphed trace, which goes up when we tighten our muscles and down when we relax them.

10.3.4 Sensor Placements

Where we attach the sensors to the skin is important, because it determines which muscles are contributing to the feedback signal.

Suppose you placed the active sensors at either end of your biceps muscle – one near the elbow, the other near the shoulder. You'd then pick up activity in the biceps. If you have a knowledge of anatomy you can measure from any muscle you like, assuming it's close enough to the skin to be accessible. Muscles commonly used for biofeedback include the trapezius and scalene.

Alternatively you can use a more general placement that picks up activity in a group of muscles. In my professional practice I generally stick to these two placements:

- **Wrists** – this placement picks up all the muscles in the arms and shoulders and to some extent the neck and upper chest. (Note that many of the muscles that control the hands are actually in the forearm, so this placement also picks up tension in the hands.) These muscles are stress responsive, making it a useful placement. Certain breathing patterns can also be detected – see section 10.4.3 below.
- **Forehead** – placing the active sensors at the left and right sides of the forehead, with the ground in the middle, will give you a general measure of head tension. This is useful because most emotions are expressed facially – frowning or grimacing for example. Not only that, but many of the muscles are involved in inner speech, so it's useful for working with excessive mind-chatter (section 10.3.1).

10.4 Breathing Biofeedback

The breath is both ever-present and ever-changing. With practice we can find an incredible richness of sensation and feeling associated with the breath. It offers a unique window on the mind because it changes perceptibly in response to even very subtle mental influences – in particular emotions, but also our general state of arousal, and even the way we pay attention (or style of attention). For these reasons the breath is probably the most commonly used object of focus in mindfulness meditation.

There are a number of aspects of the breath that we can measure, hence several biofeedback parameters. We'll consider these in section 10.4.3. Chapter four gave a detailed overview of breathing physiology.

10.4.1 Breathing and the Mind-Body Connection

Typically the breath responds to negative emotions like anxiety and anger by becoming more rapid and shifting towards the upper chest and away from the abdomen. In section 10.3 we saw how stress leads to a general reflex-like tightening of muscles, a sort of bracing against the threat.

The breathing muscles are part of this response. It's most clear-cut in the startle reflex. Imagine a loud and unexpected bang – you draw a sharp intake of breath and hold it briefly (a gasp). Less startling threats tend to produce a subtler version of this: the breathing muscles such as the diaphragm don't fully release on the exhalation, meaning we don't breathe out fully. Also the breath tends to become more variable. This pattern can become habitual in people with a "defensive" mind-set.

Most importantly we're likely to tip into over-breathing, so reducing oxygen delivery to parts of the brain associated with calm clear thinking and self-possession (see chapter four for details of breathing physiology).

Conversely feeling safe, secure, calm, relaxed, peaceful etc. has the opposite effect: we release the breath all the way, the breath becomes gentler, slower and more abdominal.

Before I learned about breathing physiology I was aware that in my most concentrated and heightened states of awareness in meditation practice (which I only rarely accessed, while on retreat) my breath became so subtle as to be barely perceptible. My clients are often surprised at how little air they need to breathe. This is the opposite of hyperventilation – oxygen is maximally available to the brain. When people optimise their breathing (chemistry) in this way, they feel calm and clear-headed, self-possessed and keenly present. I've noted in my professional practice that they often feel sleepy too. I suspect this happens when people are sleep deprived – there is no necessary connection with sleep, though blood carbon dioxide levels are naturally a little higher in sleep.

There are many other ways emotions can express themselves through the breath. Consider these examples:

- a snort of derision
- a sigh of exasperation
- a sigh of bliss.

Attention and the Breath

When our attention is narrow and tightly focused (as opposed to broad and open) this tends to have a similar effect on the breathing as anxiety – i.e. it tends to become faster, more chest-based and more variable. Conversely when the attention is broad, open and spacious, the breathing is calm, gentle and slow. (Remember the focus can be broad and open but still incredibly clear, rapt even. Relaxation doesn't have to feel hazy or sleepy.)

Of course breathing regulation should be automatic – e.g. your body should optimise carbon dioxide levels without you being aware of it. Most of the time you won't want to be aware of your breathing (e.g. in bed at night, or when you're at work). (In terms of the dual intelligence model, it's the body intelligence that knows how to breathe well, not the thinking mind.) There's a danger that just by paying conscious attention you can interfere with this sub-conscious regulation – indeed I see this a lot in my professional practice. Breathing work is very prone to the quicksand trap. In particular, over-breathing is very easy to induce. The challenge is to be aware of the breath at the same time as letting the body breathe itself. Broad, open, non-grasping attention seems to facilitate this.

When breathing is optimal it feels easy, comfortable and smooth – even pleasurable. This sense of pleasure in the breath is a sort of internal feedback – I encourage my clients to look for it, trusting the body to create it, as a counter-measure to the tendency to over-control.

10.4.2 Summary of Applications of Breathing Biofeedback

Because breathing physiology is so fundamental, breathing biofeedback is relevant to all aspects of mind training:
* emotional balance
* concentration and focus
* cognitive performance
* energy, motivation and sleep.

10.4.3 Measuring the Breath

There are several measurable or calculable parameters relating to the breath. Chapter four reviewed breathing physiology in depth.

I consider the most important measure of breathing to be carbon dioxide, because it tells us about over-breathing or hyperventilation (which remember is not black and white but ranges on a spectrum). It's worth repeating the key point of breathing chemistry: over-breathing reduces oxygen delivery to the brain – in extreme cases by up to 60%. In my practice I commonly see people 10 or 20% below optimal – if you're in this category you probably don't know it. Optimal breathing means maximising blood carbon dioxide levels and thus oxygen supply to the brain.

Over-breathing can be habitual (chronic) or context-dependent (e.g. stress-related).

Capnometry Biofeedback

As we saw in chapter four, a capnometer is an instrument that measures carbon dioxide in the breath. It can thus detect degree of over-breathing and as such is an excellent biofeedback device. A study of breathing training using capnometry biofeedback showed that four weeks of training significantly benefited panic and anxiety, even over one year later[97].

Technically, the capnometer measures the partial pressure (PP) of carbon dioxide in exhaled air. Of most interest is the peak or end-tidal PP carbon dioxide, because this correlates with the blood concentration of carbon dioxide, which is the physiologically significant parameter. Most commonly the units reported are millimetres of mercury (mm Hg). That might sound esoteric – for practical purposes all you need to know is that the aim is to maximise the height of the peaks. 40 to 45+ on the the mm Hg scale is optimal, 35-40 is average, anything below is a degree of over-breathing. Figure 10.1 below shows the trace generated by a capnometer – there is a peak in the trace at the end of each exhalation. There is a brief period of over-breathing about a third of the way from the left, where the peaks are lower.

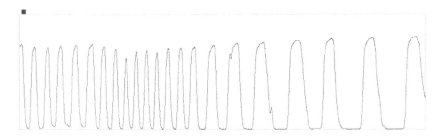

Figure 10.1   Showing the partial pressure of carbon dioxide trace from a capnometer

Clients often get confused over the fact that a low reading reflects over-breathing, not a high reading. In chapter four (section 4.2.1) I explained this using a water tank metaphor.

Even if you don't have a capnometer (and unfortunately most of them are rather expensive) you still need to keep in mind the possibility of hyperventilation, because in my experience it is very easy to induce it, when working with breathing, in which case you're probably doing more harm than good. Remember to keep the breath as gentle as possible.

In my experience of training people with a capnometer, most people can learn to optimise their breathing relatively quickly – at least when they put their mind to it. The problem is, often they go back to their habitual way of breathing as soon as their mind is elsewhere. The only solution to this is to learn a new habit through lots of practice, and lots of remembering to do it.

Breathing Rate

Breathing rate can vary widely, from about 4 breaths per minute (bpm) to upwards of 30 bpm. (If 4 bpm sounds very slow to you, you'll probably be surprised how easy it is, though it may take practice to be comfortable for some people). Slow breathing generally feels calmer, more relaxed. 6 bpm is in some sense an optimal rate, for reasons given in the next section on Heart Rate Variability. But remember the name of the game is flexibility: the ability to rapidly shift into the psychophysiological state most appropriate to the context. Relaxed is not always most appropriate.

Faster breathing rates tend to go with more energy. If you need to be keyed-up, for example you're giving a presentation, then a faster breathing rate is likely to be more conducive.

Whether you breathe fast or slow, it's possible to breathe optimally in terms of carbon dioxide levels (avoiding over-breathing).

Inhalation to Exhalation Ratio

Another variable is the time ratio between the inhalation phase and the exhalation phase of the breath. For most people in a relaxed state, the exhalation phase is longer, giving a ratio less than one (about 0.75). James Austin reports that at least some experienced meditators (in the Zen tradition) significantly reduce the relative duration of the inhalation (to 25%) – he believes this helps to quieten the brain[98].

I'm not aware of any context where it's clearly more adaptive to breath at a ratio greater than one (longer inhalation).

Breathing Sensors

We've already mentioned the capnometer, which can measure carbon dioxide and also breathing rate (but not inhalation to exhalation ratio).

In biofeedback, probably the most commonly used sensor is a strain-gauge belt – a stretchable belt that goes round the chest or abdomen (or both) which can measure the expansion as the body inhales. It should be possible to measure breathing rate and inhalation to exhalation ratio.

Another simple device is a temperature sensor or thermistor, which can be placed just at the nostril, where it can detect the difference in temperature between inhaled and exhaled air. In my experience this method is more consistent and reliable for calculating breathing rate and inhalation to exhalation ratio, though it won't give you any sense of the size of each breath.

Muscle Tension in Relation to Breathing

Quite significant changes in breathing can be effected by using different muscles. Breathing falls somewhere on a spectrum from chest-based breathing to abdominal breathing. These two styles were first described in chapter four, but to recap:

- **Chest-based breathing** uses the upper chest muscles, more, while the diaphragm is relatively immobile. It tends to involve a lifting movement of the thorax – the shoulders can be seen to go up and down. It's likely to be faster and air is exchanged at the top of the lungs which is less efficient. The upper chest should ideally be reserved for exertion and extra breathing capacity, rather than habitual breathing. In section 10.4.1 I explained that chest-based breathing is associated with a defensive style of breathing that is a response to stress and threat, also resistance.
- **Abdominal breathing** is more diaphragmatic, and likely to be slower. Movements are sideways and outwards more than up and down. Air is exchanged at the bottom of the lungs, so is more efficient, and more natural to calm relaxed states.

It's possible to differentiate these two styles of breathing using two strain-gauge belts, one around the chest, the other around the belly. But you can also do it using EMG (for muscle tension). Placing the EMG sensors on the wrists will pick up muscle activity in the arms, shoulders and upper chest, but not the diaphragm or lower rib muscles, so chest-based breathing is seen as a regular up-down rhythm in the EMG signal while abdominal breathing is much flatter.

In practice working with the breathing muscles is an important part of optimal breathing training. That means making sure the diaphragm is strong and fluid, so that you can let the breath all the way out. In habitual chest-breathers, who often live with a mild but enduring sense of threat, the diaphragm can get stuck in a tightened, immobile state, and as a result can become weakened.

10.4.4 Optimal Breathing Training

By now you'll have realised what a richly complex process optimal breathing training is – and that's before we've covered heart rate variability which is also related to breathing.

In my client work I cover breathing training in three phases using each of these biofeedback parameters in order:

1. **EMG** biofeedback – ensuring that breathing is abdominal and that the client can let the breath all the way out by fully releasing muscles on exhalation.
2. **Capnometry** biofeedback – ensuring that breathing is naturally gentle, subtle and calm (the opposite of over-breathing). At this stage I like to see the client can breathe flexibly, with optimal carbon dioxide levels at a range of breathing rates.
3. **HRV** biofeedback – this is covered in the next section.

The point here is that the three parameters form an *integrated* system – there is one method, but you can use different forms of feedback.

Note, in section 10.5.2 below I discuss a free breath pacing (software) tool, that is helpful in regularising your breathing rate.

10.5   Heart Rate Variability Biofeedback

Everyone knows that the heart responds to our emotions – a pounding heart in anxiety and a fluttering heart in high excitement are probably the most obvious examples. But if we are to exploit the connection in biofeedback, we need a way of quantifying the relationship, especially for more more everyday states of mind. Heart rate alone is too crude a measure, too changeable. Rather it's the pattern of variation that counts. Heart Rate Variability (HRV) has been found to correlate with emotional and physical well-being, and also cognitive performance. In fact it is a uniquely powerful measure. In her book "Maximum Willpower", Kelly McGonigal describes HRV as the best measure available of willpower[99].

Perhaps counter-intuitively, the more variation in your heart rate, the better. Even when you're sitting doing nothing in particular, the heart has a natural beat-to-beat variation. A metronomic heart beat is the hallmark of an unhealthy heart (both physically and emotionally). Perhaps a metaphor will help: in a fast motorbike, a mere touch of the accelerator will produce a roar of the engine and a surge of power and acceleration, while in a clapped-out old banger you can put the peddle to the metal and nothing much really happens. You'd want a heart more like the fast motorbike.

For training purposes, we are especially interested in a pattern of HRV which has been termed Heart Coherence (HC). Coherence means the quality of cohering – as when the parts of a system relate to each other in a meaningful and consistent way. In coherence, the heart speeds up and slows down in sync with the breath. An example is shown graphically in figure 10.2 below.

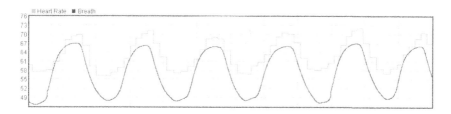

Figure 10.2 Showing relatively coherent heart rate variation over a one minute interval. The stepped trace (slightly higher of the two) is heart rate and the smooth trace (slightly lower) is breath (the upward movement is inhaling, downward is exhaling). You can see the two are synchronised.

It's not just the heart and breath that come into coherence with each other – several other body systems fall into step in some way, for example brain waves (more technically, EEG) follow the lead of the heart. You may have heard that if you put a lot of pendulum clocks in a room together, they will fall into step – the smaller ones follow the lead of the largest. When one system falls into step with another in this way it's known as entrainment. In the body the heart generates easily the largest electromagnetic field – it extends well beyond the body and can even be sensed by other people. So the heart can in some sense entrain the whole body – it seems that coherence sets up a particularly efficient state of body functioning. Coherence is not just a state of relaxation but of optimal functioning – for example it's been shown that reaction times are lower in coherence.

Physics and engineering have developed ways to quantify coherence as a relationship between two signals, and we can do the same in physiology. We'll go into the details of how this can be done later, but here we'll note that high ("good") coherence is characterised by:

- Large changes in heart rate between the beginning and end of each exhalation and inhalation. In graphical terms, what I call the heart wave (the stepped trace in figure 10.2 above) has a large amplitude. This change can easily be equivalent to 20 to 30 beats per minute or more (e.g. if HR is 50 bpm at the beginning of an inhalation, and 80 bpm at the end of the inhalation, that would give a "heart wave amplitude" of 30 bpm).

- Regular or consistent HR swings over successive breaths. A 30 bpm swing followed by a 5bpm swing followed by a 15 bpm swing etc. would be less desirable than a consistent 20 bpm swing breath after breath.)
- Tight coupling between the breath and the heart wave – the peaks and troughs occur together in the graph (as in the in figure 10.2).

Heart coherence is a natural and reflex-like phenomenon – you don't have to think about it, the body will just do it – as long as you don't get in the way. Certain mental and emotional influences will block the rhythm, as we'll see in section 5.3.

Good coherence is facilitated by slow regular breathing. To some extent, there is a sort of "resonance point" at which coherence is maximised, at a breathing rate of around 6 breaths per minute. (This is quite slow for most people, the average adult rate being something like 12-14 bpm, but usually not uncomfortably slow.) The reasons for this 6 bpm optimum are rooted in the physiological mechanisms that drive HRV, discussed in section 5.1. Breathing is by no means the only factor that contributes to good coherence – positive emotions seem to enhance the pattern.

10.5.1 Physiology of HRV

The main physiological driver of heart rate variation is the Autonomic Nervous System (ANS), first introduced in chapter 3. Let's summarise our understanding of the ANS.

The ANS influences what we might call our visceral functions (such as heart beat and digestion) both as part of ordinary physiological "house-keeping" (e.g. keeping warm but not too warm) but also a mediator of emotional responses. The polyvagal theory posits a hierarchy of three levels within the ANS:

- Old vagal – the lowest and evolutionarily the oldest system, it is one of two systems that make up the Parasympathetic

Nervous System (PSNS). It ramps down metabolism at the cellular level – it mediates the immobilisation response.

- Sympathetic Nervous System (SNS) – the middle level and mediator of the mobilisation or fight-or-flight response. It helps us deal with sudden-onset stress, for example encountering a sabre-toothed tiger by preparing us for action. For example it speeds up heart rate.

- New vagal system – newest and highest level, and second branch of the PSNS, it is capable of suppressing the lower two systems in favour of the highest level brain systems, geared towards social and other high-level cognitive functions. (It's influence has been termed the pause-and-plan response, also the rest-and-digest response.) It slows heart rate.

It's the new vagal system that has the dominant influence in driving heart coherence (which as a simple biological phenomenon is also known as Respiratory Sinus Arrhythmia or RSA). When active, its influence is applied to the heart only during exhalation, while during inhalation its influence is blocked. The result is the heart speeds up on inhalation and slows down on exhalation.

When we feel alarmed or threatened, the new vagal influence withdraws and the SNS comes to the fore (remember the SNS generates the fight-or-flight response). The HC rhythm is blocked and heart rate flattens out or varies chaotically. HRV biofeedback training aims to restore the full new vagal influence, and thus open up pathways to enhanced cognitive performance and emotional positivity.

When the breathing is slow, the rhythm is augmented by another physiological mechanism called the baroreceptor reflex. This is a mechanism that maintains stable blood pressure – we don't need concern ourselves with the detail but the important point for our purposes is that it is strongest at around 6 bpm hence this breathing rate is a kind of resonant frequency for HC.

The ANS is not the sole determinant of heart rate variability – hormones such as oxytocin (the "love hormone") play a role too.

HRV has been shown to correlate with prefrontal cortex (PFC) activation – that's one of the reasons it's such a useful training parameter.

10.5.2 HRV and the Mind-Body Connection

Negative emotions such as fear, anxiety, anger, frustration, and resentment tend to block the HC rhythm – they either flatten out the heart wave or send it into a disordered or chaotic variation. Negative emotions tend to trigger a fight-or-flight response (mediated by the SNS). I remember seeing this for myself several years ago, when I first started practising HRV biofeedback – one night on the way home I'd been stopped for a random check by the police, the result of which was that I had to take my driving licence and insurance documents to the local police station. The next morning in my (biofeedback-assisted) meditation practice I got stuck in simmering resentment about it, and my inner dialogue took the form of a bit of a rant against the police and why couldn't they find something useful to do with their time, etc. My heart coherence, which is normally quite good, was practically nil that day – my heart rate trace was pretty much a flat line.

Much of the lower-level on-going stress we experience in modern life (e.g. you don't get on with your boss) doesn't necessarily trigger an active fight-or-flight response, but it may well promote the withdrawal of the new vagal influence, leaving you in a state of SNS dominance. Remember the new vagal system engages our higher level social skills. Without it we are left in a state of emotional withdrawal or defensiveness, feeling wary, on-edge or even hyper-vigilant, and just not having much fun.

Training Coherence

Most people can demonstrate some coherence quite easily and quickly – for some people it's quite a good level straight away while for others it takes quite a bit of consistent practice. In either case, regular practice can strengthen the ability to access coherence.

A pattern of slow, regular, diaphragmatic breathing is a vital foundation for developing coherence. Without it, any measured coherence will be limited, as will be the higher level benefits. Techniques for developing coherence which have no recourse to the breath will only work to the extent that the breath spontaneously and naturally slows and becomes regular.

Even so, developing good coherence is not a matter of mechanically applying some breathing technique. Accessing coherence isn't a strongly volitional act – as I've said it's more reflex-like. In terms of the models developed earlier in the book, HC is in the province of the body intelligence, and can't be achieved by force of will – indeed using too much willpower tends to create a quicksand scenario – pushing you further to the right and down the slope of the human performance curve. Rather, it calls for the calm, open, interested but non-grasping and non-reactive mindset (if that sounds like mindfulness, well it's no coincidence). You invite coherence to come, then trust the body to deliver. Coherence feels good, having some of the qualities of flow. You patiently wait for it to arise, you can imagine what it's going to feel like, and you can savour it when it does come, but you can't force it or grasp after it because to do so would make it more elusive, as with sleep. (Think of coherence as feedback not the goal.) In coaxing heart coherence you need to be more like the sun than the north wind. Attention needs to be broad and open – overly-narrow focus can block it (we'll take a closer look at this idea in chapter 12).

In summary, HC training is a combination of mindfulness plus breathing in a certain way (slow and regular). (In chapter 11 I make the case that mindfulness and biofeedback work very well together.) There's some evidence that in meditation practice, as you develop integrated concentration (what Buddhists call access concentration, meaning access to higher states of consciousness) then coherence develops naturally. Researchers in Thailand investigated HRV changes in experienced meditators as they practised[100]. They recorded heart rate firstly while the practitioners were sitting quietly but not applying their minds to meditation, and then again during meditation practice in which they aimed to access a state of "samadhi" or meditative absorption. Though they practised breath awareness they weren't instructed to breathe in any particular way and they did not have the benefit of biofeedback to guide them – they were just recorded. Compared to their baseline, and also compared to inexperienced control subjects, the meditators demonstrated a clear difference in HRV – during samadhi they spontaneously entered what we're calling heart coherence.

Clearly coherence is not merely a relaxation technique. As I said earlier, HC correlates with cognitive performance, and can be experienced as mental clarity and sharpness – not a sort of soporific "laid-backness" but a relaxed focus and mental poise that is the basis for optimal performance.

Positive Emotion

In human culture the heart is not just a physical pump but the seat of the soul and the conduit of love. Science is now demonstrating that the long-perceived connection between the heart and emotions is much more than just poetic.

The Heartmath Institute[101] is a non-profit organisation devoted to research, education and training in HRV biofeedback which deserves much of the credit for the current popularity of coherence training. They base their teaching not on breathing techniques but on methods of accessing positive emotions. They find that positive emotions bring coherence in their train, and that in turn coherence helps to amplify positive emotions.

In my personal experience there's one emotion that boosts my coherence perhaps more than any other. I think the best name for it is anticipatory enthusiasm. When I think about my future plans – things I want to do, things that are worth doing not just for my own sake but for the benefit of others, and things that will be so rewarding to achieve, I feel like a racing car revving up on the starting grid. I feel a light pleasurable tension in my belly and lower chest and in my jaw and I can't wait to get moving with those plans. At those times (and if my breathing is slow and regular too) I see large consistent swings in my heart rate.

HRV and Over-breathing

A word of warning here: I've seen many people induce in themselves a degree of over-breathing as they try to master heart coherence. In the most clear-cut cases you can make yourself light-headed, but a lot of people will not be aware they're doing it. I think if this happens you stand to lose more than you gain.

When it happens I see it as a sign the person is over-controlling the breath: they are trying to "figure it out", and in terms of the dual intelligence model the breathing is driven by the thinking intelligence rather than the body intelligence as it should be.

To guard against it, keep in mind the breath needs to be as gentle as possible. Your rate of breathing might be constrained by the 6 bpm "resonance point" but you still have a degree of freedom in the size of each breath, or tidal volume. Allow this to be as small as you can. (In my professional practice I almost always introduce clients to capnometry biofeedback before HRV to minimise the risk.)

Breath Pacing

I've said that coherence is maximised with a slow regular breath at about 6 bpm. My experience with clients is that many of them find it hard to regularise the breath (in the sense of finding a steady consistent breathing rate). It's as though their breathing reflects the agitated and scattered state of their mind. If this is the case it can be all the more helpful to find a consistent breathing rate, and there are tools available to help.

With clients I use an audio breath pacing software tool – it's available free of charge as a download from my website (*www.stressresilientmind.co.uk* and follow the products link). The software produces a sound that gently rises and falls in pitch, and the idea is that you follow it with your breath, inhaling on the rise in pitch and exhaling on the fall. You can set the breathing rate and also the inhalation to exhalation ratio. It takes a little getting used to but with some practice your mind can follow the sound relatively effortlessly (without conscious control – remember we're not aiming for a mechanical conscious-mind-based breathing but a natural body-based breathing). The software even has some built-in brain stimulation technology (namely, binaural and isochronic beats) that you might try out if you're interested.

Other breath pacing products are available too, and some biofeedback products have breath pacing built into their software.

10.5.3 Summary of Applications of HRV Biofeedback

As I've said, HRV correlates with measures of emotional well-being, and cognitive and physical performance. Biofeedback is founded on the idea that if you re-create the physiology of optimum states, you'll make it easier to access those states. HRV biofeedback training can help with:

- stress and anxiety management
- emotional positivity
- focus, concentration and cognitive performance
- motivation and energy
- physical health and performance.

In other words there are few people who wouldn't benefit from HRV training!

It often takes some time to understand the influences on HRV and real-world benefits may only emerge gradually. In terms of the change dynamics I discussed in section 2, the insight component is relatively minor, the skills component is undoubtedly important, but the exercise component is considerable too.

10.5.4 How Is HRV Measured?

How do we measure and quantify HRV? Clearly we need a means of measuring heart rate, and it helps to measure breathing as well. Then, for biofeedback purposes, we need a computational process that can quantify the degree of coherence.

HRV Sensors

In most cheaper HRV biofeedback devices the heart sensor is a photoplethysmograph or PPG. This device clips onto the finger tip or ear lobe, and sends a beam of light through the finger or earlobe, which it detects at the other side. Clearly much of the light will be blocked by the earlobe or finger, but exactly how much depends on how much blood is present, so the transmission of the light varies with the pulse.

Other biofeedback devices uses ECG, which is the electrical signature produced by the heart. ECG gives a more accurate measure of the inter-beat time, but the difference is not really significant for biofeedback (more so for analysis). ECG is similar to EMG in requiring three sensors – two actives and a ground. The actives need to be placed either side of the heart – the wrists are usually a convenient site.

Breath can be measured by the means described in section 4.3.4.

Quantifying Coherence

To an extent we can see how coherent the heart is just by looking at the heart rate trace, especially if we can see it together with a breath trace as in figure 10.2. But it would help if we had a way to quantify the degree of coherence – then we could for example compare how we are today with yesterday and last week.

Most HRV biofeedback software quantifies coherence using some variant of a method called spectral analysis. Spectral analysis involves some complicated mathematics, which you don't need to understand in order to benefit from training. (You just need to know that the end result is a number that it higher or lower depending on the degree of coherence.) For those interested, in appendix A I've attempted an explanation of the method in terms I hope most people could grasp – don't worry no equations!

Away from biofeedback, spectral analysis is the basis of assessment and analysis of the ANS in many commercial medical systems used around the world.

One advantage of the spectral analysis method is that it doesn't require reference to the breath, which means that simple HRV biofeedback devices that only measure heart rate (and not breath) can use it. On the other hand, seeing the two traces together as in figure 10.2 gives you a fuller picture.

When I first started experimenting personally with HRV biofeedback, I thought there must be a better way of quantifying HC if you have the breath data there too. So began a development process that resulted in a software that I currently market from my website. It offers two HRV parameters for feedback which I call coherence score and synchrony. Both depend on measuring both breath and heart rate, and as far as I'm aware (at the time of writing) nothing like them is available in other software.

Synchrony is simply a measure of the time lag between the peak of the heart wave (stepped trace in figure 10.2) and the peak of the breath (smooth trace in figure 10.2). The more tightly coupled the two are, the lower the synchrony and in some sense the "better" the coherence. Based on my own experience of using synchrony biofeedback in a context of meditation practice, my sense is that low synchrony correlates with a clear but relaxed focus and alertness. Once you've gained experience in HC biofeedback I think it becomes a really useful parameter.

Coherence score captures other aspects of coherence: the size of swings in HR (or "amplitude" of the heart wave) and also the consistency. (A more precise definition is available in the software's user guide, freely available on my website, *www.stressresilientmind.co.uk*.[102])

In practice you can see what you need to see from the equivalent of figure 10.2 in any biofeedback software. Personally I think it helps to have the breath measure there too, but low cost HRV devices don't have this. Measures such as coherence score and synchrony are useful for other forms of feedback such as audio feedback.

10.6   Electrodermal Activity Biofeedback

Electrodermal Activity (EDA) is the physiological basis of the lie detector test well known in film and television. (Strictly speaking it's just one of several measurements made in the "polygraph" test.) EDA is also known as Electrodermal Response EDR), Galvanic Skin Response (GSR) and also as skin conductance (conductance is the inverse of electrical resistance).

Remember that a good biofeedback parameter is responsive to everyday mental goings-on – well EDA is perhaps the most clearly and rapidly responsive physiological parameter in regard to emotions (which is why it's used in the lie detector).

10.6.1 Physiology Underlying EDA

Technically EDA is very basic – it's simply a measure of how well the skin conducts electricity.

Why would skin conductance change when you respond emotionally? The answer in a word is sweating. Sweat is essentially salt water, which conducts electricity. The outer layers of skin don't really conduct electricity well at all, but when your sweat pores fill up with salt solution it creates an electrical bridge to the deeper layers which do conduct. So sweating increases skin conductance markedly. As the sweat evaporates, conductance drops back again.

In the skin of the hands, the sweat pores are highly responsive to emotional influences. (That's why you get clammy hands when you're nervous.) More specifically, it's the Sympathetic Nervous System (SNS) that triggers sweating, as part of the arousal response, or fight-or-flight response.

It's not entirely clear why this sweat response evolved – presumably it has proved adaptive at some point in our evolutionary past.

We've already seen that heart rate variability gives us one window on SNS activity, but it turns out that EDA is a measure of a different branch within the SNS. The nerves that stimulate sweating are technically speaking post-ganglionic cholinergic neurons. Cholinergic means that they secrete the neurotransmitter acetylcholine, unlike the rest of the sympathetic neurons which secrete noradrenalin. It's not clear how significant this distinction is, but there is some evidence that the SNS is capable of much more specific actions than was once thought[103]. Under some circumstances the cholinergic SNS may activate separately from the noradrenergic SNS. The only targets of cholinergic neurons are the sweat glands and the adrenalin-producing cells of the adrenal glands, so it could be that EDA offers us a much better measure of the adrenalin response than other biofeedback parameters such as HRV.

10.6.2 EDA and the Mind-Body Connection

The SNS response is triggered by stress, and any sense of threat, but not only these. Think of the SNS as mobilising energy, which in itself is neutral (neither positive or negative). In the negative sense it is fear, or the fight-or-flight or stress response, which prepares us physically for defensive action. But there are positive expressions of arousal too – the most obvious is excitement.

The mind is capable of generating the arousal response imaginatively (not necessarily volitionally). This is really an aspect of what I've been calling "simulator mode" – for any thought or image or idea that comes to mind, part of us asks "what would that feel like if it were really happening?" – and the body gives us the answer. Suppose you have a fear of flying and your partner proposes a foreign holiday. As you picture yourself in the departure lounge, your mind gives you here and now the same feeling as you'll have when you're in the departure lounge, albeit in a weaker form but still detectable with a EDA device.

This power of imagination is why humans get into such difficulty with anxiety. It also makes biofeedback training much more viable and relevant. Ultimately we're creating and strengthening a pathway in the mind (and brain) from an unhelpful problem state to a productive solution state (e.g. anxiety to calm). That happens through mental rehearsal.

One thing that reliably kicks off the SNS response is resistance – inwardly rejecting or struggling against some part of your experience that you don't like (e.g. pain).

Rises in the signal are short-lived – they soon fall back, as you see in figure 10.3 below, which shows a typical EDA graph. Note the sequence of sharp rises, corresponding to bursts of SNS activity, followed by gentle falls.

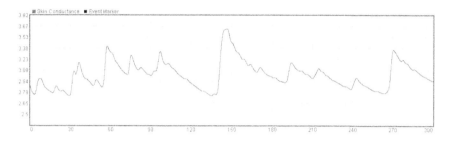

Figure 10.3   A typical EDA or skin conductance trace, showing a sequence of sharp rises, corresponding to bursts of SNS activity, followed by gentle falls

EDA biofeedback can show us clearly something of the real nature of emotions, which is that in themselves they are short-lived. (We discussed the time-course of emotions in section 2.5.2 of chapter two.) Understanding this has practical import: you don't need to actively get rid of negative emotions, you can trust the body will let go of them.

The famous Swiss psychotherapist Carl Jung was one of the first to use EDA biofeedback. He used it not as a method of training the mind but as an objective detector of emotionally charged or significant material that came up during the course of his therapy sessions[104].

10.6.3 Applications of EDA Biofeedback

I find EDA biofeedback very useful in my professional practice because it demonstrates very clearly:

- The reality of the mind-body connection: even passing thoughts trigger bodily reactions that can be both experienced subjectively and measured objectively.
- That emotional responses on this level are largely involuntary: we don't decide to have them and we can't choose to just switch them off.
- The danger of the quicksand effect: not appreciating the automatic nature of emotional responses and attempting to directly control them is likely to make things worse. What I called resistance in earlier chapters (put simply, rejecting or suppressing emotions) is one of the key processes that triggers the SNS response, creating a spiral process in which you get more of the very thing you want to get rid of.
- That emotions at this level are very short-lived. Putting it more positively, the body intelligence's capacity to relax will soon kick in automatically. We are talking just a few seconds. When emotions seem to be stuck, we are usually mistaking a cycling process of reacting to our own reactions, for a static state.
- That emotional responses are influenced by other mental processes such as how we pay attention, so creating the possibility of our indirectly guiding them even though we can't do so directly.
- These insights are the foundation of emotional intelligence: understanding what emotions truly are, in a mind-body context, and the processes that shape their arising and passing away.

In section 10.2 I described three modes by which biofeedback creates change, and it will be apparent that EDA fits well with the first, that is, insight. But because EDA changes are largely involuntary, it doesn't make a very good training and exercise parameter. In my own practice I use EDA for demonstrating the nature of the mind-body connection but not for training.

10.7   Skin Temperature Biofeedback

Skin temperature biofeedback is usually done by attaching a thermistor or temperature probe to the skin of a finger. How does skin temperature variation relate to the mind-body process?

The chief mediator of skin temperature variation is peripheral blood flow, or how much blood is flowing through the vessels at the base of the skin. If the blood flow increases the skin temperature rises because blood is warm.

Like EDA, peripheral blood flow is governed by the sympathetic branch of the Autonomic Nervous System (ANS). As part of the fight-or-flight response, the SNS diverts the blood towards the large skeletal muscles needed in fighting or fleeing, and away from lower priority tissues (including skin but also your digestive system for example). Blood vessels have muscles in their walls which when tightened, constrict the vessel and reduce blood flow. These muscles are controlled by the SNS (that is to say, automatically and non-volitionally, unlike skeletal muscles). Even minor arousals associated with mental processes (thinking and imagining rather than any real physical threat) can cause detectable changes.

Again like EDA, sympathetic (fight-or-flight) responses aren't necessarily "bad" or stressful – excitement can do the same. But we can say that with skin temperature biofeedback, to raise skin temperature we need to engage the relaxation response.

Over-breathing may also cause constriction in the peripheral blood vessels, though it practice the effect is much stronger in the brain than in peripheral areas.

Skin temperature biofeedback differs from EDA in being much slower to respond. Whilst EDA signal changes are marked and very apparent within around a second of their triggering event, skin temperature changes much more smoothly. EDA is useful for revealing specific triggers, but skin temperature variation is much more like an averaged trend. So while EDA is a better "insight" parameter, skin temperature is stronger as a training or skills-development parameter.

Another point of difference from EDA biofeedback is that blood flow changes are mediated by the noradrenergic SNS, and not the cholinergic SNS which stimulates sweating. There is some evidence that these two components of the SNS response may differ between specific emotions such as anger and fear.

Of course mental and emotional goings-on are not the only factors that bear on skin temperature. For example if the room is cold the body will reduce peripheral blood flow to conserve heat. So for skin temperature biofeedback to be meaningful in measuring the relaxation response, you need to avoid such confounding factors as draughts and air currents, the room being too hot or cold, or the trainee not having adjusted to the ambient room temperature (e.g. you've just come in from the cold).

10.8   Hemoencephalography Neurofeedback

Hemoencephalography or HEG[105] is a basis for neurofeedback, which is to say it is a way of measuring brain activity. More specifically it measures changes in metabolic or energy-consuming activity in the cells of the brain.

The brain consumes more energy when you engage in mental activities. Of course different parts of the brain activate depending on the activity. In HEG training the sensor is normally mounted over the forehead, where it detects changes in the prefrontal cortex (PFC). The PFC was introduced in chapter three as the key brain centre in executive function, which, to recap, encompasses these functions:

- Focus – the ability to hold the mind steady and maintain clarity of perception and awareness.
- Body regulation – the ability to balance both over- and under-arousal, by modulating the Autonomic Nervous System (ANS).
- Emotional balance – the ability to temper over-arousal and over-stimulation, and to summon and maintain energy and clarity in the absence of external stimulation.

- Emotional resilience – quickly recovering from knock-backs and sustaining positivity.
- Motivation and emotional drive – the ability to formulate goals, purposes and values.
- Self-monitoring – being conscious of what you say and do, and knowing that it is appropriate.
- Self-organisation – the ability to make decisions, to formulate a considered plan of action, and to hold to it in the face of distractions, as well as to update it appropriately. The ability to check impulsiveness.
- Empathy – the ability to appreciate the minds of other people, and to understand how our own behaviour impinges upon them. Ultimately this includes our moral awareness.

So HEG neurofeedback is a tool for training all these aspects of executive function, by exercising the brain at a physical level. HEG neurofeedback seems to induce lasting change – it's thought to stimulate neuroplasticity in the brain.

I think HEG neurofeedback works predominantly through the exercise mode of change (see section 10.2). HEG is like weight-training for the PFC – lasting benefits develop over a time-scale of weeks to months. That doesn't mean you have to do HEG for ever more – rather, you'll be exercising your executive function in other ways.

There are two variants of HEG, known as nIR and pIR (for near infra-red and passive intra-red, respectively). They are different physiological measurements (described in section 10.8.3 below) but they appear to be functionally equivalent to a large extent, both in terms of the experience of training (how to do it) and the benefits that accrue in time.

10.8.1 HEG and the Mind-Body Connection

The HEG signal is particularly simple – it goes up when you apply mental effort or intent (calling for PFC activation), and down when you relax mental effort, and when the mind wanders (when the PFC drops off in activation).

Most people find that the signal movements correlate to subjective experience (though there is also "noise" in the signal, meaning that some of the changes don't seem to make sense). I would say the response time-frame is around 2 to 20 seconds.

Figure 10.4 below shows a HEG training session broken into segments, interspersed with watching TV. The active training blocks are the yellow bands. The graph clearly demonstrates the HEG signal's responsiveness to intent.

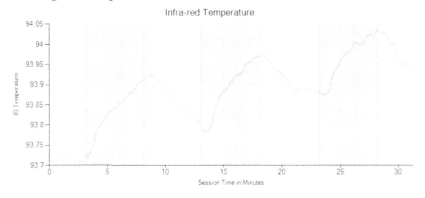

Figure 10.4   A HEG session divided into 3 minute bursts of active training (shaded bands). The signal clearly responds to the intent of training, then falls back during the intervals.

Though in general the intent of training is for the HEG signal to go up, it's worth saying that when it drops that's not necessarily a bad thing. As with biofeedback training generally, the goal is flexibility or adaptability. You want to access the physiology most appropriate to the present context, but not for any longer than is necessary. Getting stuck in a state of hyper-vigilance or over-focus is not fun. Indeed research has shown that creativity and insight are associated with a drop in PFC control (taking the brakes off, so to speak). So in HEG training don't just expect the graph to go one way – inevitably at times it drops back. You could compare HEG training to weight lifting – the exercise comes with repeated lifts, it's not about getting the weights as high as you can and keeping them high. Though your software may report your "net gain", don't attach too much significance to it.

What kinds of influences can trigger drops in the signal? In my experiences two kinds of processes:

- The mind becomes bored or fatigued, and drifts towards a dull, vague, low-energy state. It loses its edge. If allowed to continue this process would lead to a slothful, day-dreamy, foggy or even sleepy state.
- Negative emotion, perhaps triggered by a passing thought or memory, or perhaps by a negative judgement of your own performance. Recall the incident I described in chapter three section 3.10 in which I got angry with a bunch of kids and in so doing deactivated my PFC – this happened in the context of HEG training.

Again, these processes are inevitable: the practice is not to avoid them but to respond effectively to them as they arise, so that you return the mind (and brain) to its cutting edge as quickly as possible.

The following section addresses the question of how to train with HEG, or how to apply your mind to increase the signal.

How to Activate Your PFC

Put very simply, you need to engage (and maintain) a clear and vivid focus, backed by positive motivation.

Expanding on this, you aim to feel intensely awake, alert and present. Imagine that something very significant is about to happen, something that you'll want to remember all your life. The mind is rapt, poised, expectant, with all the senses "peeled", and yet calm and still. In other words, HEG training calls for the state of relaxed concentration we discussed more theoretically in chapter eight.

You need some emotional commitment behind your intent. You have to really want that graph to move upwards. And yet this motivation must remain positive – if it tips over into frustration or self-criticism or "performance anxiety" then this will work against you. Appreciate that your brain has limitations. The HEG signal will not always head upwards – at times your brain will tire.

Imagination can play a role in training too. You can imagine you can move the graph by the power of your intent, as though you had a psychic power. A useful metaphor can be found in the "Star Wars" series of films, in which Jedi knights such as Luke Skywalker learn to channel the mystical "force" to achieve psychokinetic effects. Another way is to imagine life-giving blood surging to the front of your head and rousing all the cells into concerted action.

HEG and Mindfulness

We've seen that training with most biofeedback parameters throws up the possibility of what I've been calling the quicksand trap – over-controlling or making the wrong sort of effort makes the signal move in the wrong direction. What's needed is something of the mindfulness mindset – calm, open, interested but non-grasping and non-reactive. You hold the intent for the feedback to move in a certain direction but you remain detached about whether it actually does or not.

HEG neurofeedback is much more about will and conscious intent than other biofeedback parameters, but even so, getting into mental quicksand is still a possibility, especially around your "emotional attitude". As I said earlier, performance anxiety (fear that you won't be able to do it) or frustration or being harsh with yourself will work against you. So you still need some mindful openness and non-reactivity – you can't afford to get overly attached to results and outcomes.

10.8.2 Summary of Applications of HEG Biofeedback

Clearly HEG training is applicable to anyone who wants to improve their executive function. HEG biofeedback can deliver:
- improved focus and concentration
- better energy and motivation
- emotional balance and stability, and greater positivity and resilience.

10.8.3 Physiology of HEG

When you engage in mental activity, those parts of the brain directly involved with the task become more metabolically active, meaning they burn more energy – just as a car engine burns more fuel when you put your foot on the accelerator. In the case of the brain, the fuel is primarily glucose, a simple sugar, but can also be fat-derived molecules called ketone bodies. This energy is used to drive electrical signalling between brain cells, but ultimately it ends up as heat.

Neurovascular Coupling

We know that computational processing that embodies thinking, remembering etc. is carried out by neurons, but in the brain these cells are actually out-numbered by another cell type: glial cells. Glial cells perform a lot of complex support functions in the brain. One type of glial cell, the astrocytes, monitor activity of neurons so that they can help deliver to the neurons the raw materials they need. Astrocytes communicate with the blood supply, which in the brain is a rich, dense network of small capillaries. The result is a system that can very rapidly deliver precisely localised increases in blood flow, exactly where and when they are needed. Energy consumption and regional blood flow are thus tightly coupled in the brain – this is known as neurovascular coupling. It's important because it means that if you measure changes in regional brain blood flow you are indirectly measuring changes in neural activity. Several brain scanning technologies are based on this link, perhaps most notably functional magnetic resonance imaging or fMRI.

Most importantly this whole system responds to conscious intent.

HEG and Over-breathing

Recall that hyperventilation results in a constriction of brain blood flow (due to a lowering of the carbon dioxide level). In theory therefore, hyperventilation would induce the HEG signal to drop. This is something that I've tried out in a small-scale self-experiment. My simple procedure was to record HEG, first for a few minutes baseline, then for a few minutes of forced hyperventilation, then for a few minutes recovery. The HEG signal does indeed tend to drop, though only a little during the actual hyperventilation. Interestingly, I found there was a much more significant drop *after* the hyperventilation period (i.e. in the recovery period) lasting up to several minutes. (I can promise you the hyperventilation was pretty severe and left me feeling pretty groggy.) I know that my carbon dioxide level recovers pretty quickly after a forced hyper-ventilation – within a minute it is back up to a fairly optimal level. So it goes to show that PFC regulation is more complicated than you might think. The effect reminded me of some clients who can meet with a sudden stressful situation, get through it reasonably well, then crash for the rest of the day or even longer.

In any case, with clients I prefer to train optimal breathing before introducing HEG neurofeedback so as to avoid mental exertion accompanied by "huff and puff" (which I have seen happening in some cases).

Measurements

As mentioned there are two forms of HEG, nIR and pIR. Both can detect short-term relative changes in brain activity only. That means they can't be used to measure static brain state in any meaningful way, nor can you use HEG to compare your brain as it is now to how it was last week or last month or last year, and nor can you compare two brains. Both forms only detect changes in the outer parts of the brain (close to the skull). Nonetheless they do both meet the criteria for being good biofeedback parameters.

nIR HEG

Near infra-red (nIR) HEG is historically the first form. Its inventor, Dr Hershel Toomim, adapted a method called Infra-red Spectroscopy[106]. His original contribution was to realise that the signal he was measuring could be consciously influenced and hence was useful for biofeedback training.

The nIR device directs a light source into the head, most typically at the forehead (in part because hair obstructs the signal making the forehead the most convenient site, but also because behind the forehead is the PFC). The light is a mixture of red and infra-red wavelengths. A proportion of this light is bounced back out (by a physical process called scattering) and measured by the device. The method is possible because the scalp, skull and brain matter are relatively translucent to light of this wavelength. As local blood flow rises in response to neural activity (and also as the level of blood oxygenation changes) the scattered light detected by the sensor changes. Dr Toomim found a good correlation with fMRI which is founded on the same brain blood flow response.

pIR HEG

Passive Infra-Red or PIR HEG is conceptually much simpler. It was invented by Dr Jeffrey Carmen, who adapted a technique called thermoscopy[107]. The sensor detects light (or electromagnetic radiation) of a particular wavelength - a small band within the infra-red part of the spectrum. This IR signal is essentially heat being radiated from the brain. Changes in this heat radiation are assumed to result from changes in the brain's metabolic activity. It's not clear to me whether the heat radiation is directly from metabolic activity, or from the increase in (warm) blood flowing, or both, but for practical purposes it doesn't matter.

Differences between nIR and pIR

The two methods are substantially equivalent in terms of the benefits of training but there are minor differences. The nIR HEG sensor measures from a smaller area of brain than Dr Carmen's sensor. The latter will give a more generalised measure of PFC activation. Dr Carmen advocates training from only one sensor location, which is the centre of the forehead. Dr Toomim trained from other locations, hair permitting. (I would advise sticking to the centre of the forehead, unless you know what you're doing). PIR HEG-like devices are available from other manufacturers and it is not clear to me what their field of view is.

Dr Carmen reports that his pIR sensor picks up a bigger emotional component than nIR – in other words pIR signal increases are more strongly dependent on emotional quietude in addition to mental effort.

Practitioners have reported that the pIR HEG signal needs a few minutes to stabilise when the sensor is first mounted, and they don't train actively during this time, whereas with nIR this may not be the case.

10.8.4 HEG versus EEG Neurofeedback

Most neurofeedback training is based on EEG (electroencephalogram, also known as brain waves) rather than HEG. Although EEG neurofeedback is powerful and effective modality I've chosen not to cover it in this book, for two main reasons:

- **Complexity** – EEG, being an oscillation, is an extraordinarily complex phenomenon holding a great wealth of information. A trainer must decide what particular aspect of the EEG to train, and not only that but where on the head (EEG varies across the scalp)[108]. This decision is far from easy[109] – be careful if you are a home user. Making a bad choice could mean the training is ineffective, or worse outright harmful (though I doubt you can do any lasting damage). Furthermore the EEG signal is easily contaminated with artefact (meaning what you're measuring is not coming from the brain).
- **Relationship to subjective experience** – the EEG component being trained doesn't always make sense, that is its variations don't necessarily correspond to any perceivable subjective changes. To my mind this makes training somewhat unsatisfying – in effect you're exercising the brain rather than training the mind. It's not as though you acquire a skill that you can then go out and use in your life.

HEG has several advantages:

- Easier to set up and measure, and less prone to artefact (though not free of artefact).
- Much simpler signal – it either goes up or down.
- For this reason there's no need to decide what particular aspect of the HEG signal to train.
- Discernible connection to subjective experience.
- Probably safer (though you shouldn't over-do training – you can easily fatigue the brain and this isn't particularly helpful or pleasant).

10.9   Evidence Base for Biofeedback

This book is aimed at a general readership rather than those with medical conditions, but of course biofeedback has been used as a therapeutic tool as well as a performance enhancement tool. Evidence for its efficacy goes right back to the 1950's and a considerable body has built up. A lot of the research studies have targeted specific medical conditions such as hypertension (high blood pressure). I haven't offered any references to research work, so instead I will give some sources for those interested in checking out the evidence base for biofeedback. Besides the resources listed below, you can always search the internet directly for papers. Good options are google scholar and PubMed (*www.pubmed.gov*) – run by the US National Library of Medicine (National Institutes of Health).

10.9.1 Professional Organisations

AAPB – Association for Applied Psychophysiology and Biofeedback *www.aapb.org*
AAPB is an international society (US-based) supporting professionals working in the field of biofeedback, and disseminating information about biofeedback. It was founded as a research society and still has an emphasis on science and research.

Their website has a list of disorders that biofeedback can help, each disorder having a rating of the strength of the research

evidence base as judged by the AAPB – see
www.aapb.org/i4a/pages/index.cfm?pageid=3404

AAPB publishes a scientific journal (see
www.aapb.org/i4a/pages/index.cfm?pageid=3283) a magazine for
members, and many of the older editions are available from the
AAPB website (see previous link).

BFE – Biofeedback Federation of Europe *www.bfe.org*

BFE is sort of a European equivalent to AAPB. They also
produce a magazine, "Psychophysiology Today", available from
the BFE website (from their homepage, follow the 'publications'
link). There are also articles and expert opinions.

ISNR – International society for Neurofeedback and Research
www.isnr.net

This is another professional membership organisation, this time
devoted to neurofeedback (mostly, EEG biofeedback). They
publish a comprehensive bibliography of neurofeedback evidence,
organised by medical condition, freely available from their
website: *www.isnr.net/resources/comprehensive-bibliography.cfm*

10.9.2 Books

Books that have extensive references to research include:

Biofeedback: A Practitioner's Guide, edited by Mark S.
Schwartz and Frank Andrasik

This is rather hefty tome, and accordingly priced. There are
chapters by medical condition, each with references. It's aimed at
professionals – not really light reading.

Handbook of Mind-Body Medicine for Primary Care, edited
by Donald Moss et al.

Like the Schwartz and Andrasik book, this is aimed at
practitioners and has chapters for common disorders, a little
lighter in weight.

The Clinical Handbook of Biofeedback by Inna Z. Khazan

Though it's likewise aimed at professional practitioners it's
much more accessible, and covers biofeedback used in
combination with mindfulness.

New Developments in Blood Flow Hemoencephalography, edited by Tim Timius

This short book is essentially a reprint of a journal issue (Journal of Neurotherapy) and is a collection of papers on HEG neurofeedback, including some by leading figures in the field such as Hershel Toomim and Jeffrey Carmen. It's a few years old now, and frankly is not the highest quality research evidence, and there are no doubt better studies that have been published since.

10.10 Summary of Key Points

- Biofeedback is based on monitoring physiological parameters that are easy to measure, show a recognisable relationship to subjective experience, and are relatively easy to influence.
- Biofeedback creates change in three main ways: it provides a context firstly for insight into the mind-body connection and how it works, secondly for developing skills in self-regulation, and thirdly for exercising the brain and nervous system.
- Biofeedback often gives rise to the quicksand trap: trying too hard or applying the wrong sort of effort leads to the signal moving in the opposite direction to intended.
- EMG or electromyography is a measure of muscle tension. It's a useful starting point for biofeedback as it's easy to work with.
- Breathing offers a unique window on the mind. Several biofeedback modalities relate to breathing, perhaps the most important of which is capnometry. Capnometry can detect any degree of hyperventilation and can show how to optimise breathing chemistry.
- Heart Rate Variability (HRV) correlates with several aspects of the mind including emotional balance (more specifically ANS balance), cognitive performance and even "willpower". HRV biofeedback is used for training emotional well-being, optimal mental and physical performance.

- Heart Coherence (HC) is a particular pattern of HRV in which the heart rate rises and falls in sync with the breath. HRV biofeedback aims to develop coherence.
- Electrodermal Activity (EDA) biofeedback is an excellent means of demonstrating the nature of the mind-body connection but is less useful as training tool.
- Skin temperature is a cheap and simple means of training relaxation.
- Hemoencephalography or HEG measures changes in metabolic activity in the prefrontal cortex, and so offers a means for training and exercising executive function.

11 How Biofeedback Supports Mindfulness Practice

11.1 Introduction

Let's sum up where we've got to so far. Our project is to develop mind-body intelligence, which is the foundation of:

- emotional resilience
- focus, clarity and stability of mind
- engaged energy and motivation
- mental flexibility – the ability to easily shift state according to the needs of the moment.

We've looked at two powerful tools for developing this skill-set, namely mindfulness and biofeedback. In this chapter, we'll consider how these two tools support and complement each other.

Mindfulness has been around for thousands of years. People have been using it effectively and productively in all that time. Why should practitioners need biofeedback now? Well, certainly we must admit they don't *need* it. If you already have an established mindfulness practice in your life, chances are you won't be that interested in biofeedback. But if you've tried mindfulness and found it difficult or unrewarding, I'm hoping to convince you that biofeedback has something to add – that it can make mindfulness practice more effective by making it in some sense easier, and thus more gratifying.

Lots of people have followed a mindfulness course, benefited from it, and yet don't maintain a regular mindfulness practice significantly beyond the end of their course. Let's face it, maintaining a daily mindfulness practice is not easy, all the more so if your experience of practice is not particularly gratifying. For most people, consistent mindfulness practice takes effort, discipline – in the modern age of information overload, probably more so than ever. (At the same time, the need for mindfulness is greater than ever.) If practice becomes too much of a chore, chances are we won't persist. In this chapter we'll look at how biofeedback can make mindfulness more engaging and more gratifying.

11.2   What Is Effective Mindfulness Practice?

Before we ask how biofeedback can make mindfulness more effective, we need to step back and reconsider just what it means for mindfulness to be effective.

In chapter nine I made the case that the purpose of mindfulness is to create change: to stabilise the mind and develop qualities such as tranquillity, clarity, emotional positivity and freedom. Mindfulness practice is effective to the extent that we are successful in transforming the mind, in achieving these aims.

The question then arises, over what timescale should we judge efficacy? Should every session of practice increase these qualities?

I think what counts the most is that you should experience relatively more of these positive qualities in your life as a whole (not limited to session time). It could be that on some particular day your mind is highly distracted and you spend the whole session bringing it back to your focus, only to drift off again moments later. I think as long as you are persistent in bringing the mind back, you're likely to be laying groundwork that will bear fruit later. But if you're sitting daydreaming and only occasionally remember your intention to focus, your practice is going to be much less effective.

This raises a further question – does it matter if we're continually distracted and never seem to achieve a stable focus? I think there is a perception within the MBT community that it doesn't matter, because the mechanism for change is the continual returning to the object of focus. Personally I don't find this very satisfactory. I suspect that results follow from actually being calm, still, focused, etc. If you're constantly battling distraction and for week after week, month after month, you never develop any stability, never seem to make any progress, then I think something is missing and you need to reassess your practice.

11.2.1 Is Your Practice Gratifying?

This question matters for the very pragmatic reason that, if your experience of practice is predominantly of negative qualities such as agitation and dullness, it wouldn't be much fun. Inevitably your belief that meditation is worthwhile, somehow "good for you", will be somewhat shaken, and you probably wouldn't persist. Meditation practice needs to be enjoyable, gratifying, rewarding.

In chapter nine we looked at the difference between the purpose of mindfulness and the intention you hold in mind when you practice, and the rather paradoxical mindset this throws up: the purpose is to calm the mind, yet we hold it as a matter of indifference whether it actually is calm.

This impartiality towards the results of practice needs to be balanced with the pragmatic need to enjoy practice, and to feel like you're making progress (developing skill). As ordinary human beings, we're not really indifferent to serenity, stillness, clarity, openness, etc. – we rather desire them. Nor are we indifferent to agitation, anxiety, frustration, craving, fogginess, dullness, etc. – we'd rather like to get rid of them. Maybe advanced spiritual beings have that kind of detachment, but for most of us it's not realistic.

Wanting more of good feelings and less of bad feelings is natural enough, but can be counter-productive if it leads to either craving, or resisting current experience. My point here is that we need to balance on the one hand acceptance of negative feelings and non-grasping of positive experience, and on the other, the positive drive to succeed, learn, grow (not all desire is a bad thing).

11.3   Optimal Conditions for Effective Mindfulness

For formal mindfulness meditation practice it's best to find a quiet place where you won't be disturbed, and to find a posture that allows you to be comfortable but not sleepy. It's good to prepare for practice appropriately, rather than say, playing violent video games or viewing pornography. The point is to create supportive conditions for effective mindfulness practice. People go on meditation retreats because the retreat setting offers more supportive conditions – and indeed most people find their practice is more effective in the sense that they experience relatively more of positive qualities such as stillness, contentment and clarity and relatively less of negative qualities such as agitation or dullness. Supportive conditions don't guarantee results, and they aren't necessary conditions for effective practice, but they are helpful.

Moreover, supportive conditions don't stop at the environment, they extend inside the body. If you over-eat, especially sugary foods, it's likely the mind will be dull and sleepy.

Biofeedback can be seen as a tool for developing more conducive internal (physiological) conditions for effective mindfulness practice. Let's restate some of the particulars of optimal physiology for meditation:

- soft, loose muscles – to facilitate physical stillness and psychological acceptance, and to counter the tendency to wilfulness
- slow, regular and gentle abdominal breathing – supports optimal breathing chemistry and heart coherence (see next two points)

- optimal breathing chemistry (carbon dioxide regulation) – to ensure maximal oxygen delivery to brain cells and thus mental alertness
- heart coherence – supports calm, parasympathetic-dominant body physiology, positive emotion, and optimal prefrontal cortex (PFC) function
- well-functioning PFC – supports intense alertness and stable undistracted attention and emotional positivity.

Again I stress these are helpful but not necessary or sufficient conditions, just as a quiet environment is.

11.4 Biofeedback, the Quicksand Trap and Acceptance

Methodologically, the practice of mindfulness is merely to observe the mind, and to let go of judging, of struggling against unwanted experience, and of craving and grasping after other experiences. If you don't let go of these things, you'll get more of the things you're struggling against (e.g. restlessness) and you'll be further away from the experience you desire (e.g. tranquillity). This is a restatement of what I called the quicksand trap.

When I talk to experienced mindfulness practitioners, they object to the idea of biofeedback because they think it would involve being judgemental (e.g. my experience of muscle tightness is "wrong"), that it would promote struggle (e.g. trying to get rid of muscle tension), and that it would also promote grasping (e.g. wanting soft, loose muscles). Therefore it's not consistent with the basic principles of mindfulness.

My answer is that it promotes the very opposite, for the simple reason that the same mental dynamics arise in biofeedback as in mindfulness and many other life contexts. This is a key point: the quicksand trap arises in biofeedback, as it does in mindfulness practice, and moreover it is often abundantly clear in biofeedback training, whereas it is typically subtle in mindfulness practice.

Let's say you're practising muscle tension biofeedback. The "goal" is soft loose muscles, but if you set about it with the "wrong" mindset, you'll get more tension, not less. In earlier chapters we've looked at what the "wrong" mindset is – in terms of the dual intelligence model, it's wilful effort coming from the "thinking intelligence". Biofeedback can show you very clearly that this doesn't work. Conversely the "right" mindset is letting go and acceptance. Biofeedback can show you very clearly when and how this does work.

To "succeed" with biofeedback you need the same sort of methodology as mindfulness: the intent is to maintain an active, open, curious, non-reactive awareness without attachment to results.

11.5   Mindfulness as Flow

In chapter five we took an in-depth look at the concept of flow states, first developed by psychologist Mihaly Csikszentmihalyi to describe states of effortless engagement and absorption in activities we love to do. In flow states the mind is integrated – our energies flow together.

Flow states are quintessentially gratifying. They are what we live for as human beings. We are happy to the extent that we experience flow in our lives. Naturally, wouldn't we want our mindfulness practice to be states of flow? In chapter nine we touched on the Buddhist concept of dhyana, which is in a sense a flow state. Dhyana can be seen as a higher state of consciousness, a state of bliss and effortless absorption. (It's worth repeating a point I made before: dhyana is not the purpose of meditation practice, nor is it the intent, but it is perhaps useful feedback that you're effectively working with your mind.)

11.5.1 Why Is Mindfulness Difficult?

My sense is that for a lot of people, the experience of flow in the context of mindfulness practice is relatively rare. Why is it that so?

The Nature of Distraction

Mindfulness practitioners know that sooner or later the mind will wander off into distraction (and for a lot of people it tends to be sooner rather than later). I find this quite a fascinating process – at one time there you are, present and attending to the present moment, aware that you are aware. At some time later you come to, you "remember yourself", your awareness pops back into full intensity, and you realise for the preceding time something wasn't there. Your mind was "on auto-pilot". It's a little like waking from sleep, except that you weren't so far gone as to be properly asleep. Your self-awareness (awareness of awareness) somehow faded and fogged out, and with it went your intention to stay alert, stay focused on the breath (or whatever your object of concentration).

What made you come back? You didn't consciously decide to do it, because in a sense "you" weren't there, you weren't (fully) conscious. (Just as you didn't decided to become fogged out in the first place.) It just sort of happened, or your brain did it for you. You can be glad that it did, because that's what mindfulness practice actually consists in – bringing the mind back when it wandered. Yet what a strange state of affairs, that the very heart of the practice is something that "you" don't actually do.

Now if you're expecting me to come up with some startling elucidation that will suddenly resolve this paradoxical situation, then I'm sorry to disappoint. All I can do is make a couple of general comments.

- The mind's capacity to recollect itself is related to the strength of your resolve to maintain your focus. Even so, no amount of resolution is necessarily going to keep the mind from wandering.
- Stability of focus is a function of integration, while distraction is a sign of the mind's energies flowing in different channels. Integration is a high-level goal of both mindfulness and our project of managing the mind more generally, but it cannot simply be a conscious choice, no matter how strong your

resolution, because only one part of you would be making that choice.

Interest

We can also say that interest is important. If you're watching the most interesting film or reading the most interesting book, then the mind doesn't wander (at least if you have a healthy brain it doesn't). For most of us, the breath doesn't evoke the same level of interest, but to the extent that we can engage our interest our focus will be the more stable.

Interest is on the list of positive emotions that we encountered back in chapter two. Curiosity is a variant of it. It will certainly help our practice if we can feed our interest, and create the conditions that favour the arising of positive emotion generally, but we also have to admit that interest (like all the positive emotions) can't just be turned on at will, and tends to be rather fleeting.

Preconditions of Flow

Let's return to Csikszentmihalyi's characteristics of flow states listed in chapter five, and three in particular which I described as preconditions of flow:

- clear goals – we know what we're trying to do
- clear and immediate feedback – we can see where we are in relation to the goal, and we can see the effects of how we apply ourselves
- challenge – the right level, not too stressful, not too boring.

I think it's difficult to access flow in mindfulness practice because these three elements can be somewhat lacking.

Having a clear goal facilitates flow because it naturally hones focus and stimulates interest – as long as it's achievable, and in the near-term. In meditation the immediate "goal" is to maintain attention on the object of focus. Let's say that's the breath. Once you're focused on the breath, what do you do then? It's not entirely clear. The textbook answer might be that you don't *do* anything, you just *be*. But it seems to me the everyday mind is always wanting something to do, or to achieve, with the right level of challenge, and if it doesn't have anything it will start thinking about what there is to do later.

We might somehow try to "improve" the breathing – but traditionally we're taught to accept it as it is without trying to change it. Yes, the point of mindfulness is ultimately to let go of the doing mind and just be, but what I'm talking about here is a pragmatic strategy for getting there. Remember in chapter nine I drew the distinction between samatha or tranquillity meditation and vipassana or insight meditation. In the Buddhist tradition you start with samatha because without at least some basis of stability and clarity, insight is not really within reach. So what I'm suggesting here is that as a means to an end we need to engage the doing mind in achieving stability of focus, etc.

Feedback is also problematic. Ideally feedback would enable us to see when we've become distracted, but the very nature of distraction is that we don't see it. I personally find it very easy to spend several minutes at a time in distraction without realising it (and that's after a twenty year career of regular meditation practice). In order to spot the distraction you'd have to not be distracted in the first place. Furthermore, it's not always clear why you got distracted – were you too wilful or too lax in effort? For feedback to facilitate flow, it needs to be a clear and immediate link between what you do and the effect that it has, and in meditation that link is not always obvious.

The sense of challenge in meditation is also somewhat nebulous. It's not clear what you need to do in order not to lose awareness, nor is it clear what you need to do to get better at staying focused. In playing sport or music, the clear goals and immediate feedback naturally stimulate our interest and motivation – our desire to improve – and we also have a clear sense of what improvement actually amounts to. But in meditation we don't really have a notion of getting better at breathing (indeed we're told not to attempt to change breathing.

Actually I think it helps to engage our interest if we do actually think in terms of "getting better at breathing" (meaning becoming more effective at creating optimum breathing physiology as outlined earlier). I realise that mindfulness purists won't like that statement. But whatever methodology we employ in meditation practice is a means to an end, and I think the pragmatic interest of making mindfulness easier and more rewarding for people who struggle with it is an important consideration.

One of the clearest triggers for flow is risk, which certainly creates a sense of challenge. It's most obvious in "extreme" sports such as free climbing (no ropes), but it doesn't have to be literal danger – it could be psychological threat (e.g. losing your tennis match, or making a mess of your solo violin performance). Meditation practice doesn't carry much risk.

11.6 Combining Biofeedback and Mindfulness Practice

In summary, accessing flow in the context of mindfulness practice is not easy. Biofeedback can help by addressing the difficulties listed in the last section. It can expand our conception of the "goal", though we still need to hang loose to the need to achieve goals. It can provide clearer feedback, obviously. And it can create a clearer sense of challenge, and thus engage our interest more fully.

11.6.1 Practical Considerations

In mindfulness practice the object of focus is you, or some particular aspect of your experience such as the breath. Not a computer screen, or gadget screen. If you use biofeedback, it needs to enhance your self-awareness not detract from it. The software needs to present the feedback as unobtrusively as possible. Equally the user needs to keep it at the periphery of awareness rather than centre-stage.

A lot of biofeedback software presents feedback in the context of games. There is a place for this, but it isn't mindfulness practice.

I personally find that well-conceived audio feedback (rather than visual) is particularly conducive – not least because it allows for eyes-closed practice.

11.6.2 Biofeedback as Distraction Detector

Let's return to the idea that mindfulness practice consists in repeatedly returning the mind to the object of focus when you notice that it's wandered off. As we've said, it's not easy to notice when you've wandered off.

Our mind-body perspective suggests that there is an optimum state of physiology for effective mindfulness practice, and furthermore, that in the process of becoming distracted we move away from this optimal physiology. If we can detect this (subtle) physiological shift using biofeedback equipment, then we have a means of independently and objectively detecting distractions as they arise. With this help, we can return to focus sooner and more consistently.

Threshold-based Feedback

I think the best way this can work is with threshold-based feedback. In the software you set a limit for your measured physiological parameter, and when (and if) the signal crosses it, the software produces some warning like a bell sound. This is an excellent way of keeping the feedback unobtrusive and in the background – you don't have to pay it any attention, and it only impinges on your awareness when you drift out of your desired psychophysiological zone, at which point you respond by returning to your focus.

Can Biofeedback Actually Detect Distractions?

It's a nice idea, but does it work in practice? In my own practice I've been investigating this question for several years, and my answer is yes biofeedback can detect distractions

The Nature Of Distraction

Recall from chapter nine our discussion of the particular forms that distraction can take. I listed a set of dimensions rather than mutually exclusive categories – to recap:

- energy – distractions range from restlessness and agitation to tiredness, listlessness, sleepiness
- emotional valence – positive to negative
- thinking or self-talk
- mental imagery, including visual, auditory and kinaesthetic (bodily) also fantasising and craving.
- resistance or inner conflict
- wilful or over-controlling versus passive, lazy or under-controlling.

Let's consider each of the main biofeedback modalities and how they can detect specific forms of distraction. Each has its own strengths and weaknesses.

EMG (Muscle Tension)

Useful for detecting high energy distractions – energetic mental activity tends to manifest as muscle activity (the mind-body connection again). Conversely, stilling and quieting the mind means stilling the body's muscles.

Also useful for picking up thinking distractions – insofar as thinking is a process of inner self-talk involving the speech muscles.

Conversely EMG is weak at detecting low energy distractions, as the muscles naturally go loose when we drift towards sleep.

Being strongly wilful is unlikely to be effective in lowering muscle tension – in fact it may increase it (which may be helpful if you're battling against sleepiness.)

Heart Rate Variability

Useful for detecting negative emotions such as anxiety and frustration as they disrupt the coherence rhythm. Working to develop positive emotions is an effective antidote to unhelpful emotions as they tend to be mutually exclusive.

Being over-controlling or overly wilful is actively counter-productive to developing heart coherence. It's not the conscious will that creates coherence, but rather your "body intelligence". The kind of mental application needed is one of allowing and entrusting, rather than willpower (at the same time we're still actively applying the mind).

<u>HEG</u>

Useful at detecting low energy distractions (mind wandering, or daydreaming) because the pre-frontal cortex (the brain's executive control region) tends to deactivate. (However we shouldn't assume that all drops in the HEG signal are necessarily a bad thing.)

Also useful for detecting negative emotions, as they tend to cause deactivation of the PFC.

Low energy states are not easy to turn around in the short-term. Working with HEG neurofeedback helps in the longer term as it works in part by an exercise paradigm, somewhat like regular work-outs at a gym – we are building up the "muscle" of our executive function.

11.7   Summary of Key Points

- If you spend much of your mindfulness practice time in distraction, it can feel like a chore. The more gratifying you find your practice, the easier it is to maintain. Biofeedback can help make mindfulness practice more effective and thus more rewarding.
- Mindfulness practice is effective to the extent that it develops positive qualities such as stillness, clarity, stability, calmness, emotional positivity and a sense of freedom.
- Though the methodology of mindfulness suggests we cultivate a degree of detachment from both positive and negative qualities, in practice we can make use of our natural interest in developing positive qualities.

- A mind-body perspective suggests there are optimal physiological conditions for effective mindfulness, i.e. they are more favourable to the development of positive qualities. As conditions they are neither necessary nor sufficient, nor are they the goal of practice, and we need to avoid grasping after them.
- The quicksand trap is a metaphor for the mental dynamic of making things worse by trying to hard. It can arise in mindfulness practice, when it is often subtle, but also in biofeedback, when it is usually quite obvious. To "succeed" in biofeedback, you need an open, curious, non-reactive and non-grasping mind-set (just as in mindfulness).
- We would naturally like mindfulness practice to embody the qualities of flow, and indeed it does when we become deeply absorbed. Flow characteristics are not the goal of mindfulness but are useful feedback.
- The process of becoming distracted then recollecting yourself is rather mysterious because by definition we aren't really aware of it happening and it is non-volitional. Yet this recollection is the heart of practice.
- Interest (or curiosity) is a positive emotion that helps to stabilise focus, so we should cultivate interest in present-moment awareness to the extent we can.
- Three characteristics of flow that are somewhat unclear in the context of mindfulness practice are (i) clear goals, (ii) clear and immediate feedback and (iii) the right level of challenge. Biofeedback can help augment these.
- Biofeedback should enhance subjective awareness not detract from it. Threshold-based feedback can help by making feedback less intrusive.
- Distraction may be reflected in a shift away from optimal physiological conditions. Threshold-based biofeedback can therefore act as an independent and objective distraction detector. Different biofeedback parameters have their own strengths and weaknesses in detecting specific forms of distraction.

Part 4

The Skill-set of Mind-Body Regulation

12 Attention

12.1 Introduction

William James famously said "The faculty of voluntarily
bringing back a wandering attention, over and over again, is the
very root of judgement, character, and will. No one is *compos sui*
[master of himself] if he have it not. An education which should
improve this faculty would be the education par excellence. But it
is easier to define this ideal than to give practical directions for
bringing it about."[110] Clearly the ability to control and direct
attention is right at the heart of mind-body intelligence, not just in
its own right but because how we pay attention has a profound
influence on other aspects of mind we've been looking at –
emotions, thinking, motivation, etc. In this chapter we'll look at
how this is so, and also begin to address James's important and
difficult challenge: practical instruction for training attention.

12.2 What Is Attention?

I can't do better than to quote William James' answer:
"Everyone knows what attention is. It is the taking possession by
the mind, in clear and vivid form, of one out of what seem several
simultaneously possible objects or trains of thought. Focalization,
concentration, of consciousness are of its essence. It implies
withdrawal from some things in order to deal effectively with

others, and is a condition which has a real opposite in the confused, dazed, scatterbrained state which ... is called distraction"[111].

So attention is directed awareness. It can be directed outwardly (to sensory experience) or inwardly onto the contents of the mind (thoughts, images, feelings, etc.). It acts as a kind of filter to the mind – excluding some things while *amplifying* other objects of awareness. Aldous Huxley (in his book The Doors of Perception[112]) viewed the brain as a kind of reducing valve on reality, restricting consciousness in order to enhance awareness in specific ways. Certainly it's true that what we give our attention to tends to grow to fill our awareness. Sustaining attention seems to enhance our sensitivity, revealing unsuspected richness. You can see this for yourself by spending a few minutes taking in a part of your body – say your hand or your breathing.

Attention also works like a filter in the sense that we tend to see what we look for, or what we are (perhaps sub-consciously) disposed to look for. You might look at a tree and see either an object of natural beauty or a year's supply of firewood, or if you know something about trees you might see that it is an oak and not an ash.

12.3   Neuroscience of Attention

As you might expect, neuroscience has distinguished different aspects of the faculty of attention.[113]

12.3.1 Selective Attention

Attention can work like a spotlight: you can see clearly what is at the focus, while things at the margins are in the darkness of non-awareness. Attention also works like a zoom lens: the focus can be shrunk or expanded in size, so that you either take in a small area in rich detail or a larger area with some loss of precision. These visual metaphors are most easily related to visual attention but auditory and kinaesthetic attention are similar.

An engineering metaphor may also help: attention enhances the signal to noise ratio. It makes the object of interest (e.g. the voice of the person you're in conversation with) stand out above the background noise (e.g. of all the other conversations going on in the café you're in). In this example both sounds are entering the ear, and registering with the primary sensory neurons (the ones at the very bottom of bottom-up processing) but somehow only one sound is *selected* for further processing all the way up to the level of speech comprehension.

In broad terms the brain achieves this selectivity by damping down the activity of some neurons while amplifying activity in others. The originator of these inhibiting and amplifying signals is the prefrontal cortex (PFC) which we've already met as the brain's executive control region. (This is why PFC function is critical to attentional control.)

Suppression

While you're listening to your friend in the café you're (hopefully) not distracted by thoughts about what you're going to have for dinner that evening or what you should have said in an earlier conversation. Generally, mind-chatter doesn't arise while we're paying active attention. The brain regions responsible for generating mind-chatter (collectively called the default mode network) are likewise inhibited by the focus centres within the PFC. It's not something you have to think about or put effort into, it's an automatic function of selective attention. It's different from other kinds of suppression, a point we'll return to later (section 12.6.1).

12.3.2 Alertness

Suppose you're a caveman foraging in the ancient African savannah, and you catch some movement in the corner of your eye. Perhaps it's a sabre-toothed tiger. At this point it will serve you well if you forget what you were just doing and have your eyes peeled for signs of danger. Not just your eyes but your mind

– you need to rapidly come to a peak of alertness and clarity. This function is called orienting and a key aspect is the ability to heighten alertness or intensify awareness. Whilst nowadays we needn't worry about tigers very often, we do rely on this faculty a lot. Suppose you're watching a TV detective drama – there are likely to be key points where you want to ramp up your attention so you fully take in what's happening, otherwise you won't be able to follow the plot.

Many of my clients complain of "brain fog" by which they mean they struggle to achieve peak clarity and instead are stuck in a kind of fuzziness.

12.3.3 Executive Attention

When the caveman noticed the sabre-toothed tiger, his attention was grabbed by an external trigger. This is an example of bottom-up processing – an automatic response, as opposed to a top-down or executive decision to shift attention (an example of the latter might be, it's one o'clock and you decide to break for lunch). Executive control of attention is important when there are competing demands for attention (e.g. you go online to research a work project but an advert catches your interest – do you click?). The key brain regions are the PFC and anterior cingulate (see chapter three).

In practical terms, *sustaining* attention (for tasks that take some time) is key – when people complain of poor focus it often comes down to an inability to sustain. This is an aspect of executive attention.

12.3.4 Neurochemistry of Attention

Key to the brain's ability to modulate attention are a class of chemicals called (appropriately enough) neuromodulators – we first met these in chapter three. The best known examples are serotonin, dopamine, noradrenalin and acetylcholine. These substances are produced in nuclei in the brainstem but distributed widely around the brain, where they adjust (modulate) the normal firing patterns of neurons. Noradrenalin seems to be one of the most significant for attention – a squirt of it seems to rouse us to a state of vigilance, heightening the signal-to-noise ratio and quietening any mental chatter. Dopamine is also important – remember (from chapter three) that the mesolimbic dopamine pathway is like the PFC's power-supply. It's thought this pathway is compromised in people with Attention Deficit Hyperactivity Disorder (ADHD)[114].

12.3.5 Short-term Memory

Suppose a TV advert grabs your interest. They give you a web address, and you decide to check it out. As you wait for your computer to boot up you have to keep the web address in mind – this is short-term memory. It's very much connected to attention, because you have to keep your focus internally on the web address. As your browser comes up, if you decide to check your emails first the web address is likely to be forgotten because it has been displaced from your attentional focus.

A related concept is working memory – an extension of short-term memory. In a working memory task you have to be able to use or manipulate the items you're holding in short-term memory – mental arithmetic is a good example.

Again poor short-term memory is a common practical concern for people. You can see that it's connected to the inability to sustain attention, and to less than optimal capacity to hit peak alertness. So all the problems that I've mentioned – fogginess, inability to sustain concentration, poor short-term memory – call for attention training.

12.4   Attention and the Mind-Body Connection

The mind-body principle implies that to pay attention effectively your brain needs to access the right neurophysiology. For example if your brain is imbalanced in the neuromodulators we mentioned earlier (noradrenalin, dopamine, etc.) then attention will be compromised. In chapter six I adapted the human performance curve to the context of attention – it's worth reproducing it here (as figure 12.1 below).

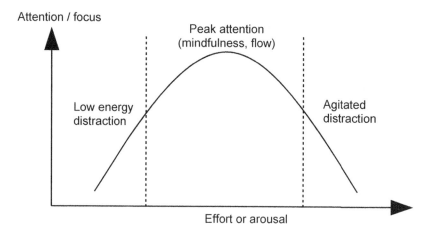

Figure 12.1 The "Human Attention Curve"

The curve expresses the idea that optimal focus or attentional performance is supported by physiological flexibility or adaptability. Training physiological adaptability is a way of training your focus and concentration.

Actually this cuts both ways – training attention is a way of training physiological adaptability (and thus benefiting your emotional balance and resilience, stress tolerance, even your energy and motivation). That's because there are different ways or styles of paying attention, with commensurate variations in underlying neurophysiology – in fact not just brain physiology but whole body physiology. We'll explore what these variations are in the next section.

12.5 Styles of Attention

It's not just what you pay attention to, but *how* you pay attention that matters – in other words, the style of attention[115]. Consider the following examples of different modes of attention.

- An accountant has found a glitch – his sums don't add up as they should. He must carefully go through his records looking for the source of the problem. His focus needs to be tight and narrow, or one-pointed, and sustained. He hardly registers background noise in the office, and new emails arriving on his computer. His brow is rather knitted, as he fixates on the screen.
- A woman is playing tennis. She needs to keep her attention very much on the game – if she gets distracted she'll likely play a bad shot. She watches the ball closely. There are lots of things to keep in the background of awareness – the position of her feet, her grip on the racquet, her opponent's position on the court, the balance of her weight as she moves into each shot. If she over-focuses on any one thing, something else is likely to go awry.
- A man is giving a presentation. Not being very confident, he's self-conscious. His awareness is on how his body feels (tight and nervous) and he's thinking about how he must appear to his audience. To the extent that he's not focused on what he needs to say and what his audience want to hear, he doesn't do a very good job.
- A hiker is out for a day in the hills. It's a lovely day, the sky is blue. It doesn't take much concentration to go for a walk, but after a few hours her mind seems to expand to reflect the broad vistas she's taking in. Her awareness feels open, expansive, spacious. Her mind feels quiet and stable – not flitting from one thing to another as minds usually do, but simply present in an open and relaxed way.

12.5.1 Dimensions of Attention

These examples show there are wide range of attentional states that we can access, all appropriate in their own contexts (and often quite unhelpful in other contexts). To analyse these, I find it helpful to think in terms of a set of *dimensions* of attention – qualities that vary between two poles. Let's list them.

Ego-centric vs. External and Sensory

In ego-centric awareness, attention is directed inwardly, inside the mind, onto mental contents such as thoughts, feelings, images and memories, that revolve around the psychological self – what I'm going to do later on, or the conversation I had earlier, or what I think and feel about a particular topic.

External attention is sensory based and necessarily present-moment centred, as opposed to ego-centric which is usually not focused in the present moment. These two modes of attention are embodied in distinct brain circuits which mutually inhibit each other.

In the examples above, the nervous presenter is caught in ego-centric focus, while the others are more external and sensory-based.

Broad vs. Narrow

Narrow mode attention is like the accountant in the above example. Attention is like a spot-light, illuminating just a small area. Background things are in the darkness of non-awareness. When the mind is in narrow mode it's as though it grasps hold of the object of attention, fixing it steady.

The physiology that backs up narrow attention tends to be tight. You can imagine the accountant's furrowed brow, maybe hunched shoulders or clenched hands.

Anxiety can take us into a very narrow attention almost to the point of tunnel vision. The nervous presenter is like this – his view is dominated by the manifestations of his nervousness. His physiology is fight-or-flight mode. Likewise thinking can become narrow, black-and-white, overly-simplistic.

Broad mode is the opposite – the attention is spread over a wider field. It's like a zoom lens that has been zoomed out. The mind takes more in. In broad mode, the mind is receptive rather than grasping – it's like allowing perceptions to come in to us, rather than chasing and grasping after them. (In other words a closely-related dimension of attention is receptive versus grasping.) Our hill-walker (in the above examples) is in broad mode. The physiology of broad attention is the opposite too: relaxed, open, loose muscles.

Most of us spend a lot of our time in narrow mode, and need to be because of the nature of the work we do (like the accountant). Narrow mode attention certainly has its place but it's a problem if we get stuck there. You can end up forever looking for the next thing for the mind to grasp hold of, which doesn't feel very good. If your mind is doing this while lying in bed at night trying to sleep, it doesn't serve too well.

Monkey Mind

Monkey mind is a metaphor that describes the way the mind can flit from one thing to another. The image is of a monkey in the tree-tops, who sees a piece of fruit, goes and grasps it, but no sooner has he taken one bite than he sees another fruit elsewhere, drops the first and goes chasing after the second. And so on.

Monkey mind shouldn't be confused with genuine broad attention. Monkey mind is more like the spot-light that shifts rapidly between all the characters on the stage. Genuine broad attention shines equally in all directions like the sun.

Absorbed vs. Self-conscious or Associated vs. Dissociated

In absorbed attention we lose the sense of ourselves as separate from the activity. There is just the doing of it. In self-conscious mode it's as though a part of us has stepped aside from ourselves and is looking in, judging and evaluating (am I doing it right? etc.). In psychology this state is sometimes known as dissociation. It's possible to be dissociated from different aspects of yourself, for example emotions (i.e. you don't really experience them) or your immediate sensory experience (in which case you are absent-minded).

Our nervous presenter is in self-conscious mode while the tennis player is in absorbed mode.

Being in absorbed mode is tantamount to being in flow. On the other hand being dissociated is not always a bad thing. Suppose you're getting some critical feedback from your boss – it's useful to be able to step away from your emotions and view things objectively. Again, adaptability is the name of the game.

Pleasure – pain

Many people have an attentional bias towards the painful and negative aspects of experience – they focus on the unpleasant or painful sensations in the body or on what might go wrong. They probably do this in an attempt to guard against things getting worse or bad things happening, but what they actually get is more of the very experience they don't want (remember attention amplifies what you focus on).

Conversely you can set your attentional filter towards the pleasurable or positive. You will tend to find them.

Top-down vs. Bottom-up or Active vs. Receptive

Top-down attention is executively controlled attention, involving conscious decisions about what to attend to, while in bottom-up attention you are receptive to whatever grabs your mind. The accountant is paying top-down attention (which normally goes together with narrow attention) while the hill-walker is in receptive attention. Note that receptive attention can still be intensely aware, I don't mean to imply it's simply day-dreaming.

Intensity of Awareness

We've already touched on this aspect of attention in section 12.3. In experiential terms, awareness ranges in quality from dull, foggy and sleepy, to clear, sharp, alert, awake and vivid. If something important is about to happen (e.g. you're about to receive your exam results), the "intensity" of awareness naturally would ramp up. High intensity attention is also a feature of flow states, enabling heightened sensory perception.

An important part of self-regulation is the ability to ramp up intensity on demand. In meditation this is what we're looking to do (at least in most forms of meditation).

Again the ability is rooted in neurophysiological adaptability. If you've smoked too much cannabis you might not be able to do it.

12.5.2 Accessing Flow

Flow states involve peak attention. Accessing flow on demand is something of a holy grail of self-regulation – not easy because of an inherent contradiction: you're consciously and deliberately attempting to lose self-consciousness. In chapter seven we looked at some of the preconditions and triggers of flow – here I'd like to add another: attentional flexibility. Specifically, I find that cultivating broad, receptive attention helps to let go of intense self-consciousness (in the sense of separateness) that is an obstacle to flow.

12.6 Resistance and Avoidance

We've already discussed resistance and avoidance in earlier chapters. At the most subtle level, resistance is not wanting even to be aware of something. This can create problems. Imagine you're giving a presentation, which you're rather nervous about. You tell yourself, "whatever happens don't blush", or perhaps "just don't think about blushing".

Sometimes we focus on unpleasant experiences in an attempt to guard against them – keeping them at arms length, so to speak. For example, people who suffer from panic attacks can get caught up in looking out for the first signs of anxiety. Sometimes we try to continually distract ourselves from something (for example a pain) but we keep getting drawn back to it – as though the mind wants to know, has it gone yet?

These are of course examples of a subtle quicksand effect. You get more of the very experience you don't want. Trying not to be aware of something or not to pay attention to something is especially prone to the quicksand effect because of the nature of attention as filter and amplifier.

12.6.1 Suppression Again

Earlier I emphasised the importance of the ability to suppress mental contents, such as competing demands on your attention. But isn't suppression just a form of resistance? Can't it backfire?

I think the answer to this potential paradox is that it depends where suppression is coming from. There are different forms of suppression.

Don't think about blushing! Of course you have to, even to understand this sentence. It seems that when we frame directions to ourselves in the negative form (i.e. don't do X) we're likely to fail. Why is this? Here's one theory that makes a lot of sense to me[116]. The brain handles the task of thought suppression using two systems, called the operator and the monitor. The operator directs attention away from X. The operator requires a good deal of brain resource. The monitor looks for evidence of failure or transgression (did X just come up?) and it needs relatively less effort or resource – it is more automatic. As time goes on, the operator flags a little, or gets diverted. The monitor is still working in the background, and this somehow feeds energy into X making it more likely to pop into mind.

So deliberate thought suppression doesn't tend to work, at least when the suppressed thing carries emotional significance. But suppression does work when it's a natural part of active selective attention. For example, you spend all day at work trying not to think about the presentation you have to give tomorrow, yet it keeps popping up. Then you go home and spend an hour playing with your four-year-old child, and don't realise till later that you never thought about it. Here's another way to think about it. When you deliberately try to suppress something, then (in terms of the dual intelligence model) the active agent is the thinking or conscious intelligence. But in active selective attention it's more like the suppression is done automatically for you by the brain. You don't have to think about it, you don't have to "try".

12.6.2 Broad Attention, Letting Go and Acceptance

Letting go of resistance can be easier said than done. Particularly when working with body awareness, it can be difficult to let go and trust in body intelligence at the same time as paying close attention. I think the difficulty has to do with the tendency to go into narrow awareness. Suppose you're working with breathing, hoping to access optimal breathing – which is something that's very much in the sphere of body intelligence. In narrow attention mode, it's as though you're too close to the breath to let go. I find that practising broad attention creates a sense of mental spaciousness that facilitates letting go, and at the psychological level, acceptance. For this reason I think broad attention practically speaking is one of the most important modes of attention.

12.7   Attention and Positive Emotion

In chapter two we discussed Barbara Fredrickson's "broaden and build" theory of positive emotion. She posits that positive emotions confer on us the benefit of broadening our attention. Her research backed this up: she found that people literally notice more – particularly in terms of peripheral awareness – when they had been primed to experience positive emotion compared to controls who hadn't been so primed.

Could the reverse also be true? That is, if we consciously broaden and intensify our attention, would we be more disposed towards positive emotion? I'm not aware of this having been tested experimentally, but my guess is that we would be. I'm reminded of a famous experiment in which researchers asked subjects to hold a pen in their mouths, some of them using their lips but not teeth, others their teeth but not lips. The latter group then rated a cartoon as funnier than the former group did. The explanation is that the teeth-only group actually reproduced something resembling a smile, while the lips-only group looked rather glum. Remember, in Damasio's thinking, the *feeling* (in this case, of amusement) is the perception of the changes that are the embodiment of emotion, and not something that causes those changes. The experiment offers support for Damasio's theory, showing that even just a kind of feigned emotional expression affects how we feel. I'm suggesting that since an attentional shift is part of the change that embodies emotion (just as a facial expression is), consciously practising attentional shifts will affect how we feel.

Put in simple terms, practising broad, open, receptive, clear attention creates the conditions for positive feelings to arise, or makes them easier to access.

12.8   Attention Training

Finally we return to the challenge posed by William James: how to train the faculty of attention. In part 3 we looked at the two main tools, mindfulness and biofeedback. Mindfulness essentially is attention training. The core of the method is noticing when the mind has drifted away from its focus, and returning it again and again. Research shows that mindfulness does indeed improve attentional performance. We've seen that the PFC is the seat of the attention faculty within the brain, and mindfulness has a physical effect on the PFC – but it's not the only tool to do so. A number of the biofeedback parameters we looked at in chapter ten strengthen attention by strengthening PFC, notably:

- **HEG neurofeedback** – directly measures changes in PFC activation and thus offers a means of strengthening PFC functioning.
- **Capnometry biofeedback** – training optimises breathing chemistry. Remember from chapter four that over-breathing reduces oxygen delivery to brain cells, in part by causing vasoconstriction in the brain. Capnometry biofeedback reverses this, and thus enables the cortex to fully activate.

- **HRV biofeedback** – slow, regular breathing with openness and emotional positivity maximises the pattern of heart rate variability known as heart coherence, which is known to correlate with PFC activation and executive function.

Traditionally in Buddhism, mindfulness of breathing practice is seen as the ideal vehicle for training attentional stability. With the understanding of optimal breathing that we've developed over the course of the book, you can begin to see why this is true. In chapter eleven I made the case that biofeedback is an ideal tool for supporting mindfulness methodology.

Two methods of attention training not previously discussed are:

- **Dual N-Back Training** – dual N-back is a computer based training method that strengthens working memory. The beauty of the method is that the gains have been shown to be generalisable, i.e. you don't just get better at the dual-n-back game but your general executive functioning improves in parallel. You can download free software for dual N-back training[117]. Regular practice is needed (ideally, daily).
- **Open Focus** – a method developed by Dr Les Fehmi designed to facilitate broad open awareness and thus attentional flexibility. Originally Dr Fehmi used a special form of EEG biofeedback (called synchrony training) to guide open focus practice, but later he developed exercises that can be done without biofeedback. A good place to start is the book "The Open Focus Brain" by Dr Fehmi with Jim Robbins[118] – the book includes an audio CD of introductory exercises.

12.9   Summary of Key Points

- Attentional control is core to the skill-set of self-regulation, and influences just about every aspect of mental life.
- Attention is directed awareness. It acts as a filter in the mind, excluding some things while amplifying others within awareness.
- Selective attention works like a spot-light, and enhances the signal-to-noise ratio with reference to sensory data. It

naturally suppresses extraneous perceptual input – this is different from conscious suppression, which tends to be much less effective.

- Executive attention is top-down or conscious control over attention – the ability to make decisions over what you attend to. It is important for sustaining attention.
- Short-term memory, or the ability to hold things in mind, is dependent on attention – focus is directed internally onto mental contents. Poor attentional control leads to poor short-term memory.
- The mind-body principle suggests that good attentional control is reflected in optimal neurophysiological functioning, and vice versa.
- How you pay attention (style of attention), also flexibility or adaptability in style of attention, is also important. We can characterise different styles of attention in terms of several dimensions of attention.
- Resistance, or wanting to exclude certain aspects of your experience from awareness, can be counter-productive, creating a subtle version of the quicksand trap, meaning that you get more of the very thing you wish to avoid.
- Positive emotion facilitates broadening of attention, and it may be that the inverse is true (that deliberately cultivating broad attention helps develop positive emotion).
- The attention faculty can be trained and developed with consistent practice. Mindfulness and biofeedback are two useful tools.

13 Motivation

13.1 Introduction

In chapter one I listed three core domains of self-regulation, the second of which is motivation, drive and energy. Many self-control challenges involve difficulties with motivation including:

- Procrastination – you know what you want but don't have the drive or staying power to follow through. You're too easily distracted from your longer term goals by immediate temptations.
- Addiction and habit problems – your motivation towards your wider goals and purposes is out-weighed by cravings.
- Depression – often depression is not so much an active misery as a kind of lassitude of the will, a hopelessness, a lack of interest in doing things. Nothing seems to offer the prospect of real, worthwhile reward. Everything seems pointless.

The former two are traditionally viewed as willpower challenges. Willpower is clearly related to motivation – I'll say more about willpower in section 13.4 below.

Motivation can be seen as a high-level mental faculty underpinned by core functions and resources such as:

- Sustained attention – to reach long-term goals you have to be able to maintain focus on them, and avoid distraction and procrastination.

- Ability to access positive emotion (lacking in depression). Positive emotions, most obviously hope, move us to act.
- Ability to let go of immediate desires and cravings – this is a mind-body skill. Life will always throw up temptations. The solution is not about gritting your teeth and beating them in a battle of willpower, but containing them in such a way that the energy behind them shifts, the wind goes out of their sails.
- Growth mindset – the view that we can develop our skills and abilities with training.

Clearly there is a lot to say about motivation – whole books have been written on the subject. In this chapter I'll focus mostly on mind-body aspects: motivation is underpinned by biology, and we can make progress with motivation problems by creating supportive physiology and developing mind-body skills and resources such as those listed above.

13.2 What Is Motivation?

Motivation is what moves us to act in the pursuit of our goals or interests. Motivation is related to desire, but while desire has a stronger connotation of feeling, motivation is the urge to *act*. Desire is typically connected to basic biological appetites for food, liquid, sex etc. and is triggered by the sight of those objects, but motivation has a more psychological or internal locus – motivation comes out of your personal goals and values, e.g. you work hard because you want to support your family and gain respect, etc.

13.2.1 Motivation and Feeling

Motivation is fundamentally related to feeling. Put simply, we are motivated to avoid feeling bad (pain), and towards "good" (positive or pleasurable) feelings.

Some examples:

- A gambler goes to a casino because it gives him a buzz, a sense of excitement and anticipation of reward (towards a good feeling).
- A city banker applies for a more senior job, because his imagined future sense of importance and respect from his friends and colleagues feels good, and perhaps also because he gets the buzz of anticipating spending the extra money on a new car (towards a good feeling).
- An alcoholic goes another day without drinking, because he remembers the trouble that will be his again if has even one drink (away from a bad feeling).
- A stressed office worker gets out of bed on time on Monday morning in spite of not feeling like it, because the thought of being late for work scares her (away from a bad feeling). On Saturday morning it was much easier to get out of bed with the pleasurable anticipation of doing the things she most enjoys (towards a good feeling).

When we move towards a good feeling, we need to see that performing the action (say, applying for a new job) will lead to feeling good. We rely on our internal mental "simulator" – first introduced in chapter three as that part of the mind that simulates in the here-and-now what it will feel like (to get the job, etc.). We need to experience some of that good feeling here and now, before we actually act, in order for it to work. In depressed people, the good feeling often doesn't happen and they don't act.

It's similar with "away from" motivation – we need some of the painful feeling here and now before we act. It's the energy mobilised in response to the here-and-now feeling that leads to action. As marketers and political spin doctors know, "away from" motivation tends to be stronger – because of the brain's inherent negativity bias, negative emotions (particularly fear) tend to be easier to trigger and more intense. So "away from" motivation can certainly work for you but if you relied on it exclusively for getting things done, life would be pretty bleak.

Instead, in this chapter I'm going to focus mainly on good feelings and how you can use them to support motivation.

13.2.2 Intrinsic and Extrinsic Motivation

When we are intrinsically motivated it means that the thing we're motivated to do is enjoyable or pleasurable in itself – it just makes us feel good. When we're extrinsically motivated we're in it for some promised consequence. The doing of the thing is not intrinsically enjoyable, and indeed might even be unpleasant, but the consequence or reward will make us feel good. For example, you can promise a child some chocolate if he finishes his homework on time. This might be enough to motivate him to get on with his homework which he doesn't want to do for its own sake.

Punishments can also serve extrinsic motivation – e.g. if the child doesn't finish his homework, his pocket money will be withdrawn. He's then motivated to avoid the punishment.

In his book "Drive: The Surprising Truth About What Motivates Us"[119], business writer Steven H. Pink shows us that intrinsic motivation is a much more powerful driver than extrinsic motivation, at least for non-mundane activities. He draws out three key elements of intrinsic motivation:

- Autonomy – we feel happy and fulfilled when we can direct our own lives, following our interests and satisfying our desires.
- Mastery – we feel a natural urge to get better and better at the things that matter to us, and that we enjoy doing. We develop our skills and expertise.
- Purpose – we enjoy activities that are meaningful, and that are in service of something larger than ourselves.

Needs and Values

These ideas relate to concepts we first introduced in chapter two: firstly emotional or psychological needs, and secondly values. Speaking more generally, we can say that activities are intrinsically motivating when they help us meet our psychological needs, and when they are in harmony with our values.

Recall I summarised the psychological needs we all seem to share as human beings like this:

1. Safety, security
2. Autonomy, control, freedom of choice
3. Stimulation and challenge – opportunity to learn and develop, and contexts for experiencing flow.
4. Sense of competence / achievement – growing out of 3 above
5. Social connection – having these elements:
    ○ giving and receiving attention
    ○ giving and receiving affection
    ○ understanding and acceptance (warts and all)
    ○ sense of belonging (to a family or community) – feeling part of something greater than yourself
    ○ having status and respect – being valued within the group.

Values are principles that we live our lives by, or aspire to live by. They're different from goals in that we never finally achieve success with our values – they are more like directions of travel than destinations. And they're different from feelings and emotions in that while feelings come and go, our values are constant. We can act on the basis of our values more or less independently of how we feel – we can be kind when we don't feel kind. Values may be virtuous or they may be pretty mundane – either way they don't need justification, they're just intrinsically what matters to us[120].

13.2.3 Neurobiology of Motivation

Again this is a huge topic in itself; I'll confine myself to reviewing a few points made elsewhere in the book.

Dopamine

In chapter three we touched on dopamine, which I described as the neurotransmitter of desire. A squirt of dopamine in the brain's prefrontal cortex (PFC), triggered by some particular stimulus, gives us the feeling of pleasurable anticipation, a sense that something good is coming. We eat a piece of chocolate, and it's soon followed by the dopamine hit, and we get a sort of pleasant buzz that says "do that again". Lots of things can stimulate the dopamine release – in fact pretty much anything that gives you that pleasurable buzz of anticipated reward. Addictive drugs such as cocaine are notable examples. Risk does too.

HRV and Willpower

In chapter ten on biofeedback I mentioned that Dr Kelly McGonigal describes Heart Rate Variability (HRV) as the best available measure, or biomarker, of willpower. A biomarker only suggests there's a correlation; it doesn't tell us whether strong HRV is either a cause or an effect (or both) of willpower. My own experience of working with HRV biofeedback suggests that experiencing anticipatory desire stimulates greater heart coherence. I suspect that motivation and heart coherence mutually reinforce each other in a complex feedback loop.

13.2.4 How We Deal With Negative Feelings

Negative or painful feelings arise in various forms such as:
- physical pain
- negative emotions such as anxiety, loneliness and sadness
- unrealised desires and cravings – thwarted often because they conflict with longer term or higher level goals and values – e.g. you find your boss's partner attractive
- not being able to concentrate, think clearly, calm down, get to sleep, find energy to get things done, etc. (inaccessible resources).

Over the course of the book we've looked at how trying to get rid of negative feelings (i.e. resisting, suppressing or avoiding them) can get us deeper into trouble (quicksand). But one aspect we haven't looked at too closely yet is this: we naturally look around for a good feeling that will replace the bad feeling. A couple of examples:

- Sitting at home, alone, watching TV in the evening, I feel a vague sense of emotional dis-ease – it could be boredom but there might be an element of loneliness. I reach for the chocolate bar in the fridge.
- Thoughts of my escalating credit card debt give me a horrible, gnawing sense of anxiety. To get away from it my mind turns to the anticipated excitement of buying new things – I go online to one of my favourite shopping sites.

Clearly in these examples the feelings being reached for are unhelpful, at least in the wider context. In the short term they may work in displacing painful feelings but they don't solve the underlying problem and the painful feelings are likely to return, perhaps amplified. So we need to be *discriminating* about the kinds of good feelings we look for.

13.2.5 Types of Good Feeling

In chapter three I introduced three high-level emotion systems, drawn from Professor Paul Gilbert's work:

- threat-detection and self-protection system – creates the emotions fear and anger
- incentive and resource-seeking system – associated with social emotions
- soothing and contentment system – associated with both receiving and giving care and love.

The three systems are all rooted in biology. The first is much more to with bad feelings, so I won't focus on it here. But the other two are associated with a range of good feelings. Let's look at three categories.

Anticipatory Excitement

Let's return to our gambler who gets a rush of anticipatory excitement as he places his bet. His brain gets a squirt of dopamine (clearly this dopamine pathway to the brain's prefrontal cortex is a major part of the incentive and resource-seeking system).

There's nothing inherently wrong with anticipatory excitement of course. But it can get us into problems. For one thing, whatever it is that generates the anticipation doesn't necessarily deliver on the reward. It's important to see clearly that the dopamine buzz is the promise of reward, not the reward itself. For addicts, the anticipated reward never really comes, because the addictive substance (or activity) only really delivers more dopamine-fueled "do that again" feeling. For "natural" desires the brain has mechanisms to switch off desire (e.g. thirst). But in addiction any such mechanism that could create the feeling of "that's enough now" is either broken or isn't strong enough.

As I've said, when we feel bad we naturally look for something to displace bad feeling with good. Often we turn to anticipatory excitement as it comes easiest to hand, so to speak. It does work – in the short term. You're bored so you go shopping. You're lonely so you eat chocolate. The trouble is, you're not really solving the problem that created the bad feeling. It's likely to come back.

Another problem is when the short-term buzz you're going for conflicts with your longer term goals and values. Eating chocolate can make you fat. Imagining yourself slim may create some anticipatory buzz but almost always nothing like the dopamine hit that eating chocolate gives, and saving towards a deposit for your new house doesn't create the same feeling as the idea of going shopping right now – so if your only solution to feeling bad is to go for a dopamine hit then you're probably going to get into trouble. Fortunately there are other ways of feeling good.

Peace and Contentment

Contentment is what we feel when our needs are met and we're free of desire and craving. But we're talking about much more than just the absence of desire – peace, bliss, serenity are positive feelings that take us to spiritual levels.

If the dopamine buzz is the promise of reward, peace and contentment are the actual reward. In this sense they are connected to the incentive and reward system, but arguably they are more closely involved with the soothing and contentment system. Soothing is what we need when we are distressed. At a basic level it happens when our physical needs (or desires) are met, but also at a psychological level when our emotional needs are fulfilled. As children we need it from others, but as we grow older we learn to internalise the process so that we can self-soothe.

In terms of underlying neurophysiology, we know that a class of neurotransmitter called endorphins (also known as enkephalins) are associated with feelings of bliss. Opioid drugs such as morphine and heroine work by mimicking endorphins (technically speaking, molecules of these substances all fit the same (opioid) receptor in neural cell membranes). Of course another side of these drugs is that they dissolve pain.

Clearly there is more to peace and serenity than endorphins – it is not my intent to reduce such powerful and sublime emotions to a mere matter of brain chemistry.

Love

Love undoubtedly feels good, and if popular music songs are to believed it's what makes the world go round. But of course there are different kinds of love. I find it useful to differentiate nurturing love, which is an active care-giving love such as a parent's love for a child, and attachment love (including romantic love) which is more to do with wanting and being receptive to others' love. Of course a loving relationship (between adults) is likely to involve both.

Undoubtedly the biology of love is complex and far from fully understood. Probably the most well-known player is oxytocin, a hormone involved with attachment and bonding. It's released at child birth in the mother, and during sex in both men and women. It seems to facilitate empathy, trust and social behaviours while reducing fear. Oxytocin is mainly produced in the pituitary gland although interestingly the heart also produces it. It increases heart rate variability (HRV), and moreover it's possible that the converse is true: increasing HRV through training may increase oxytocin.

13.2.6 Positive Emotions

Emotions are complex multifaceted entities, positive emotions perhaps even more so. One of the most significant aspects is the feeling they bring – and positive emotions do feel good.

Let's look again at Barbara Fredrickson's list of ten positive emotions in the light of the three categories of good feeling I've just listed.

- Love and generosity – associated mainly with the soothing and care-giving system, they move us to *give* care.
- Hope, interest, inspiration and pride – these emotions are more related to the incentive and resource-seeking system. I expect they would stimulate some dopamine release.
- Serenity, joy, amusement, awe – within the orbit of the soothing and contentment system, but they are more to do with receiving than giving.

13.2.7 Flow States

Some activities don't seem to require any effort – they are their own reward, or in other words they are intrinsically motivating. These occasions are opportunities to access flow.

Flow states are undoubtedly enjoyable – with hindsight. In the midst of flow you're probably too absorbed to notice. Flow states are *gratifying* but not necessarily *pleasurable*. Remember we made the distinction between pleasure and gratification back in chapter seven. Pleasures are independent of will and effort (that is, we are passive recipients), they are fleeting, and are subject to habituation (that is, with repeated experience the pleasure fades, as when you eat a whole bar of chocolate). We can crave pleasures, and they can be addictive.

Flow states require our active participation. You can experience it in the context of relatively mundane activities, such as working. It would be strange to say that flow states are the object of craving and addiction.

My point here is that it is easy to be motivated by pleasure-seeking, but it's not necessarily the best option. Positive psychology research suggests people find it much more rewarding, and gain much longer lasting benefit, when they seek gratification rather than pleasure.

When we find ourselves in a situation where our immediate experience is dissatisfying, the easy and unthinking option is to seek pleasure, particularly in the form of the dopamine buzz (the anticipation of pleasure) even if it's only in imagination. A harder choice is to cultivate flow. It's not necessarily easy to find flow, but it's going to be the more rewarding in the long run. The more often we experience flow states, the more fulfilled we feel in our lives.

13.3   The Inner Dialogue of Motivation

It's common to use self-talk or inner dialogue to motivate ourselves (especially to do things we don't really want to do). In this section we'll take a closer look at how this works (or doesn't work, as the case may be). I think this offers a helpful and relevant context for reviewing the nature of the mind-body connection, and in particular the relationship between thoughts and feelings. (It might be useful to re-read section 6.2 in chapter six which explored this relationship.)

When we attempt to talk ourselves into or out of something, we tend to use words like "should", "must", "have to", "can't", etc. When we use sentences with these words, e.g. "I have to go to the dentist", we get a feeling response, created by our internal mental "simulator" – the part of the mind that predicts what any given hypothesised scenario would feel like were it to actually happen.

Let's take an example. As a business owner, I need to spend time marketing my business, otherwise I won't get any clients. Like a lot of health coaches, I don't really enjoy doing it. Sometimes I tell myself "I should be spending time on marketing". Remember what it was like as a kid, being told "you should be doing your homework" (or whatever). As an adult I rarely get told what I should do, so I have to tell it to myself. But the feeling tends to be the same, albeit muted. My body tends to drop down,as though it is deflating. My head may drop a little, my facial expression might grow long. I might let out a sigh. Putting it into words, it's the feeling of *not wanting to*. It's not a pleasant feeling.

13.3.1 Judgements

Often when we use the word should there's a judgement going on in the background. For example, if you watch football on TV you'll often hear the pundits say things like, "he should have scored". What do they actually mean? Something like this: a footballer possessed of adequate talent, fitness, focus and judgement, and making sufficient effort, would have scored. He didn't, therefore he is lacking in one of these regards.

Often the should comes in the negative, e.g. he shouldn't have missed, he shouldn't have tried that. The same kind of judgement lies behind it.

For our internal shoulds, the judgement is often a quasi-moral one, e.g. "you shouldn't have eaten the chocolate", or "you should have known that". Imagine how you'd feel if someone were to say something like this to you, with all the implied judgement. Much more commonly we say these kind of things to ourselves, but the feeling is much the same – generally painful.

Returning to the topic of motivation, and my example that I should spend more time marketing, I think to be honest there is something of a judgement of my own inadequacy, but the main part of it is that I don't want to. Either way, the should is followed by feeling bad – that's the key point. What will this do for my motivation? Remember I'm motivated towards good feelings and away from bad. In this case I don't have a good feeling, I only have a bad. "Away from" can work if I have to do something to avoid the bad, but that doesn't fit in this case. "I should spend more time on marketing" doesn't really help, as I'm more likely to do something that will make me feel good.

Imagine that instead I say to myself, "I can spend time marketing", "I can succeed at marketing", or "I want to learn how to do marketing". These tend to lead to thoughts about getting more clients, helping more people. That makes me feel good. My body picks up instead of dropping down. Energy is mobilised.

When I imagine the feeling of actually doing marketing work I get a bad feeling and I'm less likely to do it. When I imagine the end results and beneficial consequences of having done marketing work, I get a good feeling and I'm more likely to do it. You can substitute your own example and probably see a similar pattern – e.g. when you imagine actually doing the washing up you get a bad feeling and don't want to do it. When you imagine a stack of gleaming kitchenware on your draining board, and now you can get on with things you actually enjoy with a clear conscience, then you get a good feeling and you're more likely to do the washing up.

13.3.2 Self-criticism

A lot of people have an inner dialogue of self-criticism that's either so harsh, or so habitual and persistent that it becomes a problem itself, something they want to get rid of. They want to get rid of it because it leaves them feeling bad.

At times we say things to ourselves that we wouldn't dream of saying to others. Why would you be so harsh on yourself? I think most people would say, they want to drive themselves to do better. Certainly, when you want to do well, and you're told you're not, you can be spurred to greater effort. But does it help to be so harsh as to call yourself stupid or a failure? Self-criticism is often more like self-punishment than encouragement to do better.

As children we were probably all punished at some time or other, even if only with a harsh tone of voice. Arguably punishing a child is useful in teaching it not to do wrong. But I think it's unlikely to be helpful in turning good performance into better. Yet many of us learned to internalise punishment as a way of achieving that, as a harshly critical inner voice, or in extreme cases, even as physical violence.

In self-control challenges it's common to have lapses. Suppose you're on a diet and you succumb to the temptation of a bar of chocolate. Does harsh self-criticism help to prevent repeat lapses? This is something that has actually been tested experimentally, and the answer is resoundingly no[121].

How do you work with unhelpful self-critical inner dialogue that has become habitual? How do you quieten the inner critic?

Throughout the book I've been emphasising a strategy of embodying a desired change at the physiological level. If we can shift physiology away from that which supports the problem state and towards that which supports the solution state.

I've noticed in both my personal and professional experience with biofeedback that inner dialogue (saying words to yourself in your head) can actually engage speech muscles, in a subliminal sort of way. You may have noticed that children when they're cogitating sometimes move their lips. Conversely, fully relaxing the muscles of the mouth can offer a way of quietening inner dialogue. Just as it would be difficult to speak with fully relaxed mouth and tongue, so it's a little tricky to internally string words together into thoughts. Of course thought is still possible – but subtle rather than gross.

When internal dialogue carries emotional weight such as harshness, again this needs to be embodied. For example harshness may be expressed in something of a frown. Again, fully relaxing facial muscles can work to take the emotional heat out of the inner dialogue. In chapter ten we saw how EMG (muscle tension) biofeedback can help in detecting subtle and easily-overlooked facial tension – the first step in becoming aware of and changing this pattern.

13.4 Willpower

Willpower is clearly related to motivation, but while motivation seems to come from the deeper self, or the emotional self, willpower is traditionally seen as the strength of the conscious mind needed to overpower the emotional or instinctual mind.

There are two types of willpower challenge, both characterised by a kind of inner conflict:

i. Following through with actions you committed yourself to, and which you've judged are in your long-term best interests, but which in the short or immediate term you don't feel like doing (because they're not intrinsically rewarding). For example you've decided to go jogging regularly to improve your health and fitness, but this morning it's cold and wet and you'd rather stay in bed.

ii. Resisting temptation – holding back from acting on your immediate desires when they're in conflict with your long-term goals and interests. For example you've decided to diet in order to lose weight but right now you've got a strong craving to eat some chocolate. The skill of resisting temptation and delaying gratification has been shown to be among the most powerful predictors of success in various walks of like including academic achievement and physical and emotional health[122].

13.4.1 Willpower as a Muscle

Psychologist Dr Kelly McGonigal draws comparisons (based on research) between willpower and muscle power[123]:

- By regularly exercising your willpower you strengthen it, or increase its fitness.
- Over-exercising willpower causes it to fatigue – in other words if you continually face willpower challenges such as temptations to eat unhealthy foods, it's going to literally deplete your energy, making it much more likely that you'll succumb.

This suggests that in the longer term an effective strategy for dealing with willpower challenges is a balance between on the one hand exerting yourself with relatively easy tasks, for example brushing your teeth after every meal, and on the other hand a healthy kind of avoidance of temptation. For example if you're prone to binging on ice cream it may be better to not buy it in the first place, so that it's not in your home and easily available at the moments when you're tempted.

13.4.2 Component Skills of Willpower

Following precedents from earlier in the book, we can see willpower as a high-level composite skill-set founded on a number of lower-level mind-body skills:

- **Acceptance and letting go** – when we experience craving the best strategy is not to engage in battle with it and defeat it with the superior strength of will. Resistance tends to feed the energy of craving. Acceptance creates mental space, enables us to see the craving as a small part of a much wider backdrop. As we saw in chapter eight, acceptance as a psychological skill is founded on letting go (of muscle tension) as a mind-body skill. Effective willpower is not about gritting your teeth and bearing it, as we might naively think.
- **Self-forgiveness** – research shows forgiving yourself for lapses in willpower is more effective than being harsh on

yourself in preventing future lapses. Self-forgiveness is a form of acceptance and again is supported by the mind-body skill of letting go[124].

- **Distress tolerance** – at the same time acceptance does not mean giving in. We must be willing to feel discomfort for at least a short time, without inner resistance or struggle, but knowing that distress tends to dissipate in time if not resisted.
- **Sustained attention and executive function** – helps us keep focused on our goals (especially longer term goals and values), and pause before unthinkingly acting on the basis of momentary impulses, desires and distractions, creating the space for conscious choice. Strengthening executive function, and the "muscle" of executive function (the prefrontal cortex) should support willpower.
- **Accessing positive emotion** – which mobilises the energy needed for motivation and action. As we've seen, positive emotions are not summoned by will, but arise naturally in response to the right triggers and conditions, including mental simulations. Mental imagery, supported by an open, curious and playful mind-set, is effective. Also we need to allow our body to express the physiology of positive emotion, as we'll see in more detail in chapter fifteen.

13.5   Summary of Key Points

- Self-regulation challenges relating to motivation include procrastination, addiction and depression.
- Motivation is underpinned by core mind-body functions including sustained attention, ability to access positive emotion and ability to let go or to lower arousal.
- Motivation is driven by feeling – we are motivated to avoid painful feelings and access good feelings.
- The most effective form of motivation is intrinsic motivation, where the activity is its own reward because it fulfils our human needs such as autonomy, mastery and purpose or

meaning (i.e. it connects us to our values, and to service to something bigger than ourselves).

- When we feel bad we tend to look for sources of good feeling to displace the negative feelings.
- Three principal categories of positive feelings are (i) anticipatory excitement, (ii) peace and contentment, and (iii) positive emotions such as love and gratitude.
- Anticipatory excitement is underlain by the "dopamine buzz" which offers the promise of future reward and is connected to craving and addiction. The problem is, it doesn't necessarily deliver on the anticipated reward (as is the case in addiction).
- Instead of seeking pleasures, which are fleeting and subject to habituation, an alternative strategy is to seek gratification or flow.
- How we use inner dialogue in relation to motivation is important. "Shoulds" often trigger negative feelings in practice, and thus may be counter-productive.
- Imagining finishing a chore usually feels good and thus builds motivation, as opposed to imagining the doing of it, which usually feels bad and diminishes motivation.
- Being harshly self-critical tends to lead to more self-control failures – a more helpful response is self-forgiveness.
- Willpower is the ability to act on the basis of long-term goals and values rather than passing emotions and desires which may be in conflict. The ability to delay gratification is highly predictive of success in life and is thus worth training.
- Willpower is like a muscle in that it can be strengthened by exercise, but fatigued by over-exertion. Effective willpower training balances regular gentle exercise with avoidance of excessive temptation.
- The most effective willpower strategy is to let go of the inner battle of will that we normally think of willpower, and be accepting of desires and impulses by using the mind-body skill of letting go and allowing them to dissipate naturally.

- Forgiving yourself (a form of acceptance) for willpower lapses is more effective in preventing future lapses than being harsh and critical with yourself.

14 Thinking

14.1 Introduction

A lot of the time, when your mind is a source of trouble it manifests in thinking. By thinking I particularly mean the internal use of language – inner dialogue – though mental imagery also plays a role in thinking.

When my clients raise concerns about thinking it's usually a matter of there being too much – especially at inopportune times such as when they're trying to get to sleep or concentrate on a book or a film. In other cases it's the particular form that thinking takes. Either way, what makes it a problem is that thinking feels out of control – it can't be quietened down or slowed down or switched off.

In this chapter we'll pull together some of the themes that have been running through the book, and apply them in the context of thinking. There won't be anything particularly new, but I think it's always useful to review understanding – after all, repetition is the key to all learning, as I like to say repeatedly.

In my experience it's quite hard to change thinking on its own level – that is, you can't really think your way out of thinking problems (especially if the problem is too much thinking). Instead we'll look to our understanding of the mind-body connection for solutions. The strategy throughout the book has been to effect subjective change by working to shift the underlying physiology.

As we've seen, thinking is intimately related to emotion and feeling. By feeling I mean the direct experience of physiological changes (in body and brain) associated with emotional responses, unmediated by language (though of course feelings can be labelled with words). Let's review our understanding of the relationship by reproducing a schematic from chapter six.

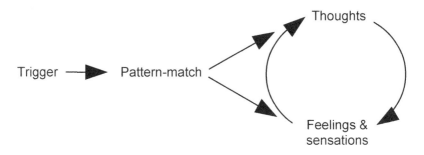

Figure 14.1   Relationship between thoughts and feelings

The key notion here is that thoughts and feelings mutually condition each other in a cyclic, feedback-like manner. An example should help. Suppose you ring a friend – she doesn't answer so you leave a message. After some time, she still hasn't called back. What goes through your head? In figure 14.2 below I've laid out a possible interplay between thoughts and feelings – in this case an example of depressive thinking.

Cognitive-Behavioural Therapy (CBT) is based on the idea that our thoughts and beliefs condition how we feel, which is undeniable. But I think CBT is in danger of missing the other side of the loop. We can end up believing things that ordinarily we'd know aren't true, because what we believe is conditioned by how we feel.

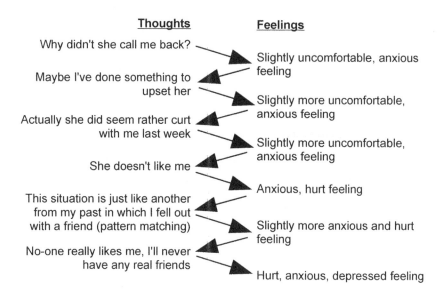

Figure 14.2 Example interplay between thoughts and feelings

14.2 Thinking Challenges

There are several ways that thinking can feel out of control or problematic, many of which we've already encountered. Let's review them.

14.2.1 Incessant Mind Chatter

Probably the most common thinking problem is endless mind-chatter, racing thoughts, that seem to keep us in a state of agitation, unable to relax. Mind-chatter is not deliberate, not directed, not useful – it's as though someone left a radio playing in the mind. It's repetitive and unproductive.

Patrick McKeown, in his book "Anxiety Free: Stop Worrying and Quieten Your Mind"[125], estimates that 95% of thinking is in this category – repetitive and useless.

A lot of insomniacs have this problem at night when they get into bed.

In chapter three we saw that mind-chatter is associated with a set of brain regions collectively called the default mode network. This system becomes active when we're not engaged in directed, focused activity (e.g. day-dreaming) and is inhibited by mindful, alert focus.

14.2.2 Obsessive Thinking

Obsessive thinking is dominated by some particular theme – the mind keeps returning to it in spite of our best efforts to distract ourselves. The extreme form is Obsessive Compulsive Disorder (OCD) but severity can be on a spectrum starting with everyday worries. Worry is slightly obsessive thinking that is motivated by anxiety – the thought is of some possible scenario that we want to avoid.

14.2.3 Ruminative Thinking

Rumination is similar to obsessiveness in the sense that it's stuck on some particular content or focus, but whereas worry tends to be concerned with possible future, in rumination the focus is negative feelings and experiences from the past. While worry and obsessiveness carry an edge of anxiety, ruminations are more typically associated with depression – though they can be anxiety laden as well. As such ruminations tend to be slow and dull in style.

14.2.4 Self-critical Thinking

We've already looked in some detail at the inner dialogue of self-critical thinking in chapter thirteen in the context of motivation – in particular the way *shoulds*, *musts*, etc. affect us. Self-criticism can be useful if it's constructive and helps us to avoid mistakes in the future, but more often it's unhelpful self-punishment, so overly harsh that it amounts to a kind of self-prejudice (you wouldn't speak to other people in the same way).

14.2.5 Pessimism or Negative Thinking

Pessimism is the tendency to focus on the negative aspects of things, or to assume that the worst outcome is more likely to happen. Pessimistic thinking may actually be more realistic but it's not very adaptive because it is associated with negative emotion.

14.2.6 Flawed Thinking

CBT aims to identify and challenge flawed thinking, or cognitive distortions[126]. Cognitive distortions are different ways of leaping to unwarranted conclusions that go beyond the known facts. They tend to arise in inherently ambiguous situations, of which there are lots in life – we saw an example earlier which started with wondering why your friend didn't call you back.

There are several categories including the following:

* **Mind reading** – thinking you know what others are thinking and feeling, or why they acted as they did. Examples: "She laughed because she thinks I'm stupid". "She said that to hurt me." "If I ask him for help he'll think I'm weak.".
* **Over-generalisation** – extending inferences way beyond what's reasonable, or treating general tendencies as inviolable rules, for example "you can't trust anyone in a position of authority", or "everyone hates me".
* **All-or-nothing thinking** – also known as black-and-white thinking, this is assuming things fall into discrete categories when the reality is a continuum (shades of grey) – for example "I'm just not intelligent" or "If you're not with us you're against us".
* **Personalisation** – this is assuming that things happen and other people act as they do because of you, as though you were the centre of the universe, e.g. "the boss looks angry – he obviously didn't like my report". This kind of thinking stems from the mistake of assuming everyone around us is paying us attention, when in truth they're not.
* **Catastrophising** – making negative predictions about how things will turn out (an exaggerated form of pessimism) e.g.

"she'll find me really boring and won't want to go out with me".

- **Emotional thinking** – assuming your thoughts must be true because they feel true, or fit with your emotions, e.g. "I feel like a failure" (therefore I am a failure). This often results from a lack of clarity and consequent inability to distinguish thoughts and feelings.
- **Mental filtering** – the tendency to focus on only one aspect of a situation, and not see the whole picture, e.g. you get one low rating on your performance appraisal, and think you're no good at your job, even though several other ratings were much higher. This often happens because we magnify the negative and minimise the positive. You may think your positive qualities don't really count for anything.

Cognitive Biases

The cognitive distortions listed above come from the CBT tradition which is concerned with mental and emotional health problems, but the truth is we're all guilty of flawed thinking at times, and to a greater or lesser extent. Psychologists have studied what are called cognitive biases, which are systematic thinking errors people tend to make, resulting in flawed decisions and judgement. An example is the confirmation bias – where we tend to look for data that supports our preconceptions, rather than open-mindedly and objectively finding out what actually is the case. There are lots more examples – see "Thinking, Fast and Slow" by Daniel Kahneman[127] for more.

Why Do Cognitive Biases and Distortions Happen?

This is a complex question that could become a whole book in itself – here I'll just touch on a few themes. The key point is that cognitive biases are normal and natural processes rather than fundamentally aberrant or pathological – it's just that at times we overdo them, we go beyond what is adaptive.

Firstly there are relatively benign reasons: the world as we experience it is fundamentally ambiguous and we need to rapidly make judgements and decisions based on insufficient data and from a limited perspective – e.g. we don't actually know why the friend didn't return the call. So to some extent we have to make assumptions, leap to conclusions and project our interpretations onto the world. This is natural, and adaptive at least some of the time, but the process has an emotional dimension – we don't like not knowing, it makes us feel uncomfortable, and this can drive the process of projection, sometimes beyond what is reasonable. (Actually, the ability to tolerate uncertainty is quite a significant component of mind-body intelligence.)

Distortions are much more likely to happen if we have a fixed mindset as opposed to a growth mindset. Remember a growth mindset is a deep-rooted view that change is possible: whenever you encounter "failure", you simply resolve to learn to do better next time. A fixed mindset is likely to lead to distorted explanations such as "I'm not clever enough".

Another fundamental basis of biases is our fundamentally egocentric nature – we tend to assume the world revolves around us, that people act as they do because of us. Again this is natural and probably to some extent adaptive.

A fourth key theme is emotional thinking. It seems that the stronger our emotions are, the less logic plays a part in our thinking. This seems to be a prevalent idea in our culture, to the extent that emotion and reason are seen as opposite and incompatible, as exemplified in "head versus heart" dilemmas. I think it's unfair – earlier in the book (chapter three) I argued that practical thinking and decision-making actually relies on feeling – logic doesn't dictate (completely) what you should have for dinner, for example. Reason and emotion need to work in partnership, serving each other. If either one over-predominates, problems follow. Emotional thinking is not in itself a problem, except in a matter of degree.

One way that emotions affect thinking is by introducing attentional biases – another fundamental aspect of cognitive biases. An attentional bias acts like a filter on awareness, meaning that we see things in ways we're predisposed to, and this can be limited. Negative emotions especially tend to narrow attention. If you think you're not good enough at your job, you'll watch out for signs your boss has realised this. If you have an anxious disposition you'll tend to focus on things that could go wrong. If you're angry you tend to see what others do and say as slights and personal attacks. And of course in all these examples you end up behaving in such a way as to make them so – e.g. the angry person retaliates first and so creates conflict.

Attentional biases can be an expression of deep-rooted beliefs we have about ourselves and the world, which in CBT are called core beliefs or schemas. Examples of (negative) core beliefs are that I'm unlovable or that other people can't be trusted. For more on core beliefs and how they affect us, see "Mind Over Mood" by Greenberger and Padesky[128].

Related to the topic of cognitive biases is the important question of why we believe the things we believe. I'm talking about everyday little preconceptions and even prejudices we all have to an extent – things like "politicians are devious and self-serving" and "salesmen are manipulative and out to rip you off". We touched on this question back in chapter five. To reiterate what I said there, the research suggests that we tend to believe things when we've heard them enough, so that they become familiar. There's a mind-body dimension here – familiarity is a feeling or a felt sense. We judge things as true or admissible if they invoke this sort of pleasurable, comfortable feeling of familiarity, while unaccustomed notions produce a feeling of unfamiliarity that is somehow jarring or discordant – and we disbelieve them or more likely just ignore them.

Let's take an example: suppose a politician says that immigrants are abusing this country's benefits system. If you've heard the idea lots of times before (perhaps it comes up in the newspaper you read) you may feel favourably disposed to this politician who dares to speak the truth. On the other hand you might have a preconception that members of such-and-such political party are closet racists and you may see this sort of statement as confirmatory evidence.

14.3   Solutions

We need to start with the question, is the problem thinking flawed thinking? Not all problem thinking is flawed. Probably in most everyday cases, if there is flawed thinking it's not central to the problem. Rather, the salient point is that the thinking is unwanted, excessive and out-of-control, and unhelpful in that it interferes with for example sleep or focus.

The question is important because while flawed thinking can be addressed at the level of thinking, a lot of problem thinking can't be. As I said in the introduction, you can't think your way out of thinking problems. Rather, the challenges are to quieten the mind, and to change your relationship to the thinking.

We'll start with this more general problem and return to flawed thinking later.

14.3.1 Resistance and the Quicksand Trap

Resistance has been a recurring theme in the book, and of course it can apply to thinking. Obsessions are the most obvious example – almost by definition there is resistance to the obsessive thought. Where there is resistance, there is the possibility of getting into what I've been calling the quicksand trap – your efforts to suppress the problem have the opposite of the intended effect, merely feeding the energy behind the thought, making it more likely to resurface later.

Resistance is usually at the core of problem thinking and needs to be addressed.

14.3.2 Cognitive Defusion

Cognitive Defusion is a term used in Acceptance and Commitment Therapy (a form of mindfulness-based therapy) to describe the process of stepping back from or detaching from thoughts, creating space around them so that you're not sucked into and swept away by them. There are numerous techniques for cognitive defusion[129], which don't attempt to change your thoughts or your degree of belief in them, but rather aim to change your relationship to thoughts. Defusion means seeing them as thoughts about the world rather than as reality; it's looking *at* thoughts rather than seeing *from* thoughts. Defusion allows resistance to melt away; it is acceptance applied to thinking.

What defusion techniques share is that they expand or shift *attention* so that the thought becomes an *object* of focus, rather than part of you as the *subject*. A very simple example: instead of mindlessly thinking repetitive self-critical thoughts such as "I'm so stupid", you think "I'm having the thought that I'm stupid". Another common technique is to use a metaphor as a way of seeing thoughts, such as that thoughts are coming from a sort of radio playing in the mind, or that thoughts are like leaves drifting by in a stream. Defusion has the effect of almost externalising thoughts – as though in some sense it wasn't you that thought them.

To actually use defusion techniques in practice, you have to first recognise the need for defusion, or recognise that your thinking is problematic. This mirrors the challenge of mindfulness practice, which is to notice when the mind has wandered off. This process is rather enigmatic – in chapter eleven we reflected that it happens spontaneously and non-volitionally – all we can do is prime it to happen more often through the strength of our intent and through regular practice. Suffice it to say at this point that the more mindful you are, the more effectively you'll be able to apply the tools of cognitive defusion.

14.3.3 Attention Shift

We've considered cognitive defusion as a kind of cognitive attention shift, i.e. a change in attention to thoughts themselves. More generally, attention can be a useful tool in shifting thinking patterns. Actually it's common to try to deal with unwanted mind-chatter by distracting yourself – focusing elsewhere. This can work well – we've seen that active external and sensory-based focus activates the PFC and quietens the default mode network (which is associated with egocentric mind-chatter). On the other hand it may be ineffective if you have poor attentional control (perhaps due to weak PFC functioning) or if it's attempted in a spirit of resistance, or if there is unresolved emotion that is feeding the thinking. In that case it probably will only provide short-term respite.

In the longer term, practices that strengthen attention (and PFC function) should increase the efficacy of distraction as a means of quietening the mind.

Another kind of attention shift is a change in *style* of attention. In chapter twelve we looked at different modes of attention, such as narrow versus broad attention. Zooming out the focus from narrow to broad can help because to an extent it circumvents resistance – you're not trying to exclude or suppress anything from awareness, you're just creating more space. It can also facilitate physiological change – which we'll turn to in section 14.3.4.

A further aspect of shifting attention relates to the time dimension. If the problem thinking is stuck in the past (e.g. rumination) then a useful response is to focus on the future, and particularly a sense of hope for the future. Problem thinking taking the form of worry about the future calls for a present-moment focus.

Cognitive Bias Modification Therapy

Cognitive Bias Modification Therapy (CBMT) is a technology-based training that shows a lot of promise in reducing anxiety. It can be seen as a form of attention training – it attempts to shift attentional bias for signs of threat and danger. CBMT software shows users sets of images, and asks users to select the most positive image. For example there may be a set of faces displaying emotional expressions, perhaps angry or smiling. People with anxiety have a bias towards negative information (they would naturally notice the angry face first) but the training is designed to gradually create a new habit of filtering for positive information. Research shows beneficial effects – brain imaging studies have shown that training shifts brain activation from right to left (which is consistent with improved emotional resilience, as we saw in chapter three)[130].

14.3.4 Learned Optimism

Optimism is the obvious antidote to pessimism or negative thinking.

We must thank Martin Seligman (who we encountered earlier as the founder of positive psychology) for his powerful insights in this area. His early research focused on pessimism as "learned helplessness", which is a way of interpreting repeatedly encountered negative experiences. For example suppose you fail an exam. Three "explanatory styles" characterise pessimistic thinking:

- Permanent – it's always going to be like this; I'll never pass this exam.
- Pervasive or global – other things go similarly badly; I never succeed at anything.
- Personal – it's my fault things went badly; it's because I'm not intelligent.

By contrast optimists adopt the opposite three explanatory styles:

- Temporary – this is just a blip; I'll pass it next time.
- Specific – this is the exception, not the rule; I generally pass exams.
- Impersonal – the failure was due to circumstances; I didn't have time to study hard enough.

When good things happen, e.g. you pass your exam, explanatory styles are the opposite way around. Pessimists think success is temporary, specific and impersonal, (i.e. they fluked it), optimists think success is permanent, pervasive and personal (i.e. they deserved it).

Seligman showed that optimistic explanatory styles could be deliberately adopted or learned, and he offers techniques in his book "Learned Optimism"[131].

It's worth pointing out that working with negative thinking in this way requires first catching yourself in the act – that is, a degree of mindfulness or self-awareness is the foundation. With this recognition comes a degree of cognitive defusion, or stepping apart from pessimistic assumptions.

14.3.5 Cognitive Reappraisal

Cognitive reappraisal, also known as reframing[132], works by shifting the context of the problem, so that we see it in a new way or from a different perspective. The facts of the matter are the same, but the meaning or significance is changed. Implicit here is the notion that the things that happen in life don't have implicit meaning, but we *create* meaning in how we interpret them, or the story we put on them.

The example I gave in the introduction of this chapter, of the unreturned telephone message, serves to illustrate. The facts of the matter are ambiguous, so we create stories to explain them. An alternative explanation might be that the friend got the message but was too busy to call back – her two children are very demanding of her attention – and then later she forgot. This story leads to a different feeling response – a much less hurtful one.

Reframing is useful for problems that seem to have no solutions. Reframing in a sense doesn't offer solutions but changes the focus. In the above example, we've created an attentional shift so that we consider the facts of the unreturned phone message in a wider perspective. Other reframes change the focus from an insoluble problem to a different, related, but more tractable problem.

Shifting Mindset

Earlier in the book I've made reference to the concept of growth mindset – the deep-rooted view that change is possible through learning, commitment and hard work. Shifting from a fixed mindset to a growth mindset is a reframe that changes the focus. Suppose you failed an exam. From a fixed mindset the problem is that you aren't intelligent enough (insoluble), while from a growth mindset the problem is that you didn't work hard enough and you need to do more next time. The focus of the problem is now, how should you do things differently next time. As a reframe this is very broadly relevant and of fundamental importance.

Stress Mindset

Another profoundly useful reframe that we've already touched on earlier in the book involves shifting your stress mindset. Remember this is how you view stress and the stress response. From a negative mindset, stress is a threat that can harm your health and your performance, and so must be avoided. The problem of avoiding stress is an impossible one. From a positive mindset, stress is a challenge to be embraced, and the stress response is your body's rising to the challenge. This shifts the task to how best to direct the energy of the stress response, and how to quickly and easily recover afterwards – a different, more constructive and more tractable problem.

We've looked at a number of cognitive techniques which work by directly changing beliefs or at least reducing the strength of belief. But as I said in the introduction, you can't always think your way out of problem thinking. Next we'll turn to a mind-body approach.

14.3.6 A Mind-Body Approach

If problem thinking can't be resolved at the level of thinking, we have to look at the wider set of conditions that create and maintain the thinking patterns. As we've seen from the model reviewed in this chapter's introduction, that includes emotion and feeling, and more generally physiology.

Review of Physiological Basis of Problem Thinking

Chapter three presented a relatively detailed account of the physiological and neurophysiological side of the mind-body connection. Here I'll review a few of the key points relevant to problem thinking.

- Pessimism or negative thinking may be reflected in a predominance of activity in the right side of the PFC over the left.
- Excessive mind wandering or mind-chatter may be the result of an under-active PFC which can't effectively inhibit other parts of the brain and the default mode network in particular.
- Depressogenic, ruminative thinking may be linked to both the above patterns.
- Obsessive thinking in its extreme form of OCD may reflect dysregulation in brain circuits linking the PFC and anterior cingulate cortex[133].
- Agitated, busy and racing thoughts may reflect a more general physiological over-arousal or sympathetic nervous system dominance.

Discharging Emotion

In cases where thinking is driven by underlying emotions, what's really needed is to address the emotion. No doubt we're all familiar with this – for example anxiety drives worry (thinking about what might go wrong). In my personal experience, anger and resentment leads to a lot of obsessive and repetitive thinking about how so-and-so has done me wrong and what I should have said to them or what I will say to them or do to them in revenge. Emotion manifested in physiology is what conditions the thinking to recur. We need to see the emotion for what it is, accept it, and allow the physiology to change – perhaps repeatedly.

Arousal

It's not just overt emotion that can drive problem thinking. When I was a student I planned a round the world trip, to begin after I'd finished my master's degree thesis. Once I'd booked my flights I had a strict deadline to meet, and the closer the time came the more my daily workload increased, so that in the last weeks I was working pretty intensively for long hours. When I came home in the evening, I found that I couldn't switch off – my mind kept spinning with all the things I still had to do. I found it difficult to relax and to get to sleep at night. I think this was probably a typical case of stress-related over-thinking. Though it was a stressful situation I wouldn't have said I was overly anxious. I wasn't particularly worrying about missing the deadline. It was just that I spent most of my time in a rather driven, hyper-focused and over-aroused state, and I got stuck in it. I didn't have the mind-body flexibility to shift out of it. Physiological over-arousal was driving over-thinking. Looking back, what I needed was the ability to calm that over-arousal.

At other times, problem thinking is associated with under-arousal (low energy). Here I have in mind day-dreaming and mind-wandering. I think it's useful to adapt the human performance curve to thinking, as I've done in figure 14.3 below. Again I've linked the optimal performance peak of the curve to flow. In flow states, thinking may be very subtle or even absent. For example a tennis player in flow doesn't need to think about footwork or racquet grip – and yet all the time he is making effortless decisions. Other kinds of flow states involve directed or creative thinking (e.g. writing or computer programming).

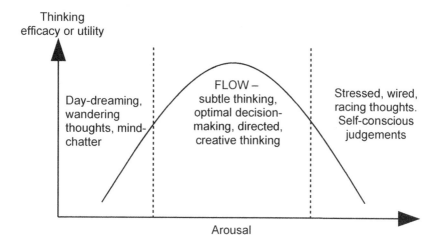

Figure 14.3 The Human Performance Curve adapted to thinking

Tolerance

Earlier I mentioned the need for tolerance of uncertainty – I find this is a common issue for my clients. Tolerance of uncertainty is an instance of a more general ability, distress tolerance. The opposite, distress intolerance, clearly is a kind of resistance, and as such generates physiological arousal, and tightening of muscles. Distress tolerance is a mind-body skill that involves reducing arousal and letting go of muscle tension.

Biofeedback

We've seen that biofeedback is an excellent tool for developing skill in psychophysiological self-regulation. In particular:
- **HRV biofeedback** can reduce arousal by activating the parasympathetic nervous system, and furthermore helps activate the PFC.
- **Capnometry biofeedback**, by optimising oxygen delivery to brain cells, strengthens cortical regulation of the brain. In my personal experience this has a powerful effect in quietening mind-chatter.

- **HEG neurofeedback** strengthens PFC function so in theory it should strengthen the capacity to inhibit the default mode network which generates mind-chatter.
- **EMG (muscle tension) biofeedback** plays a key role in training acceptance as a mind-body skill since it literally trains letting go, which, as I've argued earlier in the book, is a physical counterpart of psychological letting go or acceptance. Conversely resistance (the opposite of acceptance) manifests as muscle tension. Fully releasing muscle tension is a effective method of cognitive defusion – it's a way to take the "heat" out of thinking and begin to detach from it.

Thinking as Inner Speech

In chapter ten I made the case that thinking as inner dialogue is a subliminal version of full speech, and as such it can sometimes be detected as subliminal activity in speech muscles using EMG equipment. Learning to fully relax the muscles of the mouth (lips and tongue) using EMG biofeedback is an effective way of quietening mind-chatter.

Long-term Outlook

Mind-body solutions aren't necessarily going to give you instant fixes for your problem. Rather, they build your mind-body resources – your "fitness" level – with consistent practice over a longer timescale. This fitness leaves you better placed to respond to challenges. For example, suppose your train leaves in five minutes, but you're still ten minutes' walk from the station. If you're fit you can run and catch it, otherwise you're going to miss your train – this time.

In the short term you may have to accept your particular problem (e.g. not sleeping very well) for the time being, and that change is going to be gradual. Problem patterns are habits that have built over time with repeated experience, or conditioning. You're building new habits – new pathways in the brain – and that takes time, consistent training and exercise.

14.3.7 Conclusion

We've considered cognitive techniques, which work by changing beliefs or at least reducing the strength of belief, and also mind-body techniques which attempt to shift the physiology associated with problem thinking – not necessarily changing beliefs, but taking the "heat" out of the beliefs and introducing more of a "so what" element.

I believe these two approaches work best when combined. They complement and augment each other. For example, cognitive defusion, which is a kind of letting go of painful thoughts, works best when you can *literally* let go – that is, let go of muscle tension. And the real power of letting go of muscle tension is its application at the right times, that is, when you're experiencing resistance to your present-moment experience.

14.4 Summary of Key Points

- Thinking can become a problem when it is excessive and out of control.
- Problem thinking can't necessarily be solved at the level of thinking – you can't think your way out of problem thinking.
- Thoughts arise in dependence on conditions, and perhaps the most significant conditioning factors are feelings and emotions, or more generally, the physiological terrain.
- At the same time thoughts condition feelings – in other words there is a cyclic causal relationship.
- Sometimes problem thinking is flawed or biased thinking but not always – often the problem with thinking is it's unwanted (we can't switch it off).
- Resistance can arise in relation to thinking. Attempting to wilfully suppress unwanted thinking can make the problem worse in the longer term (an example of the "quicksand trap").
- Cognitive defusion is the process of detaching from thoughts, or creating space around them. It shifts perspective so that you can look at thoughts rather than seeing the world through

the lens of thoughts. Defusion is acceptance applied to thinking.

- Attention is another significant factor that shapes thinking. Both the *what* and *how* aspects of attention are important.
- Learning to be optimistic means learning to change three aspects of your explanatory style, or how you interpret positive and negative events. These are (i) permanent vs temporary, (ii) pervasive or global versus specific, and (iii) personal versus impersonal.
- Cognitive reappraisal or reframing attempts to shift the context of a problem so that we see it in a different way or from a different perspective, or we attach a different meaning or significance to the facts.
- Two important reframes, namely shifting from fixed mindset to a growth mindset, and moving from a negative stress mindset to a more positive one, work by shifting the focus from an insoluble problem to a related but much more tractable problem.
- A useful strategy for managing problem thinking is to attempt to shift the physiological patterns that underpin problem thinking. Optimal thinking involves balanced arousal, and is a kind of flow state. Biofeedback is a tool for achieving this in specific ways.
- Biofeedback and other mind-body methods don't necessarily offer immediate results but can work in the longer term to improve mental "fitness".
- Cognitive methods and mind-body approaches to problem thinking work best together and complement each other – for example letting go (of muscle tension) supports cognitive defusion.

15 Positive Emotion

15.1 Introduction

Research in the field of positive psychology shows clearly that the experience of emotional positivity predicts varieties of "success" in life – not surprisingly career success but also physical health and longevity. Having said that, few people need persuading that positive emotion is worth cultivating. In this chapter we'll cover some principles of how to develop positive emotion.

Most people understand that emotions can't be forced – they come from a part of the mind that is not the same as the conscious will. Indeed, attempting to over-control emotions tends to have the opposite of the desired effect. But that doesn't mean we're wholly powerless in the face of emotions, as though they are our mental weather. We need to understand which aspects of emotion are responsive to willed effort, and which are not. Our strategy will be indirect: we'll look to create the conditions that will best support the natural arising of positivity. And since emotions are mind-body phenomena, we'll review the physiological conditions for their arising.

15.1.1 What Is Positive Emotion?

Let's start by reviewing what is meant by positivity. As we saw in chapter two emotions are complex and multifaceted. Perhaps the key aspects are:

- **feeling** – the perception of the physiological responses triggered in emotion, and experienced as something to do with the body, though not necessarily as a tangible sensation
- **motivation** – emotions move us to act (also to not act in the case of certain emotions).

Feelings are largely "given" in the sense that we don't directly choose to have them or not. In the terms I used earlier in the book, feelings are the purview of the body intelligence. However we do have some indirect influence over feelings. Moreover there is a volitional or intentional aspect of emotion – we can choose to act on the basis of them, or not.

We naturally tend to assume we first have a feeling and are then moved to act – but this is too simplistic a view; the causal relations between feelings and motivation are two-way. The practical import is this: you don't have to wait for the feeling before you act. While friendliness may move you to act generously and helpfully, you can be generous and helpful even if you don't feel like it on the inside, and importantly, you are creating conditions for friendliness as a feeling to arise.

Positive emotions include love, gratitude, interest, joy, hope, amusement, pride, inspiration, awe, serenity (this is Barbara Fredrickson's list again). They can be seen as ranging between two poles: active and engaged (e.g. interest) to receptive (e.g. contentment, serenity). Generally speaking positive emotions are less intense than negative emotions – this is an aspect of the brain's negativity bias.

15.1.2 Time Course of Emotions

Back in chapter two (section 2.5.2) we saw that to fully appreciate the nature of emotion you have to look at different timescales. Emotions are fundamentally *responses* to events, and as such are rather short-lived. But it's also true to say we have background states that have an emotional quality – we can call them moods. Being in a positive mood means that you're more likely to experience positive emotional responses to events (e.g. someone smiles at you – you appreciate it and smile back – whereas in a bad mood you might hardly even notice it). You're also more likely to be outwardly and broadly focused.

15.1.3 What Makes Emotion Positive?

Positive emotions are not merely the absence of negative emotions, nor are they simply the opposite of negative emotions – positivity has its own distinct neurophysiology as we shall see.

By and large, positive emotions feel pleasurable and lead to creative and favourable outcomes. They are the ones you'd naturally want to cultivate. Arguably some emotions such as remorse are positive in the ethical sense (remorse is a healthy response if you've done something harmful) but you wouldn't naturally want to cultivate it.

Positive emotions broaden the mind – perceptually they open our senses so that we take more in, they heighten our awareness. Psychologically they open us up too – we take in a broader perspective in terms of the meanings we see. We also see more in the way of opportunity and possibility for acting. Positive emotions build our social and psychological capital, so to speak. Gratitude, for example, helps us acquire social resources in the form of positive relationships, while curiosity moves us to acquire new knowledge and skills.

15.2 What Are We Aiming For?

It's not possible to experience positive emotion all the time, firstly because emotions as responses are short-lived, and secondly because negative emotions are practically speaking inevitable – bad things happen in life. How can we express the ideal of positivity in terms of abilities we can realistically develop as part of the skill-set of self-regulation? We can outline three components:

i. having an emotionally positive baseline state (mood) which we inhabit most of the time

ii. ability to quickly and easily recover from emotional set-backs (i.e. let go of or being accepting of negative emotions and return to our positive baseline)

iii. ability to access positive emotions (as responses to stimuli) as frequently as possible.

Let's look at each of these in turn.

15.2.1 Positive Baseline

In chapter three I touched on Professor Richard Davidson's work on the brain basis of emotion[134], and more specifically, what he calls emotional style – a construct defined by six variables or dimensions, each based in its own relatively independent brain circuitry. One of the six is emotional outlook. The positive pole of emotional outlook looks like a positive and optimistic disposition or set-point, but the negative pole is in a way more revealing: it is negativity and pessimism, yes, but also lack of drive, persistence and motivation. Davidson's brain-imaging research showed that what differentiates the two poles is the ability to sustain activation of the prefrontal cortex (PFC). Positive emotional cues such as seeing a smiling face trigger the brain's (dopamine-based) reward circuit which tends to kindle activity in the PFC. This much is true in everyone, whether your set-point is positive or negative. But what happens then is pivotal: in depressed, negative people, the PFC can't sustain the activation and it quickly dwindles away, while in positive people it is much more enduring. The problem isn't really in the reward system but in a PFC unable to sustain the link. In more metaphorical terms, the seeds of positive emotions are there, but they aren't growing, they aren't flowering.

Happiness Set-Point

Research in the field of positive psychology suggests that people have a sort of happiness set-point. Life's events create perturbations in happiness but they often prove to be temporary. You may win the lottery or your partner may leave you but sooner or later you return to your set-point, and end-up just as happy or unhappy as you were before. We don't all have the same set-point: some people seem to be naturally happier than others (they have a "sunny disposition"). Probably our set-point is determined by such things as genetics and early life experiences.

My reading is that positive psychology is approaching from a different angle the same thing: what Davidson calls emotional outlook, and what I'm calling emotional baseline.

Does it mean that we can't change our set-point, and that we're stuck with our emotional disposition (outlook)? The research is pretty clear: a lot of things don't seem to permanently affect our set-point (winning the lottery for instance), but other things do. You can read more about what does and doesn't in Martin Seligman's "Authentic Happiness"[135] and other positive psychology texts. One thing that does seem to reliably boost our set-point is engaging in altruistic activity – a theme we'll return to in section 15.6 on values.

Sustaining Positive Emotion

In a sense the idea of an emotional set-point is something of an illusion, because our emotional state is changing all the time. The set-point is more like an average over time. What counts is the ability to sustain positive emotion – not perhaps the full emotion itself but at least the after-glow. Davidson's research has shown this is dependent on the PFC's ability to sustain activation in the dopamine-based reward pathway. From our mind-body perspective, it makes sense that strengthening PFC function is a useful undertaking.

15.2.2 Emotional Resilience

Emotional resilience is the ability to quickly and easily recover from emotional set-backs (i.e. let go of negative emotions and return to our positive baseline). It is another of Davidson's six dimensions of emotional style, and its neurological basis is the balance in activity between the left and right sides of the PFC, as we saw in chapter three.

The first part is to let go of negative emotions, and the physiological arousal often associated with them. This means not chopping them off or trying to eradicate them but dropping the struggle against them (resistance) and allowing them to dissolve of their own accord (remember emotional responses in themselves are short-lived). It means opening up space around negative feelings so they don't dominate our awareness to quite such a degree.

It helps to be able to physically let go (drop muscle tension), and also to broaden focus outwards to encompass awareness of more pleasurable stimuli.

Naming Emotions

Another core skill that's been shown to help with emotional regulation is the ability to name emotions. It works because to name an emotion, to some extent you have to step outside of it and see it as an object, rather than seeing the world through the emotion. In other words you separate yourself from the emotion (at least to an extent).

The ability to name emotions can be seen as a part of self-awareness, which is of course an important core skill that is prerequisite for developing the skills associated with positivity.

15.2.3 Accessing Positive Emotion

It's not enough to merely let go of negative emotions – the second part of resilience is accessing the positive.

Barbara Fredrickson has researched the "positivity ratio" - the ratio between positive and negative emotions. She found there seems to be a sort of tipping point of about 3:1, above which people really start to flourish[136]. That it is so high is another consequence of the brain's negativity bias – negative emotions have a stronger and longer-lasting effect on us, and take relatively more positive experiences to offset their effects.

15.3   Cultivating Positive Emotion

I think cultivation is the right word to use with regard to positive emotion. What gardeners do is create conditions in which plants grow – all they need is the right environment, then they will fulfil their own nature, which is to grow. Positive emotions are the same. They can't be forced but they are a natural expression of human nature given the right conditions. We need to look for positive emotions with a balanced mindset: they should be appreciated, savoured even, but not grasped, not craved. Take time and allow your sensitivity to deepen, because positive emotions can be very subtle – especially if you're starting out from a low level of positivity.

15.3.1 The Seeds of Positive Emotion

Following the gardening metaphor, we need to look for the seeds of positive emotion. The seeds are our automatic responses to events and triggers. They begin as feelings of *pleasure* – perhaps subtle and fleeting. It's important to realise these seeds are all around us, all the time – they aren't rare, but they so often go unnoticed[137]. It might be seeing someone smile, or the rich green of the grass I can see outside my window (even though it's raining at the moment) or the sensation of sunlight on the skin, or the sound of wind in the trees. Music is usually a pretty reliable trigger – though nothing is fool-proof.

Pleasure can be mental as well as sensory-based – that is, triggers can be cognitive (thoughts). For example you can reflect that tomorrow is Saturday and you don't have to go to work, or that someone went out of their way to help you.

Simply being receptive to pleasure opens the door to contentment.

Visualisation

I've given examples of sensory pleasures available in the present moment. It can also work if you mentally simulate sensory experience – you can imagine lying on a beach with the warm sun on you, maybe the sounds of the waves in the distance. There's a danger of falling into a slightly grasping sort of mindset – to avoid this, focus on recreating as much sensory detail as you can, as realistically and vividly as you can – then let the feelings of pleasure look after themselves.

Visualisation can work effectively when you focus on future experiences of gratification and positive emotion as opposed to future pleasure (imagining future pleasure might amount to mere craving) – for example finishing a course and gaining a qualification, or getting a new job. Hopefully this kind of visualisation will build your (present-moment) motivation.

Mindfulness and Imagination

Being open to pleasurable sensations in the present moment (as opposed to imagining them) is an important aspect of mindfulness. Noticing pleasure calls for a mind-set of openness and receptivity – like waiting for pleasure to reveal itself. It's clear that there's nothing to actually *do* – only be aware.

Having said that, I think imagination can play an important role in mindfulness practice. Remember mindfulness includes the quality of sampajanna (to use the Buddhist term) – awareness of purpose, of where you're going. For example, you may be aware of the soft heavy quality in your muscles, and you may notice a natural interest in this pleasurable experience, and it's a small step to wonder what it would be like to feel that even more intensely, or what it would be like if other parts of your body joined in with that feeling. So although this has an element of leading your experience, it's still in the spirit of mindfulness as long as you stay centred in, and accepting of, your present moment awareness, and as long as you hold lightly to the idea of change rather than getting attached to an idea of how you want things to be.

Visualisation and imagination work because they *invite* responses from the deeper part of the mind (or body intelligence as I termed it earlier in the book) rather than demanding or forcing responses.

15.3.2 Gratitude Diary

Positive psychology research demonstrates that practising gratitude boosts well-being[138]. One of the simplest and best exercises is the gratitude diary. The idea is to write down on a daily basis three things that you might feel grateful for, or more broadly, good things that happened. The point is not what you actually felt at the time, or what you feel when you record the event – you might not actually feel any gratitude – but you're looking for the seeds. Don't concern yourself with what you *should* feel at any point – simply "collect" the seeds and eventually the feelings will start to germinate.

At first you may find it hard to think of things, or at least different things every day, but remember they can be quite trivial things – e.g. the girl at the supermarket checkout made eye contact with you, or asked how you were doing. One of the ways the exercise works is by setting up a sort of attentional filter so that you actually notice things during the course of the day – you find yourself making a mental note of things that happen so that you can write about them later.

Once you get into the swing of it you can try out variants of the basic exercise. You can choose any positive emotion from the list, for example try an interest and curiosity diary, or an inspiration diary. These are more challenging.

In summary, the key idea for this section is that the seeds of positive emotion are all around, and the challenge is only to notice them.

15.3.3 Broad Attention

Recall Barbara Fredrickson's research finding that positive emotion literally broadens attention so that we take more in. Does it work the other way? That is, if we practice broad, open, receptive attention, does it predispose us to greater positivity? We touched on this in chapter twelve. My guess is it does. I find practising broad attention is a useful exercise for cultivating positivity.

15.4 Emotional Intelligence

Emotional Intelligence means having an awareness of and understanding of emotions in yourself and others, and an ability to use this knowledge to guide your thinking and behaviour. The concept was made popular by Daniel Goleman in his 1995 book "Emotional Intelligence"[139] but was developed as a psychology research construct in the eighties[140]. It is measurable (by questionnaire) and has been shown to predict better mental health and career success.

The most common usage of the expression is as a skill-set, involving these components:

- Self-awareness – the ability to perceive your own emotions and to discriminate and name them. A major part of this is awareness of physiological change.
- Empathy – the ability to know how others are feeling, based on perceiving their facial expressions, body language, prosody and other clues. Empathy entails being able to in some sense simulate others' emotions using your own brain systems for emotion (this is a particular application of "simulator mode", which we met in section 3.5 of chapter three).
- Understanding – knowing how emotions arise in yourself and others, and how they develop and change over time, and the factors that influence them.

- Self-regulation – the ability to effectively manage or modulate emotions, or guide them in your chosen directions. It entails being able to modulate emotions as physiological processes.
- Reasoning with emotions – using awareness of emotions to guide thinking and decision-making – in particular how to prioritise what you pay attention to and react to.

The fourth of these (self-regulation) is really a complex composite skill-set in itself, and much of the book has been about expressing what it is. Emotional resilience is an aspect of it.

15.5   Creating the Conditions for Positivity

In summary, positive emotions are like sleep in the sense that we all have them but we can't wilfully turn them on like a tap. We can, however, create the conditions in which they naturally arise, and also in which they are sustained. In part that means configuring our awareness so that we notice the seeds – this is what we're doing in mindfulness practice. But we can also work at preparing the ground, or preparing the soil, so to speak. Here I mean that the seeds of positive emotion are more likely to germinate if our physiology is in a favourable state. It's not my intention to reduce positive emotion down to mere physiology, but to make the practical point that cultivating adaptive states of physiology is likely to enhance our experience of positivity.

15.5.1 Physiological Conditions

Positive emotions are more likely to develop and be sustained in certain physiological states than others – that is, these physiological conditions are a significant part of a positive baseline emotional state. Throughout the book we've seen the pivotal role the PFC plays. Let's summarise its function in relation to positive emotion.

- The PFC can inhibit centres of the limbic system such as the amygdala which trigger negative emotions. The amygdala is over-reactive in people with anxiety and depression. Part of the PFC's normal function is to apply a tonic (or habitual) brake (independent of conscious intent), and the weaker this brake the more unruly emotions are likely to be. In emotional meltdowns the limbic centres swamp PFC control, but a well-functioning PFC can quickly dampen amygdala alarms or at least keep on top of them. This is a key aspect of emotional resilience.

- Left-right balance in PFC activation is a further neurophysiological pattern underlying emotional resilience. Several therapeutic practices have been shown to change it favourably, including mindfulness, and some brain stimulation tools (e.g. transcranial direct current stimulation) target it directly.

- The PFC plays a role in sustaining activation of the (dopamine-based) reward pathway – this is the basis of sustaining positive emotion and maintaining a baseline positivity, or a positive outlook in Richard Davidson's terms. It is key to the motivational aspect of positive emotion – translating feeling into action.

- More indirectly, PFC activation is key to focus and especially sustained focus in the present moment. By contrast the default mode network, which is associated with rather distracted non-present-moment self-oriented mind-chatter is likely to throw up triggers for negative emotion (e.g. memories of painful events or worries about possible future scenarios).

- Parasympathetic dominance is an aspect of whole-body physiology that supports the brain's social functioning. Most positive emotions are tied to the social realm. Parasympathetic dominance is reflected in high heart rate variability (HRV) and correlates with PFC activation.

The Role of Biofeedback

As we saw in chapter ten biofeedback offers a powerful set of tools for training optimal physiology. Let's review how these tools are relevant to emotional positivity.

- EMG (muscle tension) biofeedback can train the ability to fully let go of muscles, which is a physiological counterpart of

letting go of negative emotions, and of psychological acceptance more generally.
- Breathing biofeedback with capnometry optimises oxygen delivery to the brain and the PFC in particular, enabling it to fully activate metabolically.
- HEG neurofeedback strengthens the "muscle" of the PFC.
- HRV biofeedback builds the state of heart coherence which stimulates the parasympathetic nervous system, and in particular the new vagal pathway (recall Polyvagal theory, discussed in chapter three) which opens up the PFC's social circuits.

15.6 Values

We now turn more directly to the intentional aspect of emotion. Though we probably think of motivation and action as following out of feeling, what we do, and particularly the intent behind what we do, lays powerful seeds for how we'll feel in the future – that's why in Buddhism the volitional or intentional aspect of emotion is considered much more important.

Research in the field of positive psychology shows that acting on the basis of values or virtues is much more rewarding than acting in pursuit of pleasure, and the boost we get in terms of our mood lasts much longer (it's the difference between pleasure and gratification again). This is something you can try for yourself: compare the experiences of on the one hand treating yourself (to some pleasurable experience) and on the other hand being kind and helpful to others. Pick specific activities (e.g. for the pleasurable activity, take yourself to the cinema or eat some fine food) and then carry them out, perhaps on consecutive days.

Values are high-level (or deep, if you prefer) principles that guide how we live and what we do. They are what our lives are about, or at least what we'd like them to be about. We want what we do in life to be imbued with our values, or an expression of our values – though values aren't specific actions in themselves, but rather qualities of actions.

You can find out what your values are by asking yourself what is important about the things you do. Suppose you earn your living as a nurse. Being a nurse is not in itself a value, but you might do it because you care about your fellow human beings. In practising as a nurse you are expressing that care, you are acting out care. Perhaps also, in your work as a nurse you feel yourself to be part of a wider community, and that's also important to you. Working as a nurse earns you the money you need to support your family, also important. So we've touched on three values: caring, being communal, and supporting your family.

Maybe you play football in your spare time. Playing football can be an expression of all sorts of values too, for example fairness, health and fitness, being part of a team, developing your skill as far as you can.

Values are different from goals, in that they can never be "achieved", or "ticked off the list". They are more like directions – you can head west but you never arrive at "west" – it is not a destination. Specific goals are important of course, because they are particular embodiments of values. Indeed you can't live out values in the abstract, you have to find goals that express them. Getting married might be a goal, that expresses the value of living in a committed and loving relationship. A value like that needs concrete embodiment; you need to find an actual person to love.

Values are also different from feelings. I once asked a client what she wanted her life to be about. She was seeking help for anxiety and depression. Her answer was "peace" – quite understandable, but peace is not quite a value. You can act on the basis of values regardless of how you actually feel, you don't need to wait for the feeling. A value is a quality of what you do, or how you do it. You can think of feelings as useful feedback on how well you are embodying your values – if you're expressing values, positive and pleasurable feelings will naturally arise (eventually).

Again values are different from wants and needs. Maybe it's important that you have the respect of your colleagues at work, but the respect comes from them, it is in them, not a quality of what you do. On the other hand, if you act with honesty and integrity, you will naturally gain respect. Those are values because they are embodied in what you do.

Values are related to virtues and ethics, but a value does not require justification or approval. Being kind can be a value, if it is actually important to you, regardless of society's judgements about what is good and bad. That said, it's clear from research in positive psychology that other-regarding activities do boost happiness, indeed they are a trigger for flow states. Real values tend to take us beyond ourselves, or at least beyond our narrow conscious self-views and desires.

The point of this discussion of values is this: being in touch with and living out values and virtues creates positive emotion, creates abundant seeds of positive emotion. If you want to experience more positive emotion, don't go chasing emotions but act out of values and virtues, and the positive feelings will simply look after themselves – they are not the goal but feedback.

Of course that's easier said than done, and too big a topic to venture into in this book – instead I refer you to self-help books on Acceptance and Commitment Therapy or ACT. I've mentioned ACT before as it's considered a mindfulness based therapy but a major part of it is concerned with how to live a valued and committed life[141]. Many positive psychology books go into this topic too[142].

15.6.1 Loving-kindness Meditation

In chapter nine I mentioned a type of meditation practice known in Buddhism as *metta bhavana*, which translates to something like "development of loving-kindness". Barbara Fredrickson's research showed that the practice produced an increase in the daily experience of positive emotion – and not just in the context of the practice itself but extending into "normal" life.

The focus of the practice is not love as a *feeling* but as an *intent*: the heartfelt wish for the well-being of others (ultimately all sentient beings). That sounds rather abstract – in practice you bring to mind specific individuals (in different stages of the practice) including a good friend, a neutral person, and someone you find difficult. As you bring each person to mind, you look for good will, which is naturally present on some level, however impure and complicated by other emotions (sometimes including contradictory ones). Don't confuse the wish for someone's well-being with liking them – again the practice is not about the feelings. Though positive, pleasurable feelings are a natural "side-effect" of the practice, and useful feedback, they may not arise within the time frame of the practice.

The first stage of the practice focuses on oneself. This can be confusing at first – it's certainly not an exercise in narcissism but more about developing a kindly and gentle attitude in general, as a preparation for the other stages. For more about the metta bhavana practice, see Sharon Salzberg's book "Loving-Kindness".

15.7   Summary of Key Points

- Emotions are multifaceted but two key aspects are firstly feeling, which is a kind of body-sense, and largely non-volitional, and secondly intention or motivation – how emotions move us to act.
- Positive emotions broaden our perception and outlook and help us develop social and psychological resources.
- Emotional positivity expressed as a skill-set is threefold: (i) having a positive baseline state or set-point, (ii) the ability to quickly and easily let go of negative emotions and the arousal associated with them, and (iii) the ability to generate positive emotions as responses to stimuli as frequently as possible (giving you a high positivity ratio). The latter two constitute emotional resilience.
- The capacity to sustain positive emotion is important in maintaining a positive baseline, and is a complement to resilience.

- Positive emotions can't be summoned at will but there's a lot we can do to create favourable conditions for them to arise and then develop.
- Seeds of positive emotion are abundant – the challenge is to notice them. The gratitude diary is a proven tool that helps us focus on the seeds. The experience of pleasure is an important seed of positive emotion.
- Visualisation and imagination are useful tools in developing positive emotions, that work by inviting responses from the body intelligence rather than attempting to force responses.
- Emotional intelligence is a useful construct that includes resilience and the ability to self-regulate, and highlights how other mind-body skills such as self-awareness are a crucial foundation for emotional positivity.
- A well-functioning PFC is a key aspect of the physiological terrain of favourable emotional positivity. It can suppress negative reactivity and sustain positive emotions. It also helps to maintain a mindful present-moment awareness that avoids the arising of negative triggers that pop up in background mind-chatter.
- Parasympathetic dominance helps to activate the brain's social circuitry. Most positive emotions are social in nature.
- Biofeedback is a powerful tool for training and developing the physiological terrain favourable to positivity.
- If you want to experience greater emotional positivity, rather than chasing positive emotions as feelings a better strategy is to act on the basis of your core values, and let the feelings look after themselves. Feelings are not the goal but useful feedback.
- Loving-kindness meditation is a proven tool for developing greater positivity.

16 Conclusion

16.1 Introduction

Little remains other than to summarise our journey, and to take a brief look at what lies ahead.

Everyone at some time or other faces challenges in which the mind feels to some extent out of control, and so our project has been, how can we learn to manage the mind more effectively?

The typical everyday problems I'm talking about are:

- emotions – anxiety, anger, depression
- focus and concentration problems – distraction, fogginess, perhaps related cognitive problems such as poor memory
- craving and addiction
- motivation and energy – weak or inconsistent (e.g. procrastination)
- thoughts and thinking patterns – especially excessive mental chatter, but also negative thinking and obsessiveness
- sleep problems – which may be connected to any of the above.

Digging a little deeper we can discern some underlying problem dynamics:

- Lack of self-awareness – awareness is a prerequisite for conscious choice. For example you may be prone to anxiety, poor focus and tiredness because you're a habitual over-breather, but if you're not aware of it there's little you can do about it.

- Inner conflict – the mind is not integrated, and different parts of us pull in different directions. For example one part of you wants to restrict your spending so that you can save towards a deposit on a new house, but another part of you wants to go shopping.
- Inaccessible resources – sometimes you can't access the abilities you know you have. It's as though these resources lie in another part of the mind, out of the reach of conscious control. For example we all know how to sleep, but at times sleep seems to desert us, leaving us feeling powerless to access it.

Looking even deeper, we can see that all self-regulation challenges have a mind-body dimension, which is to say that our subjective experience is reflected in body and brain physiology, and vice versa. Problem states are associated with certain non-adaptive physiological patterns, and conversely solutions are associated with more conducive physiological patterns. For example, poor focus may be underlain by poor functioning in the prefrontal cortex (PFC), the part of the brain associated with executive control or executive function.

As a solution to the challenges of self-control I've proposed a hierarchical skill-set founded on mind-body regulation, or the ability to guide your own physiology towards more adaptive states. There are a number of elements to this skill-set, which we'll list in section 16.2 below. Ultimately they are inter-dependent.

The key point of looking at the solution in terms of skills is that they can be honed and developed with training and exercise. We're not necessarily accustomed to think in terms of developing say emotional skills.

We've looked at two tools for training the skill-set of regulation: mindfulness and biofeedback. I've made the case that they are complementary or mutually supporting practices. One of the key themes running through the whole book is that you have to apply the mind in the right way. Applying effort in the wrong way can make things worse (it's what I've been calling the quicksand trap).

To clarify what the "right way" means, I've developed a number of models and concepts:

- Body intelligence versus thinking intelligence: a lot of the abilities we're interested in are in the sphere of body intelligence, meaning they're not accessible to our everyday conscious will. Instead we need to use other faculties to access them, such as trust and imagination.
- Over-control versus under-control as expressed in the human performance curve (which captures the idea that optimal performance is a matter of balanced effort, or even balanced arousal).
- Flow states as states of peak integration, where energy and information flow harmoniously and coherently, and characterised by the experience of absorption and effortlessness.

Training is about skills development – getting "better" at what you practice, as when you play a lot of tennis, or the piano. With training you can become more effective in managing the mind. That means having the flexibility or adaptability to meet the challenges that life throws up – in mind-body terms there is no single ideal physiology, rather the goal is to be able to shift physiology easily, quickly and appropriately.

While I've emphasised skills development, training also creates change by building fitness through exercise (as in weight training and running), by establishing new habits or conditioning (literally new brain pathways), and lastly by generating insight and understanding.

16.2 The Skill-set of Self-regulation

Throughout the book we've discussed self-regulation as a skill-set. It's time to attempt a succinct delineation of this skill-set.

At a high level, we'd probably all sign up to these abilities:

- emotional positivity and balance
- emotional intelligence (defined in section 15.4 of chapter fifteen)

- ability to access flow
- executive function, defined in section 3.4.4 of chapter three, and including focus and attention, working memory, decision-making
- body regulation, including ability to relax (reduce arousal), to access energy (increase arousal) and access sleep.

What are the core component mind-body skills underlying these high-level abilities? The following table summarises them.

High-level Resource	Core Skills	Notes
Self-awareness	Awareness of body	Including pleasure/pain, arousal level, "energy", muscle tension, breathing, heart
	Awareness of thoughts	Being aware of thoughts *as* thoughts about reality rather than as reality itself – this entails being able to step apart from your thinking to some degree.
	Awareness of impulses, desires, urges, motivation	Also awareness of inner conflicts – different parts of ourselves pulling us in different directions (i.e. awareness of our level of integration).
	Ability to name emotions (emotional literacy)	Awareness of emotions means awareness of the above three (body, thoughts, etc.). It's also useful to be able to discriminate the three. Being able to name emotions helps you to separate yourself from them to some degree. This is an aspect of mindfulness, and also of emotional intelligence.
	Awareness of and understanding of mind-body connection	Relationship between thoughts and feelings, etc., how they mutually condition each other (as discussed in chapter six section 6.2).

Attention	Alertness	Ability to intensify or vivify awareness or awakeness.
	Stability of focus	Holding the mind steady on one thing. Basis for short-term memory – holding things in mind, or internal focus of attention.
	Selective attention (inhibition)	Ability to inhibit or suppress background noise (automatically, without having to think about it). Noise could be external-origin (sensory distractions such as literal noise) or internal-origin – mind-chatter, passing cravings, etc. As with the other attention core functions, this ability is founded on a well-functioning PFC.
	Flexibility of focus	Including style of attention, e.g. perceptual, broad vs. narrow, associated vs. dissociated, etc. (see chapter twelve section 12.5). Also at the conceptual level – e.g. seeing the details versus seeing the big picture.
Body regulation	Accessing energy / drive	Increasing physiological arousal level. Put another way, accessing enthusiasm and excitement.
	Relaxation	Decreasing physiological arousal level. We can also include releasing muscle tension. This is an important component of letting go at the psychological level (e.g. of negative emotions, listed separately below).
	Optimal breathing	Principally optimising carbon dioxide levels and thus oxygen delivery to brain cells – not over-

		breathing. Also helps ANS regulation (see chapter four for a full discussion of breathing physiology).
Emotional regulation	Letting go of or accepting negative emotions and painful feelings / sensations	This is a component of emotional resilience or "bounce-backability". Also known as "distress tolerance", includes tolerance of uncertainty, tolerance of lack of control or power.
	Accessing positive emotions	The other half of emotional resilience. Recall Fredrickson's list – perhaps the key ones are: love, joy, hope, interest. Others: gratitude, pride, amusement, awe, inspiration, serenity. Most of these are "activating" (meaning they entail accessing energy, which is listed separately in the body regulation section below) while others are "soothing" (and thus decrease arousal). Self-soothing is an important component of emotional regulation.
	Sustaining positivity	Founded on a well-functioning PFC and mesolimbic dopamine pathway (equivalent to Richard Davidson's "outlook" dimension of emotional style).
	Empathy	Ability to know what others are thinking and feeling – a special application of "simulator mode" (first described in chapter three).
	Cognitive defusion	Ability to stand apart from negative thoughts that would otherwise give rise to (or sustain) negative emotions. A form of acceptance, it is built on physical letting go, also attentional flexibility.

Motivation	Letting go of craving, desire	That is, desires that conflict with your long-term goals. This is itself built upon (i) the ability to lower physiological arousal, and (ii) flexibility of attention (broadening awareness without actively suppressing the craving).
	Attention	Sustaining motivation means keeping focused on long-term goals and avoiding distractions.
	Accessing positive emotion	This is important for accessing and harnessing energy. Most important for motivation are probably anticipatory enthusiasm and interest.

As you work your way through the table you'll realise that I've started with more fundamental (or low-level) components and progressed to higher level functions. Although I haven't spelled it out in the table, self-awareness underlies pretty much all the functions in the body regulation, emotional regulation and motivation sections (for example you can't hope to develop empathy without an awareness of your own emotions). The same is largely true of attention – e.g. to be able to let go of negative emotions you need flexibility of attention: it's useful to be able to "zoom out" to a broader focus, so that the unpleasant feelings don't dominate your whole awareness, and also to be able to step outside of yourself to a degree, or dissociate. Conversely to access positive emotions it's useful to be able to "step into yourself" or "associate" – viewing life from afar is not conducive to the experience of positivity.

Let's take a closer look at how the core skills apply in one of the high-level functions I listed, accessing flow. Suppose you're a teacher in some capacity – perhaps in a school or perhaps you lead a dance class or perhaps you teach your own child something you both like doing.

- Flow is quintessentially a state of integration – the mind is taken up with one thing, and distracting influences (which are always there on some level) don't really register. Your focus is stable, and your attention faculty naturally inhibits potential distracting influences. Your executive attention keeps you aware of what you're trying to achieve (the outcomes of the class).
- Flow states involve absorption or "associated" awareness as we described it in chapter twelve. As a teacher you need to be "inside" your experience, otherwise you'll seem aloof, flat, uninspiring. But occasionally you also need to take a step back from yourself, so that you can see where things are going, make sure you are on track and doing a good job – so flexibility of attention again.
- Positive emotions fuel the flow state, particularly interest.
- Interest (and other positive emotions) rely on physiological and neurophysiological arousal (mobilising energy).
- Another inherent feature of flow states is feedback. Teaching is a form of communication, and so involves a vital mutual awareness and empathy. Your own emotional responses are the internal feedback that help you maintain and develop the spirit of communication – of course founded on self-awareness.

16.3 What's Missing

The above list is by no means a comprehensive delineation of human functioning. There are some important areas very relevant to the sort of problems we're addressing, that I haven't covered. In this book I've focused on abilities around the mind-body interface, but it's possible to extend the hierarchy of functions both upwards and downwards.

A simple philosophy for human flourishing would be: provide everything that is needed, and avoid what is harmful, and the human organism will thrive.

Needs are hierarchical:

- **physical** – nutrients, water, oxygen, warmth, shelter, exercise (physical challenge)
- **psychological** – sense of security and safety, sense of autonomy and control, sense of competence and achievement, stimulation and challenge at the appropriate level ("good stress"), a sense of a future to look forward to, being in touch with values
- **social** – supportive and caring relationships, giving and receiving of attention.

We can make a similar list for things to avoid:

- **physical** – toxins (e.g. mercury), unhealthy foods (e.g. sugar, wheat), infections, harmful radiations, sedentary lifestyle
- **psychological** – excessive stress and negative emotion, boredom, lack of engagement and meaning
- **social** – exploitation, bullying, isolation.

We've looked at the role of physiological and neurophysiological functioning but we haven't addressed the biochemical basis. To function well the body and brain need nutrients in the right amounts, and they need to be relatively free of toxic influences. This is actually a huge topic in itself. To give an example, one of the most common drains on brain function at this level is poor blood sugar regulation, caused mainly by poor diet (excess sugar and refined carbohydrates). Blood sugar problems can lead to emotional problems, brain fog (poor focus, memory, etc.) and fatigue. Unless you address this level, practising biofeedback, mindfulness, etc. can to an extent be like pumping up a tyre that has a puncture. In my professional practice this is certainly an area that I cover (I'm trained in a functional approach to nutrition), but I can't hope to do the topic justice in the context of this book. For those interested I've given some suggested reading in this area, in the end note following this sentence[143].

Moving upwards takes us into the realm of social intelligence. Social intelligence (or interpersonal intelligence) is the ability to understand and effectively negotiate social relationships and environment, including friendships but also more "hierarchical" relationships such as with your boss at work, and group settings. Undoubtedly social intelligence is built on a foundation of mind-body intelligence – for example a core component is empathy, which is itself dependent on awareness and understanding of your own emotions. We could say social intelligence is the ability to apply mind-body intelligence in social contexts. Again it is a matter of flexibly and smoothly adapting to the changing contexts.

For a good account of the topic of social intelligence I recommend Daniel Goleman's book, "Social Intelligence"[144].

In my professional practice the most common problem my clients seek help with is anxiety, and the most common form of anxiety is social anxiety. Often these clients need help in building their mind-body self-regulation skills, and then a little more help in learning to apply them in social settings, but they have a basic social competence and understanding (they know how social interactions work, they know what is expected of them and what to expect of others) and that makes things a lot more straight-forward. But other clients never really learned basic social skills, perhaps because of parental attachment problems or perhaps because they have Asperger's syndrome – whatever the reason they have a lot more work to do. Social intelligence is beyond the scope of this book but I would say the tools and concepts we've covered are very relevant.

16.4 Where Next?

As I said in the introduction, the book is not really in itself a self-help book, but rather a preparation for and manifesto for working with mindfulness and biofeedback. I hope it's given you a sense of the possibilities offered by these tools, and the appetite to take things further. But to create any real change in your life you have to take action.

16.4.1 Mindfulness

Probably one of the easier next steps you could take is learn mindfulness. These days there are lots of courses available, many of them secular in their approach (even many Buddhist centres offer non-Buddhist courses in mindfulness). If you can't find a group in your area, there are self-help books available with included audio CDs (of guided practices) and also online mindfulness courses. I've listed some of these in the further reading section at the end of the book. But finding a local class offers advantages: the opportunity to meet like-minded people, and to practise together.

16.4.2 Biofeedback

Taking up biofeedback is likely to be more challenging. Your first option is to find a local practitioner. In the UK there aren't many of us, nor is there any register of practitioners that I'm aware of (at the time of writing) so an internet search is your best option. My own practice is based in York, but I do offer devices for home rental, and also internet coaching. In other countries biofeedback is much better established. In the US, BCIA (Biofeedback Certification International Alliance)[145] maintains a register of practitioners with accredited training.

If you want to buy your own kit, you have a rather daunting choice. Devices range from simple low-cost single-parameter gadgets to professional-grade multi-parameter devices costing up to several thousand pounds. The cheapest options are apps for smart phones costing just a few pounds – the most basic ones use the phone's camera to detect the heart beat. Devices for other modalities tend to be much more expensive. To get a sense of what's available, have a look at the websites of prominent re-sellers, such as the US-based Bio-medical (*www.bio-medical.com*).

Lastly you might check out my own offerings – by visiting *www.stressresilientmind.co.uk* and especially the 'Resources' menu where you'll find articles on biofeedback and some free offerings. As I said back in chapter one, I developed my software (Mind-Body Training Tools – see the 'Products' menu on my website) to meet my personal and professional requirements – the result is a product that I hope bridges the gap between the cheapest and most limited, and the most expensive products. It offers a richness of feedback (i.e. multiple parameters) that you can't get from basic devices, at a much lower cost that the professional-grade products.

16.4.3 Growth Mindset

If you want to overcome your self-control challenges perhaps the most fundamental requirement of all is a growth mindset: belief in the possibilities of change, and in your own capacity to learn and develop. I hope reading this book has at least strengthened your growth mindset, and your willingness to begin the work.

Appendix: Quantifying Heart Coherence Using Spectral Analysis

Heart coherence biofeedback software needs a way to quantify coherence. Most programs use some variant of a method called spectral analysis (also known as Fourier analysis or frequency analysis). Spectral analysis involves some complicated mathematics, which you don't need to understand in order to benefit from training – for practical purposes you just need the software to tell you when your coherence is higher or lower. However for those interested, I'm going to attempt an explanation of the spectral analysis method. I'll keep it as simple as I can – don't worry, no equations!

Let's start with a reminder of what heart coherence is, and what it looks like. In coherence, heart rate speeds up and then slows down again in sync with the breath. Figure A1 below shows a good example.

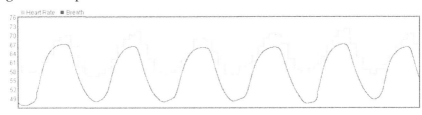

Figure A1 Showing relatively coherent heart rate variation. The stepped trace (slightly higher of the two) is heart rate and the smooth trace (slightly lower) is breath (the upward movement is inhaling, the downward exhaling). You can see the two are synchronised.

- There are large swings in heart rate – that is, the "heart wave" (which is what I like to call the heart rate trace) has a large height between the peak and the trough. Actually it can go up to 30 beats per minute or more.
- These swings are consistent, meaning that the cycle is stable over successive breaths, as opposed to e.g. a large swing followed by a small swing followed by a large swing again.
- The breath and the heart wave a tightly coupled, or closely in sync, so that the peaks occur together and the troughs are together.

The spectral analysis method is based on heart rate data alone – the advantage is that you can use it without needing to measure breath, but the disadvantage is that it leaves out the third of the above features.

In figure A1, the heart wave (stepped) looks quite a lot like a regular, "pure" wave, which mathematically is described as a sine wave. Figure A2 below shows a pure sine wave.

Figure A2 A "pure wave" known mathematically as a sine wave. Note it has constant frequency and amplitude.

A sine wave has a constant and clearly-defined *frequency*, which tells you how far apart the peaks are, and also a constant and clearly defined *amplitude*, which tells you how tall the peaks are.

Of course the heart wave isn't always perfectly sine-wave-like. Figure A3 below shows a heart wave which is less coherent than what you see in figure A1. You can see that both the frequency and the amplitude of the heart wave are not consistent.

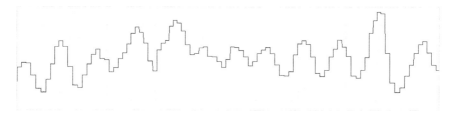

Figure A3 A heart rate trace or "heart wave" having a lower degree of coherence – though not zero. Note the amplitude and frequency are not consistent.

Summed up in broad terms, the spectral analysis method is quantifying how closely the heart wave resembles a pure sine wave.

A low coherence heart wave is more complex, and to describe it mathematically we need to rely on a theorem discovered by Jean-Baptiste Fourier, which says that (roughly speaking) any complex oscillation (i.e. one without a consistent frequency or amplitude) is equivalent to a set of pure sine waves of different frequencies and amplitudes, added together. (Ultimately you may need an infinite number of sine waves to be perfectly exact, but in practice you can be close enough with just a relatively manageable number.)

Visual examples will help here.

Figure A4 below shows three sine waves with different amplitudes (heights) and frequencies (or wavelengths).

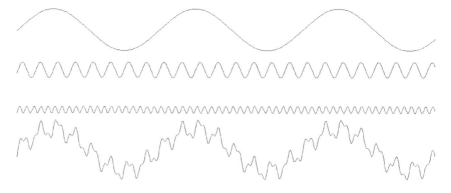

Figure A4 The three upper traces are pure sine waves of differing frequency and amplitude. The more complex trace at the bottom is simply the upper three added together.

Spectral analysis or Fourier analysis essentially does the opposite: it decomposes a complex oscillation into component sine waves. Spectral analysis delivers you another kind of graph, something like a bar graph or histogram, showing frequency along the horizontal axis. The "bar" at any particular frequency has a height that corresponds to the contribution that particular frequency makes to the complex wave you started with – in other words it relates to the amplitude of the original sine wave.

So the spectral analysis of the lowest, composite trace in figure A4 is shown below in figure A5.

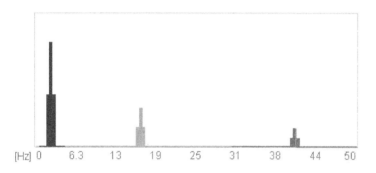

Figure A5   Spectral analysis of the composite oscillation in figure A4 above (bottom trace). The three peaks correspond to the three component frequencies.

Hopefully it makes sense that you see three peaks, one for each of the component frequencies. The leftmost peak in figure A5 corresponds to the first sine wave in figure A4, and the middle peak in A5 to the second sine wave in A4, and the rightmost peak in A5 to the third in A4).

The height of each peak in figure A5 is proportional to the amplitude of the component that we started with.

Spectral analysis is used a lot in the world of engineering and computing. A real-world example would be more complex than the three simple peaks of figure A5.

Hopefully now you can see that the spectral analysis of a high-coherence heart wave (such as that seen in figure A1) would give a relatively simple-looking chart like figure A6 below – there is one single prominent peak because the heart wave looks a lot like a single sine curve to begin with.

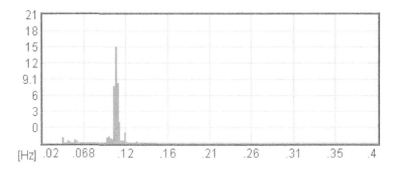

Figure A6 Spectral analysis of HR data with a fairly high degree of coherence, reflected in a single sharply-defined peak

Good coherence typically involves breathing at around six breaths per minute, which corresponds to about 0.1 Hz in the spectral analysis. (Hertz is the unit of frequency – 1 Hz is 1 cycle per second, so 0.1 is 1 cycle every 10 seconds, or 6 breaths per minute.)

Different breathing rates would create peaks at different points, most likely smaller in height recall that six breaths per minute seems to be a sort of resonance point for breathing, at which coherence is maximum. Of course in practice breathing rate is usually not constant, which would make for a more complex spectral analysis.

A low coherence heart wave would give more spread-out areas as in figure A7 below – reflecting the idea that the low coherence heart wave is not sine-like but is more complex, and would need to be analysed into lots of components.

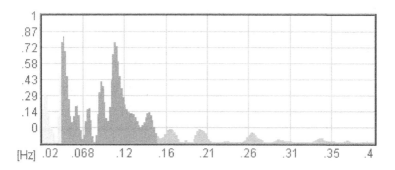

Figure A7   Spectral analysis of relatively incoherent HR data

Often in biofeedback software the area around 0.1 Hz is green, emphasising that the "target" of coherence training is a prominent peak in this range.

To come up with the final measure of coherence, the software must somehow estimate the prominent peak around 0.1 Hz as a proportion of the total "activity" in the chart. One way to do this might be to calculate the area in each part of the histogram.

A more specific example of how to calculate coherence is described in a paper by Rollin McCraty et. al. published in the journal *Integral Review*[146]. Probably the best known heart coherence biofeedback applications come from the Hearthmath Institute, who deserve much of the credit for popularising HRV biofeedback. McCraty is a key figure in the Heartmath Institute, and it's likely they use something like the method described in this paper, though no doubt the exact method is their commercial secret.

One thing about calculating coherence that I hope you can appreciate is that you need to look at at least several seconds' worth of data to see it, or at least a few breaths' worth. This is true of any software actually – it's not just giving you an instantaneous coherence but rather a sort of moving average.

That means any heart coherence measure is relatively slow to respond. It's not really working at the same timescale as emotions, which can be very fast. An emotion can pop into mind and you can feel the change almost instantly – and it might even affect the heart rate instantaneously. For example, you suddenly remember you're late for an appointment. Your heart lurches, the heart rate trace jumps upwards – but the coherence calculation is only going to follow some time later – it's going to take a few seconds to work through.

Recommended Further Reading

Science and the Mind-Body Connection

- **Sapolsky, Robert "Why Zebras Don't Get Ulcers"** (first published 1994, now in its third edition)

  Professor Sapolsky describes the biology of stress, and how its practical relevance to us in our everyday lives. Sapolsky's writing is scholarly (he's a research scientist himself) yet easy, humorous and eminently comprehensible. The book is especially good on stress hormones such as cortisol, which I've rather glossed over in this book.

- **Davidson, Richard, with Sharon Begley "The Emotional Life of Your Brain: How to change the way you think, feel and live"** (2012)

  Professor Davidson is one of the foremost researchers in the neuroscience of emotion, and more recently has investigated meditation and contemplative practice. The book is the fruit of his decades of research.

- **Goleman, Daniel "The Brain and Emotional Intelligence: New Insights"** (2011)

  Dr Goleman wrote the bestselling "Emotional Intelligence" (which I recommend too, likewise his "Social Intelligence"). This short e-book is a sort of update on the science behind emotional intelligence and self-regulation.

- **The books of Professor Antonio Damasio**

I consider Damasio one of the foremost writers of neuroscience for a general audience. His books are filled with wise insight based on profound understanding of brain science. I find it difficult to select the best of his works. His first book, "Descartes' Error", is quite a few years old now, but it focuses most directly on the interdependence of rational decision-making and emotion, a theme which runs though his more recent books.

General

- **McGonigal, Kelly "Maximum Willpower: How to master the new science of self-control"**(2012). More or less the same book is published in the US as "The Willpower Instinct"

  Research psychologist Dr McGonigal has devoted her career to investigating self-control, or willpower. Besides being a fascinating read, her book is very practical and relevant. Her later book "The Upside of Stress" (2015) is also highly recommended.

- **Seligman, Martin "Authentic Happiness"** (2002)

  Martin Seligman is considered the father of the field of positive psychology, which investigates the basis of well-being and happiness. This book is a survey of the field, and covers the concept of flow which is core in positive psychology. He includes practical tools and assessments.

- **Gallwey, W. Timothy "The Inner Game of Tennis"** (1975)

  Written many years ago now, I regard this as a classic. It's not only relevant to tennis but to any activity where the art of "relaxed concentration" is important (i.e. most of life).

- **Siegel, Daniel "Mindsight: Transform your brain with the new science of kindness"**(2010)

  Psychiatrist Dr Siegel combines an account of mindfulness and its neuroscience underpinnings, with great insight into its relevance in the field of personal development and therapy.

- **Fredrickson, B. "Positivity"** (2009)
  Positive psychology researcher Professor Fredrickson offers us an account of the science of positive emotion, with a wealth of practical relevance.
- **Kotler, Steve "The Rise of the Superman: Decoding the Science of Ultimate Human Performance"** (2014)
  Co-founder of the Flow Genome Project which aims to understand and document the preconditions in which flow states arise, Steve Kotler presents the neuroscience and psychology of flow in the context of a fascinating account of action and adventure sports pioneers.

Self-Help and Therapy Books

First, books on how to practice mindfulness – these two offer a westernised, secular approach and come with CD recordings of guided practices:

- **Burch, Vidyamala and Penman, Danny "Mindfulness for Health: A practical guide to relieving pain, reducing stress and restoring wellbeing"** (2013)
- **Williams, Mark "Mindfulness: A Practical Guide to Peace in a Frantic World"** (2011)

The next is a more personal account (from a very experienced practitioner) but still essentially a how-to book:

- **Puddicombe, Andy "Get Some Headspace: 10 Minutes Can Make All the Difference"**(2011)

Acceptance and Commitment Therapy (ACT) is a variety of mindfulness-based therapy that I personally favour (largely because it fits so well with biofeedback work). The following are good self-help books.

- **Hayes, Steven, with Spencer Smith "Get Out of your Mind and into Your Life"** (2005)
- **Harris, Russ "The Happiness Trap: Stop Struggling, Start Living"** (2007)

Video and Audio Resources

If you prefer listening to reading, there are plenty of useful online resources available. Most of the authors I've mentioned have videos on YouTube – you can just search on their name. Here are a few that I've found helpful:

- "Transform Your Mind, Change Your Brain: Neuroplasticity and Personal Transformation" *http://youtu.be/7tRdDqXgsJ0* - a talk given by Professor Richard Davidson, covering some of the same ground as his book.
- "The Willpower Instinct" *http://youtu.be/V5BXuZL1HAg* - a talk by Kelly McGonigal
- "Mindsight: The New Science of Personal Transformation" *http://youtu.be/Gr4Od7kqDT8* a talk by Dan Siegel – see also his website where he has lots more recordings available: *http://www.drdansiegel.com/*
- "Get Some Headspace" http://youtu.be/MdcXKrpbnrM - a talk by Andy Puddicombe on mindfulness and meditation, with practices.
- "Steve Kotler and The Rise of the Superman" – a podcast interview with Dave Asprey (the "Bulletproof Executive") *https://www.bulletproofexec.com/109-steven-kotler-and-the-rise-of-superman-podcast/*

The next two videos focus on biofeedback, a topic which is missing from the books I've recommended.

- "Coping with Stress" *http://youtu.be/iup0msVJeAI* – a talk on stress, how it manifests in the body, and how biofeedback helps, given at University of California by Richard Harvey.
- "Being Brilliant Every Single Day" *http://youtu.be/q06YIWCR2Js* - A TEDx talk by Dr Alan Watkins in which he discusses his use of HRV biofeedback in optimal performance training.

About the Author

A graduate of Cambridge University in Natural Sciences, Glyn Blackett first began practising mindfulness meditation as a student. After an early career as a software developer, he moved to North Wales to live and work at a Buddhist retreat centre. It was here that he first encountered biofeedback - while investigating the physiological basis of meditative states of mind, and searching for ways of making meditative concentration more accessible. Immediately impressed by the power and potential of biofeedback, he decided to make it the basis of a career as a therapist and coach.

After training in psychotherapy, biofeedback and neurofeedback, in 2005 Glyn established his current professional practice, first as York Biofeedback Centre. Later he qualified in Nutritional Therapy, adding a new layer to a holistic, integrative practice - but still focused on mental and emotional health and optimal brain functioning.

In recent years Glyn has developed a powerful multi-parameter biofeedback software product, Mind-Body Training Tools, which he uses in his professional sessions, in his personal meditation practice, and additionally as basis for home biofeedback rental for his clients.

For more information please visit: *www.stressresilientmind.co.uk*

Notes

1   Siegel, D. "Mindsight: Transform your brain with the new science of kindness" (2010). Dr Siegel advocates a neuroscientifically informed and mindfulness-based form of psychotherapy – this book is on my suggested further reading list.

2   The term "flow" was first used by Mihaly Csikszentmihalyi in his book "Flow: The Psychology of Optimal Experience" (1990)

3   Dr. Siegel discusses integration at length in his book "Mindsight" (see note 1 above). See also his website, *www.drdansiegel.com/home/* where he has several recorded talks.

4   Dweck, Carol "Mindset: How You Can Fulfil Your Potential" (2007). Dweck's website, *mindsetonline.com* gives a useful overview of her work and offers a questionnaire that measures your mindset (in terms of growth versus fixed). You can also get a taste of her work from this presentation available on YouTube: *youtu.be/QGvR_0mNpWM*

5   Hutchison, M. "Megabrain" (1986)

6   For more on this idea, see Ekman, Paul "Emotions Revealed: Recognizing Faces and Feelings to Improve Communication and Emotional Life" (2003). Charles Darwin first expressed these ideas in his book "The Expression of the Emotions in Man and Animals" (1872).

7   I'm indebted to Dr Antonio Damasio for this distinction. It is quite fundamental to his thinking, and he makes the case for its utility very well in his published books.

8   See Fredrickson, B. "Positivity" (2009). I return to this concept later in the book.

9   Russell, James (1980). "A circumplex model of affect". Journal of Personality and Social Psychology 39: 1161–1178

10   Again, see Fredrickson, B. "Positivity" (2009).

11   Rick Hanson, in his book "Buddha's Brain: The Practical Neuroscience of Happiness, Love, and Wisdom" (2009) covers the topic of negativity bias in more depth than I do, offering a few references to research. His books are well worth reading, and his website, *www.rickhanson.net*, has lots of useful resources (follow the 'multimedia' link).

12   Fredrickson discusses the positivity ratio extensively in her 2009 book "Positivity", though she was not the originator of the idea. She also has a website devoted to the topic: *www.positivityratio.com* - it has a questionnaire to test your positivity.

13   I consider Dr Damasio's books as amongst the best presentations of neuroscience for the general public. At the time of writing he has published four popular books, the first, "Descartes' Error" (1994) is about the connection between emotion and reason. His further works develop his thinking on the biological basis of emotion and feeling.

14   Darwin, Charles "The Expression of the Emotions in Man and Animals" (1872)

15   Gilbert, Paul "The Compassionate Mind" (2009)

16   My account of the brain structures involved in emotion is necessarily brief. There are of course lots of popular neuroscience books, but I think that among the most helpful are the works of Dr Daniel Amen (e.g. "Change Your Brain, Change Your Life" is one of his earlier and more general works but he's written books on specific topics such as ADHD). One of my favourite brain books is McCrone, John "Going Inside: A tour round a single moment of consciousness" (2000).

17   See for example Hoelzel, B. et al "How Does Mindfulness Meditation Work? Proposing Mechanisms of Action From a Conceptual and Neural Perspective" Perspectives on Psychological Science 2011 6: 537 *www.emory.edu/ECCS/education/Holzel.pdf*

18   Most popular writing doesn't make clear the difference between neurotransmitters and neuromodulators – essentially the former are secreted into the synaptic cleft (transmitting a signal between one

neuron and its neighbour) while the latter are secreted into the broad space around neurons, and are absorbed by many neurons and rather than effecting transmission they modulate the way that signals are transmitted. See for example Bear, Connor & Paradiso, "Neuroscience: Exploring the Brain" for a fuller account.

19 In the US noradrenalin is known as norepinephrine (and adrenalin as epinephrine).

20 This article summarises research in the neuroscience of mindfulness: Dr Michael Baime "This Is Your Brain on Mindfulness" (published in Shambhala Sun, July 2011). You can read the article here:
www.nmr.mgh.harvard.edu/~britta/SUN_July11_Baime.pdf

21 Hamilton, J.P. et al "Modulation of subgenual anterior cingulate cortex activity with real-time neurofeedback" Human Brain Mapping Vol. 32, Issue 1, pages 22–31, January 2011
onlinelibrary.wiley.com/doi/10.1002/hbm.20997/abstract

22 You can find more detailed discussion of the PFC in firstly, Siegel, Daniel "Mindsight: Transform your brain with the new science of kindness" (2010) and secondly Goldberg, Elkhonon "The New Executive Brain: Frontal Lobes in a Complex World" (2009). See also Richard Davidson's book, note 23 below.

23 Davidson, Richard, with Sharon Begley "The Emotional Life of Your Brain: How to change the way you think, feel and live" (2012)

24 This article in Psychiatric Times looks at this tDCS protocol for depression: *www.psychiatrictimes.com/neuropsychiatry/current-status-transcranial-direct-current-stimulation-treatment-depression*

25 You can find an account of mirror neurons in Goleman, Daniel "Social Intelligence: The New Science of Human Relationships" (2007)

26 Not all accounts of dopamine function in the popular literature make this distinction between pleasure and promise of reward clear. One that does is McGonigal, Kelly "Maximum Willpower: How to master the new science of self-control" (2012). More or less the same book is published in the US as "The Willpower Instinct".

27 These findings are described in Kelly McGonigal's excellent book, "Maximum Willpower" see note 26 above.

28 An outstanding book describing the biology of stress and arousal is Sapolsky, Robert "Why Zebras Don't Get Ulcers" (first published 1994, now in its third edition).

29 See Cacioppo, J.T. et al "The psychophysiology of emotion" (2000) – in Lewis, M. and Haviland-Jones, J. (eds) "Handbook of Emotions" (2nd ed, pp. 173-191) available here: *psychology.uchicago.edu/people/faculty/cacioppo/jtcreprints/cblpi00.pdf*

30 Porges, Stephen "The Polyvagal Theory: Neurophysiological Foundations of Emotions, Attachment, Communication, and Self-regulation" (2011)

31 Thayer, J.F. et al "Heart rate variability, prefrontal neural function, and cognitive performance: the neurovisceral integration perspective on self-regulation, adaptation, and health." Ann. Behav. Med. 2009 Apr;37(2):141-53. *www.ncbi.nlm.nih.gov/pubmed/19424767*

32 Again in her excellent book "Maximum Willpower", see note 26 above.

33 See Fredrickson, Barbara "Positivity" (2009), also her research paper: Kok B.E., and Fredrickson B.L. "Upward spirals of the heart: autonomic flexibility, as indexed by vagal tone, reciprocally and prospectively predicts positive emotions and social connectedness" Biol Psychol. 2010 Dec;85(3):432-6 *www.ncbi.nlm.nih.gov/pubmed/20851735*

34 Sapolsky's book – see note 28 above.

35 Kotler, Steve "The Rise of the Superman: Decoding the Science of Ultimate Human Performance" (2014)

36 See for example this blog article: *bps-research-digest.blogspot.co.uk/2012/07/does-your-heart-rate-hold-secret-to.html* – also this research paper: de Manzano et al "The Psychophysiology of Flow During Piano Playing" Emotion (2010) available here: *www.wpi.edu/Images/CMS/HUA-CIMA/2010_Manzano.pdf*

37 The Heartmath Institute is a non-profit organisation focused on research and education in the area of HRV and biofeedback. Emotional quiescence is described in their ebook: McCraty, Rollin et al "The Coherent Heart: Heart-Brain Interactions, Psychophysiological Coherence, and the Emergence of System-Wide Order" (2006)

38 Again these research findings are reported by Kotler – see note 35 above.

39 Sapolsky again, see note 28 above.

40 Daniel Goleman uses this phrase and gives a much fuller account in: Goleman, Daniel "Emotional Intelligence: Why it Can Matter More Than IQ" (1996)

41 Siegel, D. "Mindsight: Transform your brain with the new science of kindness" (2010). Another good source on the neuroscience of PTSD is Rothschild, Babette "The Body Remembers: The Psychophysiology of Trauma and Trauma Treatment" (2000)

42 For a fuller account of the chemistry of breathing, a good source is the website of Better Physiology Ltd., and Dr Peter Litchfield, who deserves much credit for developing capnometry as a biofeedback modality. See this page in particular:
www.betterphysiology.com/BetterPhysiology/AboutBr%20What%20is.htm

43 Richerson, George B., "Serotonergic neurons as carbon dioxide sensors that maintain pH homeostasis" Nature Reviews Neuroscience 5, 449-461 (June 2004)
www.nature.com/nrn/journal/v5/n6/abs/nrn1409.html

44 In the medical world the Nijmegen Questionnaire is used as a standard means of assessing hyperventilation. You can find it if you google "nijmegen questionnaire".

45 Thayer, J.F. et al "Heart rate variability, prefrontal neural function, and cognitive performance: the neurovisceral integration perspective on self-regulation, adaptation, and health."Ann. Behav. Med. 2009 Apr;37(2):141-53. *www.ncbi.nlm.nih.gov/pubmed/19424767*

46 Kim, S. et al, "Heart rate variability biofeedback, executive functioning and chronic brain injury" Brain Injury, February 2013; 27(2): 209–222 *www.heartmath.com/wp-content/uploads/2014/04/HRV_and_Brain_Injury_Study_2013.pdf*

47 Austin, James H. "Zen and the Brain: Toward an Understanding of Meditation and Consciousness" (1998)

48 See note 47 above.

49 Sukanya Phongsuphap et al "Changes in heart rate variability during concentration meditation" International Journal of

Cardiology 130 (2008) 481–484
www.ncbi.nlm.nih.gov/pubmed/17764770

50　Serenity prayer – for the full Niebuhr version see the wikipedia page: *en.wikipedia.org/wiki/Serenity_Prayer*

51　Marketers and political spin doctors know that simplistic unconscious processes more than rational consideration goes to informing our beliefs. Repetition is an important part of the process, see for example this research paper: Ozubko J.D. "Remembering makes evidence compelling: retrieval from memory can give rise to the illusion of truth" J Exp Psychol Learn Mem Cogn. 2011 Jan; 37(1):270-6 *www.ncbi.nlm.nih.gov/pubmed/21058878*

52　This work on learned helplessness is described in Seligman, Martin "Learned Optimism: How to Change Your Mind and Your Life" (1991)

53　For a good account of how these thinking patterns play out in depression and what you can do about it, see Yapko, Michael "Breaking the Patterns of Depression" (1997)

54　The human performance curve is technically known as the Yerkes-Dodson law – for more information see the wikipedia entry: *en.wikipedia.org/wiki/Yerkes-Dodson_law*

55　See his seminal work: Csikszentmihalyi, Mihaly "Flow: The Psychology of Optimal Experience" (1990)

56　A ten year study by McKinsey and Co. found executives were up to five times more productive when in flow – see *www.mckinsey.com/insights/organization/increasing_the_meaning_quotie nt_of_work*. Several corporations have put accessing flow at the centre of their corporate strategies.

57　Steve Kotler makes this comment in an interview with Dave Asprey (aka the "bulletproof executive") available online here: *www.bulletproofexec.com/109-steven-kotler-and-the-rise-of-superman-podcast/* The Flow Genome Project (*www.flowgenomeproject.com*) is committed to mapping the state of flow and the conditions for accessing flow, and making this knowledge available. Steve's book is an excellent resource (I list it in my recommended reading section) looking at flow in the context of extreme sports. Kotler, Steve "The Rise of the Superman: Decoding the Science of Ultimate Human Performance" (2014)

58 The distinction between primary and secondary suffering is an important concept in mindfulness-based therapy. It was first made by the Buddha and is recorded in a text called the Sallatha Sutta, available here: *www.accesstoinsight.org/tipitaka/sn/sn36/sn36.006.nypo.html* A fuller account is given in Burch, Vidyamala and Penman, Danny "Mindfulness for Health: A practical guide to relieving pain, reducing stress and restoring wellbeing" (2013).

59 Many CBT books are available. A good self-help CBT book is Greenberger, Dennis and Padesky, Christine "Mind Over Mood: Change How You Feel By Changing the Way You Think" (1996)

60 Human Givens is a school of brief, solution-focused psychotherapy created by Joe Griffin and Ivan Tyrrell. My understanding of the relationship between thoughts and feelings owes a lot to their APET model, which is described in Griffin, Joe and Tyrrell, Ivan "Human Givens: A new approach to emotional health and clear thinking" (2003)

61 I adapted the idea of the two intelligences from the work of Stephen Gilligan, and his book "The Courage to Love" (1997)

62 Gallwey, W. Timothy "The Inner Game of Tennis" (1975)

63 Siegel, D. "Mindsight" (2010) – already mentioned in chapter one in connection with integration

64 See Haidt, J. "The Happiness Hypothesis" (2006). This metaphor has been adopted and made famous in Chip & Dan Heath's book "Switch: How to Change Things When Change Is Hard" (2010), of which it is a central theme. Both these books are well worth a read. The wikipedia page gives a good summary of the former work: *en.wikipedia.org/wiki/The_Happiness_Hypothesis*

65 Peters, Steve "The Chimp Paradox: The Mind Management Programme to Help You Achieve Success, Confidence and Happiness" (2012)

66 Asprey, Dave "The Bulletproof Diet" (2014)

67 A similar version of this split is found in Acceptance and Commitment Therapy (ACT) where they speak of the wider self as "self-as-context" or the observing self as opposed to the thinking self.

68   Daniel Goleman has a chapter on top-down and bottom-up processing in his book "Focus: The Hidden Driver of Excellence" (2013)

69   Kahneman, Daniel "Thinking, Fast and Slow" (2011)

70   Goleman, Daniel "The Brain and Emotional Intelligence: New Insights" (2011)

71   Yoda says this to Luke Skywalker in episode 4 of the Star Wars saga, "The Empire Strikes Back", while teaching him to lift objects using the the force.

72   Gratification is discussed in Seligman, Martin "Authentic Happiness" (2002). Other psychologists make the same distinction with the terms "eudaimonic happiness" and "hedonic happiness", e.g. see this article: *www.positivepsychology.org.uk/pp-theory/eudaimonia/34-the-concept-of-eudaimonic-well-being.html*

73   Kotler, Steve "The Rise of the Superman: Decoding the Science of Ultimate Human Performance" (2014)

74   This definition comes from McGonigal, Kelly "The Upside of Stress: Why Stress Is Good For you and How To Get Good At It" (2015), which I highly recommend.

75   This experiment is reported in McGonigal's book, see note 74 above.

76   Selye's work is admirably described in Sapolsky, Robert "Why Zebras Don't Get Ulcers" (first published 1994, now in its third edition).

77   The exhaustion stage of stress is commonly known as "adrenal fatigue" in the world of natural, complementary and alternative healthcare. The term is a controversial one – most mainstream endocrinologists don't recognise it. In fairness, the issue is really a dysregulation of the adrenal control system – the "HPA axis" - rather than a physical disorder of the adrenal glands themselves, and a stress condition rather than a medical one. Saliva testing of adrenal hormones is widely used in complementary and alternative health, and in functional medicine, but not in mainstream healthcare. The same test is also widely used in research into the effects of stress . For more information see Wilson, James "Adrenal Fatigue: The 21st Century Stress Syndrome" (2001). Dr Wilson is a naturopathic doctor who has become something of an expert in adrenal fatigue. He has studied the science behind it and his book is

well referenced.

78   The UK's National Institute for Health and Clinical Excellence (NICE) recommends MBT as an evidence-based therapy for relapse prevention in depression – see *www.nice.org.uk/guidance/CG90/chapter/1-Guidance*

79   The most commonly quoted definition of mindfulness is almost certainly Jon Kabat-Zinn's. Kabat-Zinn deserves much of the credit for establishing mindfulness as an evidence-based therapy. He says "Mindfulness means paying attention in a particular way; on purpose, in the present moment, and non-judgementally." For more on his take, see any of the several books Kabat-Zinn has published on mindfulness.

80   Ellen J. Langer, Harvard professor of psychology, discusses the pitfalls of mindlessness (as routine and automatic behaviours) and the benefits of an attitude of mindfulness in many walks of life including business and social relations, in her book "Mindfulness" (first published 1989 and now in its 25th Anniversary edition).

81   I confess to not having read many Buddhist scriptures myself. I took most of these from an online talk by Dharmachari Paramabandhu of the London Buddhist Centre, available online: *www.freebuddhistaudio.com/audio/details?num=OM778*

82   Andy Puddicombe gives a much longer and better exposition of the tethered wild horse metaphor in his book: "Get Some Headspace: 10 Minutes Can Make All the Difference" (2011)

83   Kamalashila "Buddhist Meditation: Tranquillity, Imagination and Insight" (3rd Ed. 2012) - the system Kamalashila is expounding is that of his teacher Sangharakshita.

84   Mark Williams and Danny Penman use this expression in their book, "Mindfulness: A practical guide to finding peace in a frantic world" (2011).

85   Bodhipaksa, founder of the "Wildmind" online meditation resource, and author of a book of the same name, offers this article defining sati and sampajanna - *www.wildmind.org/mindfulness/four/dimensions*

86   Ray, Reginald "Touching Enlightenment: Finding Realization in the Body" (2008)

87   Fredrickson, B. et al "Open hearts build lives: positive emotions,

induced through loving-kindness meditation, build consequential personal resources" J Pers Soc Psychol. 2008 Nov;95(5):1045-62 *www.ncbi.nlm.nih.gov/pubmed/18954193*

88   Salzburg, Sharon "Loving-kindness: The Revolutionary Art of Happiness " (1995)

89   Nagabodhi "Metta: The Practice of Loving Kindness" (2nd ed. 2001)

90   I found an article online by Dr Michael Baime called "This Is Your Brain on Mindfulness" (published in Shambhala Sun, July 2011) that sums up what neuroscience has to say about mindfulness. He quotes research by Amishi Jha investigating attentional performance in mindfulness practitioners. You can read the article here: *www.nmr.mgh.harvard.edu/~britta/SUN_July11_Baime.pdf*

91   Lazar, S. W., Bush, G., Gollub, R. L., Fricchione, G. L., Khalsa, G., & Benson, H. "Functional brain mapping of the relaxation response and meditation" NeuroReport, 11, 1581–1585 (2000) *www.massgeneral.org/bhi/assets/pdfs/publications/lazar_2000_neuroreport.pdf*

92   At the same time, as we saw in chapter three it's been reported that flow states involve deactivation of certain centres within the PFC, and it's possible that this happens in flow-like states of absorption in meditation – dhyanas.

93   Again Dr Baime's article (see note 90 above) summarises these findings. See also Hoelzel, B. et al "How Does Mindfulness Meditation Work? Proposing Mechanisms of Action From a Conceptual and Neural Perspective" Perspectives on Psychological Science 2011 6: 537 *www.emory.edu/ECCS/education/Holzel.pdf*

94   Professor Davidson's work is described in his book, Davidson, R with Sharon Begley "The Emotional Life of Your Brain: How to change the way you think, feel and live" (2013)

95   The paper by Hoelzel et al (see note 93 above) gives a detailed account of the mechanisms of mindfulness change from a neuroscience perspective.

96   In the Buddhist tradition the five hindrances are desire or craving, ill-will, restlessness and agitation, sloth and torpor, and doubt. See for example Kamalashila's book, note 83 above.

97   This study used the Freespira Breathing system, and you can read

more about it here: *www.freespira.com/clinical/*

98   Austin, James H. "Zen and the Brain: Toward an Understanding of Meditation and Consciousness" (1998)

99   McGonigal, Kelly "Maximum Willpower: How to master the new science of self-control" (2012). More or less the same book is published in the US as "The Willpower Instinct".

100 Sukanya Phongsuphap et al "Changes in heart rate variability during concentration meditation" International Journal of Cardiology 130 (2008) 481–484 *www.ncbi.nlm.nih.gov/pubmed/17764770*

101 The Heartmath Institute – for more information see their website www.heartmath.org - they have a free ebook called "Science of the Heart" which is available here: *www.heartmath.org/free-services/downloads/science-of-the-heart.html*

102 For more information about the software, see *www.stressresilientmind.co.uk/mbtt/mbtt* – details of the HRV algorithms are given in the HRV Application User Guide – there is a link to the user guides in the navigation panel on the right.

103 See Cacioppo, J.T. et al "The psychophysiology of emotion" (2000) – in Lewis, M. and Haviland-Jones, J. (eds) "Handbook of Emotions" (2nd ed, pp. 173-191) available here: *psychology.uchicago.edu/people/faculty/cacioppo/jtcreprints/cblpi00.pdf* also see Shiota, M. et al "Feeling Good: Autonomic Nervous system Responding in Five Positive emotions" Emotion 2011, available here: *www.gruberpeplab.com/teaching/psych231_fall2013/documents/231_Shiota2011.pdf*

104 Jung discusses EDA, also known as Galvanic Skin Response, GSR, in his book – Jung, C.G. "Studies in Word Analysis" (1906). See also this article: *www.trans4mind.com/transformation/gsr.htm*

105 The term hemoencephalography was coined by Dr Hershel Toomim, who first developed it as a biofeedback modality. He founded the Biofeedback Institute of Los Angeles with his wife Marjorie – their website has a good collection of articles on HEG neurofeedback: *www.biocompresearch.org/#!biocomp-research/c1u6v*

106 Again this collection of articles on the BILA website is a useful source of further information (see note 105 above).

107 Dr Carmen has a couple of papers available via the BILA website –
see note 105 above. One of them reports on his experience of using
PIR HEG with migraine sufferers – Dr Carmen specialises in the
treatment of migraine and originally developed his method with
this patient group in mind.

108 The best accounts of EEG neurofeedback, that give a sense of the
complexity, are Swingle, Paul "Biofeedback for the Brain: How
Neurotherapy Effectively Treats Depression, ADHD, Autism, and
More" (2010) and Fisher, Sebern "Neurofeedback in the Treatment
of Developmental Trauma: Calming the Fear-Driven Brain" (2014).

109 Let me give an example of the difficulty of the choice: training alpha
peak frequency. Alpha is a frequency band within the EEG
spectrum that loosely correlates with the brain idling but ready.
Dominant frequency correlates with intelligence, or more generally
(as Paul Swingle says) brain efficiency – the higher the better. It
drops low in cases of dementia. So it seems to make sense to train
peak alpha frequency upwards. Yet it's also been reported that in
peak states of flow, it is slow alpha (or high theta) that is dominant.
So maybe training alpha frequency down is a good idea?

110 James, William "Psychology: The Briefer Course" (1961)
books.google.co.uk/books?isbn=0486416046

111 James, William "The Principles of Psychology" (1890)
books.google.co.uk/books?isbn=6050312192

112 Huxley, A. "The Doors of Perception" (1954) – the book describes
Huxley's experiences when taking the psychedelic substance
mescaline.

113 A good accessible account of attention including its neuroscience is
Goleman, Daniel "Focus: The Hidden Driver of Excellence" (2013)

114 Actually it's thought there are sub-types of ADHD, not all of them
primarily related to dopamine. For an accessible account see Amen,
Daniel "Healing ADD: The Breakthrough Program That Allows You
to See and Heal the 7 Types of Attention Deficit Disorder" (Revised
Edition 2013)

115 My thinking in this area owes a lot to Dr Les Fehmi, who developed
a method called open focus, initially as a neurofeedback-assisted
technique but also a stand-alone method, as described in the book:
Fehmi, Les, and Robbins, Jim, "The Open Focus Brain: Harnessing

the Power of Attention to Heal Mind and Body" (2007). I mention his work later in the text

116 I read about this in McGonigal, Kelly "Maximum Willpower: How to master the new science of self-control" (2012)

117 The version of Dual N-back I've used is called Brain Workshop – see this site (free software download): *brainworkshop.sourceforge.net* Dual N-back is described in Hurley, Dan "Smarter: The New Science of Building Brain Power" (2013) – the book is an account of Hurley's self-experiments in boosting intelligence.

118 See note 116 above.

119 Steven H. Pink, "Drive: The Surprising Truth About What Motivates Us" (2009) is an engaging and worthy read.

120 For more on values I recommend you check out ACT (Acceptance and Commitment Therapy) – a form of mindfulness-based therapy. Two good ACT self-help books are firstly Hayes, Steven, with Spencer Smith "Get Out of your Mind and into Your Life" (2005) and secondly Harris, Russ "The Happiness Trap: Stop Struggling, Start Living" (2007)

121 Kelly McGonigal takes a look at the evidence in her book, "Maximum Willpower: How to master the new science of self-control" (2012)

122 Seminal work on delayed gratification was done by psychologist Walter Mischel beginning in the late 60's, with his Standford "Marshmallow experiment". For more information see the wikipedia page *en.wikipedia.org/wiki/Stanford_marshmallow_experiment*. Also see McGonigal, Kelly "Maximum Willpower: How to master the new science of self-control" (2012)

123 Dr McGonigal's book "Maximum Willpower", already mentioned in note 121 above, is a highly recommended treatise on willpower.

124 Again this finding is discussed in "Maximum Willpower" by Kelly McGonigal.

125 McKeown, Patrick, "Anxiety Free: Stop Worrying and Quieten Your Mind" (2010). He describes the Buteyko method of breathing, which aims to reduce hyperventilation (without the benefit of capnometry biofeedback).

126 Most CBT books cover cognitive distortions. A good self-help book is Greenberger, Dennis and Padesky, Christine "Mind Over Mood: Change how you feel by changing the way you think" (1995)

127 Kahneman, Daniel "Thinking, Fast and Slow" (2011)

128 See note 126 above.

129 Two good ACT self-help books, both of which cover defusion techniques, are firstly Hayes, Steven, with Spencer Smith "Get Out of your Mind and into Your Life" (2005) and secondly Harris, Russ "The Happiness Trap: Stop Struggling, Start Living" (2007)

130 Cognitive Bias Modification Therapy is described in the book: Fox, Elaine "Rainy Brain, Sunny Brain" (2012) see also the author's website *www.rainybrainsunnybrain.com* which has some online tests etc. here: *www.rainybrainsunnybrain.com/bbc-horizon/*

131 Seligman, Martin, "Learned Optimism: How to Change Your Mind and Your Life" (1991)

132 Cognitive reappraisal is covered in lots of CBT self-help books, including Greenberger and Padesky (see note 126 above) and one I like a lot, Yapko, Michael "Breaking the Patterns of Depression" (1997)

133 Schwartz, Jeffrey and Begley, Sharon "The Mind and the Brain" (2002) offers a detailed account of the neurology of OCD and describes how Dr Schwartz was able to produce measurable benefits using mindfulness based techniques.

134 Davidson, Richard, with Sharon Begley "The Emotional Life of Your Brain: How to change the way you think, feel and live" (2012) – basically wherever I reference Davidson's work, you'll find more about it in this book.

135 Seligman, Martin "Authentic Happiness: Using the New Positive Psychology to Realise Your Potential for Lasting Fulfilment" (2002). Another excellent read is Haidt, Jonathan "The Happiness Hypothesis: Putting Ancient Wisdom and Philosophy to the Test of Modern Science" (2006).

136 Fredrickson discusses the positivity ratio extensively in her 2009 book "Positivity", though she was not the originator of the idea. She also has a website devoted to the topic: *www.positivityratio.com* - it has a questionnaire to test your positivity.

137 I'm reminded of the opening monologue of the film, "Love Actually", set in the arrivals hall of Heathrow Airport, which you can view here: *youtu.be/cUoxXpqof8A* ('It seems to me that love is everywhere. Often, it's not particularly dignified or newsworthy, but it's always there.')

138 See for example Emmons, Robert "Thanks!: How Practicing Gratitude Can Make You Happier" (2008)

139 Goleman, Daniel "Emotional Intelligence: Why it Can Matter More Than IQ" (1996)

140 For a history of the concept of emotional intelligence see e.g. *wikipedia: en.wikipedia.org/wiki/Emotional_intelligence*

141 Two good ACT self-help books are firstly Hayes, Steven, with Spencer Smith "Get Out of your Mind and into Your Life" (2005) and secondly Harris, Russ "The Happiness Trap: Stop Struggling, Start Living" (2007)

142 Martin Seligman is regarded as the founder of Positive Psychology. His work is concerned not so much with values as the related character strengths and virtues. He attempted to find a set of culture-independent virtues – read more about this in: Seligman, Martin "Authentic Happiness: Using the New Positive Psychology to Realize Your Potential for Lasting Fulfilment" (2002)

143 For practical reading on the topic of the nutritional and biochemical basis for optimal (brain) performance, see for example, (i) Hyman, Mark, "The Ultramind Solution" (2008) (ii) Kharrazian, Datis "Why Isn't My Brain Working" (2013) (iii) Walsh, William, "Nutrient Power" (2012)

144 Goleman, Daniel "Social Intelligence: The New Science of Human Relationships" (2007)

145 See the BCIA website: *www.bcia.org*

146 "The Coherent Heart: Heart–Brain Interactions, Psychophysiological Coherence, and the Emergence of System-Wide Order" (Integral Review Vol. 5. No. 2, December 2009) by Rollin McCraty et. al. - the method is described on page 23. The paper is available online at *www.integral-review.org/ issues/vol_5_no_2_mccraty_et_al_the_coherent_heart.pdf*

Made in the USA
Monee, IL
29 November 2022

19016827R00203